Zicklin School of Business Financial Markets Series

Series Editor
Robert A. Schwartz
Zicklin School of Business
Baruch College/CUNY
New York, NY, USA

More information about this series at https://link.springer.com/bookseries/7133

Robert A. Schwartz • John Aidan Byrne
Eileen Stempel
Editors

40 Years of Experience with the National Market System (NMS)

Who Are the Winners and What Have We Learned?

Springer

Editors
Robert A. Schwartz
Zicklin School of Business
Baruch College-CUNY
New York, NY, USA

John Aidan Byrne
Rockaway, NJ, USA

Eileen Stempel
Zicklin School of Business
Baruch College
New York, NY, USA

ISSN 2627-521X ISSN 2627-5228 (electronic)
Zicklin School of Business Financial Markets Series
ISBN 978-3-030-91911-5 ISBN 978-3-030-91912-2 (eBook)
https://doi.org/10.1007/978-3-030-91912-2

This Springer imprint is published by the registered company Springer Nature Switzerland AG
The registered company address is: Gewerbestrasse 11, 6330 Cham, Switzerland

Preface: 40 Years of Experience with NMS: Who Are the Winners and What Have We Learned?

Robert A. Schwartz
Zicklin School of Business
Baruch College-CUNY
New York, NY, USA

In 1975, exactly forty years ago, the US Securities Acts Amendments were enacted by Congress. As you know, the new law, amongst other measures, precluded a return to fixed commissions. But most significantly for us, the development of a National Market System (NMS) was officially mandated.[1]

At the time, nobody, not even Congress, knew anything much about an NMS. Yet that did not slow them down in their mission to implement an NMS.

While the conference title appears to have a slant towards regulation, I anticipate that our discussions today will be a good deal broader. I certainly hope so. I have talked to the moderators and speakers about broadening the discussion. Nevertheless, the conference title is, perfectly suitable for our gathering today on market structure.

We all know that, since 1975, there have been technology changes that are huge and pervasive in scope. The competitive map has been redrawn. So, today, let's not focus just on regulation. Let's also pull technology and competition into our discussion.

The conference subtitle is, "Who are the winners and what have we learned?" The winners? Look at the landscape, and at the firms still standing. New firms arise and older firms disappear, driven out in part by the regulatory changes. There is market turbulence and other turbulence, and some change is naturally inevitable. But this change appears to be more pronounced when the regulatory environment itself changes.

Let me call your attention to one set of winners you might not immediately think of. It's us academicians! We've won because the issues are so intricate, complex, subtle, and seemingly without end. That means our microstructure research can continue on and on without interruption.

[1] Federal legislation launched on June 4, 1975, to amend the Securities Exchange Act of 1934. The 1975 amendments instructed the Securities Exchange Commission to cooperate with the industry creating a National Market System along with an ambitious system for the clearance and settlement of securities transactions nationwide. The amendments also provided for the prohibition of fixed-commission rates, promulgated earlier by the SEC in its Rule 19b-3.

What have we learned? I have my thoughts, my proposals, and my suggestions. I will not go into them right now. But, from a personal point of view, I want to point out something I have learned. I've learned how complicated the issues are. There are no magic answers, no silver bullets and, of course, the questions never end. When it's complicated as it is, it says something for letting nature take its course in a competitive environment.

The opinion is widely held today that our market quality is far better than it was 40 years ago. Yes, there are tighter spreads. The evidence is that market impact costs have come down. Those are tricky things to measure, but the evidence is certainly saying that. Clearly, commissions are lower too.

At the same time, the feeling is widespread that something isn't working so well. On both sides of the Atlantic, there's a great deal of regulatory attention being given to market structure issues. Of course, of particular concern are the flash crashes, but it's not just flash crashes.

How do you know if a boat is really seaworthy? Don't assess it on a calm day. If you really want to know, see how it rides when the weather turns foul. If we are to properly assess market quality, assess it during stressful times. The market is very accommodating about this-it gives us a lot of stressful times.

Sila Alan and I published a study on this in a 2013 paper in the *Journal of Portfolio Management*, "Price Discovery, the Economic Function of a Stock Exchange."[2] Our paper can be traced back to comments made at an earlier conference in our Zicklin School series. We found evidence of extraordinarily high intraday volatility for some individual stocks on some individual days. That evidence demands attention.

Let me remind you that so many assessments of market quality have to do with spreads, market impact or whatever, and are made on the basis of averages. My warning: beware of averages.

There's a story told about a physicist, a chemist, and a statistician who went bear hunting in Maine. They went into the woods and spotted a bear in the distance. The physicist shoots first and misses, 5 feet to the left. The chemist goes next, shoots, and misses, 5 feet to the right. The statistician says, don't worry guys, on average, you killed the bear!

Highly computerized markets are great.

Here is one other thing about electronic trading. The computer doesn't think, in reality it responds to instructions. If an unusual situation comes along, a computer does not know how to handle it. I've worked with enough of the markets. I know this is a terrible concern.

The computer deals with a bunch of "*if* statements", *If* this, then that; *if* this, then that. These *if* statements, don't think behind the meaning of what's being said. This reminds me of the fellow who is working in his office late in the afternoon. He gets a call from his wife. "Honey", she says "On the way home, would you please stop

[2] "Price Discovery: The Economic Function of Stock Exchange," by Nazli Sila Alan and Robert A. Schwartz was published in The Journal of Portfolio Management Fall 2013, 40 (1) 124–132; https://doi.org/10.3905/jpm.2013.40.1.124

at the grocery and gett me a quart of milk?" The husband responds: "Sure, dear, I'll be pleased to." The wife then adds: "A quart of milk, please. And if they have avocados get me four." The husband confirms: "Sure, honey, I'll be pleased to." He shows up a short while later, walks in the front door, and his wife loudly exclaims, "My, God, what are you doing with four quarts of milk." He replies: "Because they had the avocados" (laughter)! *If* statements, guys, *if* statements. Some people here today laughed. Some didn't. If you didn't understand this joke, I have to explain it! This is a cross between a joke and an IQ test (laughter).

I want to call your attention to liquidity. It isn't just trading costs that are at stake. It is also liquidity. What is liquidity? How do you define it? How do you measure it? How might it best be provided? And do we even want it? Why do I add this? How many of you read Martin Wolf's column in the *Financial Times*, October 6th? Did any of you read it?[3] Just a couple? It's a really interesting article; it's a sparky article. After I read the piece, my first reaction was, Oh, my goodness gracious, how could he be correct?

I'll zip through a couple of quotes from the piece. "Market liquidity is likely to disappear when one needs it most, building our hopes on its durability is risky." Correct, I agree. "Market liquidity is a fickle friend;" Correct, I agree. "We should contest the conventional wisdom of the benefits of market liquidity." The benefits, hmm? That's when I slowed down. This is the last quote I'll give you from the same piece: "The economy should not be based on confidence in something likely to vanish." Fine, I can accept that.

I believe that there is truth to what he's saying about fragility and fickleness. But I would take the conclusion in a different direction. I would say you should emphasize the need to find a superior, more reliable source of liquidity. That's where I pull in the listed companies. I hope that in our discussions today we get into some of this stuff.

It is now a pleasure on my part to introduce Tom Gira from FINRA, the Financial Industry Regulatory Authority. This is your third appearance here, Tom. I am very excited to have you back again. [4]

---

[3] Beware of the Liquidity Delusion. Martin Wolf, *Financial Times*, October 6, 2015. https://www.ft.com/content/c8c2cc44-68fa-11e5-a57f-21b88f7d973f

[4] With great sadness, FINRA announced the passing of Tom (Thomas) Gira, executive vice president, Market Regulation and Transparency Services, on Saturday, June 20, 2020. He was 58.

List of Participants

Name	Company	Title
John Adam	Portware	Global Head of Product Management
Nazli Sila Alan	Fairfield University	Assistant Professor of Finance
Amber Anand	Syracuse University	Associate Professor
Gregg Berman	Ernst & Young	Principal, Financial Services
William Brodsky	CBOE	Chairman of the Board
Andy Brooks	T.Rowe Price	Vice President
Enrico Cacciatore	Voya Investment Management	Senior Quantitative Trader
Arthur Cashin	UBS	Managing Director
Stephen Cavoli	Virtu Financial	Global Head, Virtu Execution Services
Bryan Christian	BATS	Senior Vice President
Curt Engler	JP Morgan Asset Management	Head of Equity Trading, Americas
Anthony Fortunato	Instinet	Managing Director
Joe Gawronski	Rosenblatt Securities	President & COO
Thomas Gira	FINRA	Executive Vice President of Market Regulation
Bill Harts	Modern Markets Initiative	CEO
Alan Hill	Jones Trading	CEO
Pete Jenkins	CODA Markets (formerly PDQ ATS)	Managing Director
Richard Lindsey	Janus Capital Group	Chief Investment Strategist
Frank Loughlin	Alliance Bernstein	Global Co-Head of Equity Trading
Tim Mahoney	BIDS	CEO
Nina Mehta	Journalist and Author	
Bob Pisani	CNBC	Correspondent
Robert Schwartz	Zicklin School of Business, Baruch College	Speiser Professor of Finance
Gary Stone	Bloomberg Trading Solutions	Chief Strategy Officer

Name	Company	Title
Nandini Sukumar	World Federation of Exchanges	CEO
Adam Sussman	Liquidnet	Head of Market Structure & Liquidity Partnerships
Larry Tabb	Tabb Group	CEO
Dave Weisberger	Markit	Managing Director
Greg Wood	Deutsche Bank Securities	Director
John Zecca	Nasdaq	Senior Vice President

Conference Sponsors

BATS Exchange
BIDS Trading
CBOE Holdings, Inc.
Instinet
Jones Trading
Modern Markets Initiative
Nasdaq
PDQ ATS Inc.
Portware
TABB Group

Contents

Chapter 1
Thoughts and Perspectives on 40th Anniversary of the National Market System (NMS)

Thomas Gira

I want to start by thanking Bob Schwartz for inviting me to speak this morning, and for his tireless efforts to foster a greater understanding of trading and market structure. As always, Bob today has laid out a very provocative and thoughtful theme, "40 Years of Experience with NMS: Who Are the Winners and What Have We Learned?" It looks like we can expect a great conference with all the excellent panels.

Before the panels begin, I would like to share my views on the National Market System, or NMS.[1] Many of us in this business a long time will appreciate how the '75 Act Amendments to the Securities Exchange Act of 1934, and the rules by the SEC to create the National Market System, set the stage for the last 40 years of innovation in the markets.[2] The pace of change since 1975 has accelerated through the decades, leading to what are the most efficient markets in the world.

While the changes have not always been welcome, and indeed, they've been very contentious and painful for some, they have nevertheless brought a variety of positive effects for investors and issuers and have triggered a technological revolution to this day.

[1] Federal legislation launched on June 4, 1975, to amend the Securities Exchange Act of 1934. The 1975 amendments instructed the Securities and Exchange Commission to cooperate with the industry in creating a National Market System along with an ambitious system for the clearance and settlement of securities transactions nationwide. The amendments also provided for the prohibition of fixed-commission rates, promulgated earlier by the SEC in its Rule 19b-3.

[2] Ibid.

T. Gira (✉)
FINRA, New York, NY, USA

R. A. Schwartz et al. (eds.), *40 Years of Experience with the National Market System (NMS)*, Zicklin School of Business Financial Markets Series,
https://doi.org/10.1007/978-3-030-91912-2_1

To put that in perspective, FINRA collects on average 40 billion events a day.[3] On August 24 alone, we successfully collected 75 billion events.[4] To further put that in perspective, on just one day, FINRA handled more events than MasterCard processed in a year, and Visa processed in a month. That will give you a sense of the enormous size of the market, and of all the events generated in our markets today.

Because the National Market System facilitated the infusion of technology, the industry is now starting to discuss execution speeds in picoseconds, or a one-trillionth of a second. The industry also is now starting to talk about reducing latency further, by swapping out the dated fiber optic cables with microwave dishes that were so famously described in *Flash Boys*.[5] These can convey data in almost half the time, allowing high-frequency traders a way to squeeze profit from miniscule price discrepancies in assets traded around the world.

Lastly, exchange data centers are now an amalgamation of exchange trading engines and computers of broker-dealers, to reduce latency as much as possible. All these changes are grounded in the wide latitude the SEC gave to markets and market participants to determine the best structure to achieve the objectives of the National Market System.

So, in addition to Bob's questions, I would like to pose two additional questions: Did the SEC give the markets too much discretion; and, if so, is the result a market that is now out of control? It is important to note that these are not simply academic questions. The fairness and efficiency of our financial markets have an impact on investor confidence and on capital formation. Our markets are a key component of America's competitive strength within the global economy. So, it's critical that we get these answers right.

For a little more perspective on the impact of the National Market System, I would like to take you on a trip down memory lane. Before 1975, there were off-board trading restrictions that limited where investors could purchase or sell securities. Also, competition among exchanges was limited, and there were no consolidated data feeds for quotes. Options listings were allocated in lotteries much like the NFL draft; and the norm was fixed commissions with excessively high trading costs. That meant that retail investor participation in the market was a fraction of what we see today.[6]

The Securities Act Amendments of 1975, which mandated the creation of a National Market System, spurred far-reaching change in the equity markets. The five objectives for the National Market System are: (1) the efficient execution of transactions; (2) fair competition between markets; (3) the availability of quotation and transaction information; (4) the best possible execution of orders; and (5) where

---

[3] Event gathering and processing refers to the collection and management of the data associated with customer orders and other commercial transactions. FINRA, or the Financial Industry Regulatory Authority. About FINRA: https://www.finra.org/about

[4] After historic 1,000-point plunge, Dow dives 588 points at close. Matt Egan. CNN., August 25, 2015 https://money.cnn.com/2015/08/24/investing/stocks-markets-selloff-china-crash-dow/

[5] See, Flash Boys: A Wall Street Revolt. Michael Lewis (2015, WW Norton & Company, LLC).

[6] See, The History of Options Trading. Source: optionstrading.org.

consistent with other goals, the execution of orders without the participation of a dealer.[7]

With these objectives in the forefront and equipped with a flurry of proposals and approvals starting in the mid-1970s, the SEC created securities information processors, or SIPs. The SIPs were created for the consolidation of quotes and trades for equities and options.[8] The Intermarket Trading System, or ITS, was also implemented.[9] It was a rudimentary linkage among the stock exchanges that was, nevertheless, an enormous change at the time, one that allowed non-members access to liquidity on an exchange. It was designed to ensure that customers got the best prices possible.

Off-board trading restrictions were eventually lifted, and the options listing lottery was abolished for a system that rewarded market share based on market quality, not on exclusive assignment.

Later in the 1990s, the SEC adopted the order handling rules.[10] These rules required market makers to publish customer limit orders in their quotes, and abolish the two-tiered market structure where a market maker could simultaneously display a public quote and a superior non-public quote on a private electronic trading system.

Next, the shift to decimalization in 2002 led to a sea change in the over the counter market—with spreads dramatically narrowing, and firms acting as their clients' agents rather than trading with them as market makers.[11]

The implementation in 2007 of Regulation NMS, ushered in another period of incredibly rapid change, and provided a catalyst that led to enhanced technology and competition.[12] Perhaps the greatest changes were the more fulsome automation of the NYSE and the moving away from the floor-based specialist model. Also notable are the joys of access fees, maker taker and taker maker, other pricing

---

[7] Federal legislation launched on June 4, 1975, to amend the Securities Exchange Act of 1934. The 1975 amendments instructed the Securities and Exchange Commission to cooperate with the industry in creating a National Market System along with an ambitious system for the clearance and settlement of securities transactions nationwide. The amendments also provided for the prohibition of fixed-commission rates, promulgated earlier by the SEC in its Rule 19b-3.

[8] Security Information Processors (SIPs) were established to link US markets by processing and consolidating quotes and trades from trading venues into a single and accessible data feed.

[9] Network linking the trading floors of US stock exchanges to permit trading among them in stocks listed on either the NYSE or AMEX (now part of the NYSE), and one or more regional exchanges.

[10] SEC's Order Handling Rules and Beyond https://link.springer.com/chapter/10.1007/978-3-319-54588-2_1

[11] "A system in which the price of a security is quoted using a decimal format rather than fractions. For example, a decimal trading quote would be $56.25; using fractions, the same quote would appear as $56¼. The US Securities and Exchange Commission ordered all stock markets within the US to convert to decimals by April 9, 2001. Prior to 2001, markets in the US utilized fractions in price quotes. Since decimalization, all quotes appear in the decimal trading format." Source: Investopedia Read more: Decimal Trading https://www.investopedia.com/terms/d/decimal-trading.asp#ixzz56MmIr0Vz

[12] Reg NMS (Regulation National Market System) was adopted by the Securities and Exchange Commission in 2005, and introduced two years later to further advance the ideals of a national market system. The regulation includes the order protection, or trade-through rule; access rule (fair access) to market data including quotations; rules on sub-penny trading and on market data.

models, and the advent of dark pools created to facilitate the execution of block orders in a market with shrinking quote sizes. With this come the potential for greater order leakage.[13]

We have also seen a dramatic shift in where trades are executed, and how trading volume is spread across the venues. The NYSE and NASDAQ once had an overwhelmingly dominant share of the market for their issues.[14] But a substantial portion of that volume has shifted to other upstart venues, including the BATS family of markets, and the revamped Pacific Stock Exchange, now known as NYSE Arca, as well as the 40-odd ATSs that are operating today.[15]

Who are the winners of the regulatory changes over the last four decades? Clearly, investors. And because of that, issuers too. Investors now benefit from lower trading costs through tighter spreads, instantaneous executions, a wider variety of order types to achieve their investment objectives, and the availability of multiple innovative trading platforms.

However, with our National Market System, it is never that straightforward, nor is it clear-cut. While our investors have benefitted, the regulations have also created a much more complex, fragmented market, and liquidity is disbursed over many trading venues. Ironically, as the SEC has continued to seek to improve the National Market System, where their centerpiece is transparent markets, a significant byproduct of these efforts has been the proliferation of dark pools, where the lack of transparency seems antithetical to the objectives of the NMS system.[16]

In addition, we also are becoming much more of an order-driven market, with the registered market makers playing a much less prominent role in the provision of liquidity.[17]

---

[13] In a competitive program to encourage trading on exchanges, maker-taker fees, for instance, offer a transaction rebate to trading participants who provide liquidity, charging customers who take liquidity. New York Stock Exchange Systems and Trading Procedures Joel Hasbrouck.George Sofianos.Deborah Sosebee. NYSE Working Paper #93-01 http://people.stern.nyu.edu/jhasbrou/Research/Working%20Papers/NYSE.PDF. The SEC's Order Handling Rules of 1997 and Beyond: *Perspective and Outcomes of the Landmark Regulation*. Richard Lindsey, John Aidan Byrne and Robert A. Schwartz. The Journal of Portfolio Management Spring 2016, 42 (3) 56–64; https://jpm.iijournals.com/content/42/3/56

[14] At the time of writing, the dominant market share of both exchange operators had declined sharply to some 19 percent for the New York Stock Exchange and to 16.62 percent for NASDAQ.

[15] By one early count, prior to this conference, a total of 91 ATSs were registered with the Securities and Exchange Commission by late 2013, according to a story published by Reuters.

[16] The National Market System (NMS) addresses this transparency in the following ways:

> Promotes free market transparency by regulating how all major exchanges disclose and execute trades; facilitates the fair distribution of information, the NMS requires that exchanges make bids and offers available and visible to both individual and institutional investors. In 2005, the SEC issued Regulation National Market System (Reg NMS) to strengthen the NMS and account for changing technology. (Source: Investopedia)

[17] An order-driven market is one where pricing primarily comes from orders placed by investors and other market participants. In contrast, a quote-driven market is one where pricing primarily comes from market making entities obligated to maintain two-sided quotes.

This brings me back to the question I previously posed: Did the SEC give too much latitude to the markets as the NMS system developed? Were the guardrails for innovation established by NMS set too far apart? I think the answer is absolutely not, but there are many who think otherwise. Some believe high-frequency trading should be banned, or at least seriously curbed. There are those who believe the speed at which trades occur and quotes are updated, is a root cause of dramatic fluctuations in the market.

There are some who believe firmly in human intervention. But history tells us that trying to stop technology is a fool's errand, particularly market technology. Looking at all the changes the markets have experienced in the last 10 years, it is clear that we likely do not know what's around the corner from a technology perspective. But it would be dangerous to rein in the market and not make use of the available and evolving technology.

One thing we have learned about the NMS system over the years is that it is an evolutionary process, not a utopian destination point. I think there are also several other lessons learned about the NMS system that we should keep in mind as markets evolve.

First, NMS regulations in the past have tended to apply a one-size-fits all approach, where a particular rule applies to all NMS issues. Given the differences in market characteristics across issues in terms of volume, liquidity, and other attributes, it is not entirely clear that it is best to apply one set of rules designed for highly capitalized, actively traded issues to all issues. I think that it's a very positive development the SEC is conducting the tick size pilot, and potentially looking for a more nuanced and stratified approach to regulation.[18] The data this pilot provides will deepen our understanding of how tick sizes affect market quality, and help us consider new regulatory initiatives that can improve trading in all small-cap securities.

Second, by applying more data analytics to the rule making process, and conducting more robust cost-benefit analyses, we need to continue to focus on maximizing the intended consequences of regulation and minimizing the unintended consequences.

I'm not so sure that the SEC fully anticipated all the issues that have flowed from access fees.[19] It was very encouraging to hear there was consensus to develop a pilot to evaluate trading without maker-taker inducements, among SEC staff, and market participants, and at the SEC's recent Equity Market Structure Advisory Committee.

---

[18] The pilot was approved by the Securities and Exchange Commission. See, SEC Approves Pilot Program to Assess Tick Size Impact for Smaller Companies. Press Release. Securities and Exchange Commission. May 6, 2015. https://www.sec.gov/news/pressrelease/2015-82.html. See also, SEC Approves Pilot Program to Assess Tick Size Impact for Smaller Companies. Center for Financial Stability, May 7, 2015. http://centerforfinancialstability.org/wp/?p=5987.

[19] See, Capital Markets Outlook 2015: The SEC is conducting a broad review of US equity market structure, but the most important proposals are the tick-size pilot, maker-taker rebates, dark pools, and order routing transparency. *Wall Street and Technology*. Ivy Schmerken. January 7, 2015. http://www.wallstreetandtech.com/trading-technology/the-clock-for-market-structure-change-is-ticking/d/d-id/1318135.

Third, given the pace of technology changes, we need to make sure that market regulations are as nimble as possible. This is important because if you look at the National Market System rules promulgated over the last 10 years, they are becoming increasingly detailed and more prescriptive, than the broad policy rules established in the mid-'70s.

Good examples of how much more detailed the SEC's trading-based rules have become are Reg NMS, the SEC's direct market access rule, the recently implemented Regulation SCI, and the SEC's proposed consolidated audit trail.[20]

As the SEC's trading rules become more technical, it will be important for the SEC to modernize them, lest they contain standards that while acceptable now, may not be in the future.

I would like to give you just one example. Regulation NMS, as you know, contains a flickering quote exemption that allows a firm to ignore a protected quote, if the quote was displayed within 1 sec of a trade through.[21] This rule was put in place in 2007, when a second in time was not an eternity—and it probably needs to be modernized now. To the extent possible, hopefully the SEC will consider pushing more detailed rule writing down to the SROs, as was successfully the case with the limit up/limit down process.[22]

I'd also like to mention a few areas where we should consider further examination, given the evolving nature of the NMS system. First, with respect to the extreme intraday volatility that occurred this past August 24 when the Dow dropped 1089 points at the open, (the largest intraday decline in the 119 year history of the Dow) were it not for the trading pauses and limit up/limit down procedures put in place after the Flash Crash, the fluctuations would have been much more dramatic.[23] To my earlier question, this event illustrated not a market out of control, but the value of having appropriate controls in place.

---

[20] Five years later, market access controls evolve into a pyramid of preventive actions. *Bloomberg*. July 28, 2016. https://www.bloomberg.com/professional/blog/five-ears-later-market-access-controls-evolve-pyramid-preventive-actions/. Regulation Systems Compliance and Integrity (Regulation SCI) is a set of rules created by the United States Securities and Exchange Commission to monitor the security and capabilities of US securities markets' technological infrastructure. The Commission adopted Regulation SCI and Form SCI ("Form") in November 2014. https://www.sec.gov/rules/final/2014/34-73639.pdf. The Consolidated Audit Trail (CAT) https://www.catnmsplan.com/.

[21] See, footnote 10.

[22] NASDAQ Frequently Asked Questions: https://www.nasdaqtrader.com/content/MarketRegulation/LULD_FAQ.pdf.

[23] See, footnote 4.

> In June 2012, the Securities and Exchange Commission approved two proposals put forward by the national securities exchanges and FINRA to counter unprecedented volatility in individual stocks and the U.S. stock market following the 2010 Flash Crash. [One of these proposals was "limit up/limit down]. (Source: Investopedia)

However, the volatility and extended trading halts in some instruments, notably ETPs, have highlighted several aspects of the trading pause process that need to be reevaluated. Namely, there is the need for more coordinated openings across exchanges, the application of the limit up/limit down process when stocks come out of a halt, and the application of the limit up/limit down process to ETPs.[24]

Second, the execution quality reports required by SEC Rule 605 have now been in place for 14 years.[25] While this rule continues to provide benefits to investors, it was developed with a market maker model in mind, and the market was far less automated then. This is another example where a rule could be modernized to leverage better analytics for the benefit of investors.

Third, while we will talk a lot today about market structure, it is equally important to remember our regulatory structure, too. Given the level of fragmentation in today's market, in an attempt to hide their footprints and avoid detection, bad actors consciously disperse their trading activity across markets, asset classes and broker-dealers. It is absolutely critical that regulators have a bird's eye view across markets.

At FINRA, through our regulatory service agreements with exchange clients, we are able to put the pieces of the puzzle together for 99 percent of the listed equity market, and 65 percent of the listed options market. Even though the markets are widely fragmented, FINRA's ability to pull together data across exchanges and alternative trading systems, allows us to see one big virtual market, instead of a disjointed patchwork of individual markets.

With our cross-market surveillance program, we can run dozens of surveillance patterns and threat scenarios across the data we gather to look for, among other things, layering, spoofing, algo gaming, wash sales and other manipulative and distortive content.[26] These sophisticated patterns allow us to detect things that we had not been able to detect before.

For example, 40 percent of our cross-market alerts have identified potential manipulative activity by two market participants acting in concert. Oftentimes, that means that you have a customer, or a group of customers, that have multiple accounts at multiple firms, and they orchestrate their activity in a way to make it look independent, when it's really very much coordinated.

Sixty-seven percent of our cross-market alerts identify potential manipulation by a market participant on multiple markets. This statistic also shows how fragmented the markets are, and how bad actors attempt to disperse their activity across markets to avoid detection. Without FINRA's cross-market surveillance program, this conduct would not be detected, and the markets would be less safe.

However, as strong as our cross-market surveillance program is, the implementation of the SEC's proposed consolidated audit trail, or CAT, will take surveillance to

---

[24] Exchange-traded products (ETPs) are types of securities that track underlying securities, an index, or other financial instruments. ETPs trade on exchanges similar to stocks meaning their prices can fluctuate from day-to-day and intraday. However, the prices of ETPs are derived from the underlying investments that they track. Source: Investopedia. See also, footnote 17.

[25] Rule 605. http://www.finra.org/industry/sec-rule-605.

[26] See, FINRA's Surveillance: http://www.finra.org/industry/market-regulation.

the next level by having unique identifiers for accounts, better order auto trail information for options, more detailed information about each trade, and linkages between related equities and options trades, among other things.[27] Surveillance systems should be able to reduce false positives and false negatives, with the result being quicker and more exacting investigations that will better serve investors.

In addition to the equity and options markets, the fixed-income market structure is also ripe for deeper analysis. Recent developments in the bond markets raise questions about market structure, and the role of transparency. Specifically, with TRACE-eligible securities, we were seeing increased trading on Alternative Trading Systems, or ATSs, greater use of request for quote processes, and more executions of custom orders on an agency, or riskless principal basis.[28]

Among the issues we should consider is how we can apply the principles of the National Market System to TRACE—eligible securities. For example, is there a role for pre-trade transparency that will afford investors better information to assess prices and valuations?

I'd like to note that we understand that when you do have pre-trade transparency, there is a certain amount of concern about telegraphing positions. If pre-trade transparency for fixed-income instruments were to be a FINRA initiative, those issues would have to be addressed. But as the fixed-income market continues to expand, it is time we look more closely at whether we can bring the benefits of a National Market System to fixed income.

It is essential to continuously reevaluate regulations in light of rapid market changes. The changes we are talking about today will be the subject of market structure conferences for years to come. And Bob, I think your securities conferences are quite secure with all the issues that are going to be raised! But, more importantly, these changes are a sure sign that, upon its 40th birthday, the National Market System is alive and well.

Even as we continue to work on it, our markets are living, breathing, vital things that continue to evolve. And they require a smart, strong, adaptable regulatory framework to guide that ongoing evolution in the interest of investors.

I'd like to thank you for listening, and I'd be happy to take any questions you might have.

STEVEN SACHS [FBN Securities]: You talked about the Flash Crash of August 24, 2015, when the Dow dropped about 1000-some-odd points, which is statistically more than for the Flash Crash of May 6, 2010. The one area I think made August 24 a more monumental day than the actual Flash Crash was the effect on ETFs. And that has really expanded dramatically since 2010.

I follow some of these ETFs. They track not inactive securities, but some of the biggest companies like General Motors, Facebook, and Amazon. If you look at the

[27] Consolidated Audit Trail(CAT). https://www.catnmsplan.com/.

[28] TRACE is FINRA's system for collecting transactions in corporate bonds and other fixed income instruments from FINRA members and disseminating them to the public.

actual pricing, they were down 20, 30 percent.[29] So as bad as the Dow was at 8 percent move, some of these were down, as I noted, by 20, 30 percent. And what was particularly worse, in my opinion, was the significant amount of volume.

You know, some of these instruments spiked over a million shares. So, somebody was on the side making money. Unfortunately, there were also some on the side losing money. I'd like to know your thoughts, particularly on the ETF area.

GIRA: That is a very good point. I do think one difference between the Flash Crash and August 24 was this: There was more news on the 24th versus the Flash Crash. So, I think you really were looking at a pretty fundamental repricing. I do think in a lot of ways the market held up from that perspective very well. But you are exactly right in the ETP space. You do see a lot of anomalies. For example, some ETPs based on the same benchmark had different results. While the components of ETFs generally were not halted, the ETFs themselves generally remained in a halted state. I think August 24 will be remembered as a moment to reevaluate the interconnectedness between ETFs and the cash market, how these interconnections function, and there are issues to worry about.

The events of August 24 also highlighted that some indices still calculate based off of the prices on the primary markets and that, within this construct, there is the potential for confusion if a primary market opens late while other markets are open. For example, for a variety of valid reasons, the NYSE values the ability to have some potential for human intervention during hectic market openings, and this, at times, can result in trades being slowed down for index-calculation purposes when other markets are open. And so, when markets do not open simultaneously, there is the potential for confusion about what the cash market prices are, and how that impacts derivatively priced instruments such as ETFs.

SACHS: Since you mentioned the primary market, I find it fascinating today how prices are coming to us in the same way they were done hundreds of years ago from the primary market. Today, with the fragmented market, the exchanges account for maybe 10 percent of the volume at a given point in time after 9:35AM, and before 3:55PM. So, the prices that these ETFs are priced on, are based upon, really, really missing prices. And besides the pricing of the primary market, you have also the SIP.[30] We talked about the consolidated tape that has prices from all the fragmented

[29] Steven Sachs is referring to the market plunge of August 24, 2015 compared with the Flash Crash of May 6, 2010, when the Dow Jones Industrial Average dropped more than 1000 points in 10 minutes. Writing about the events of August 24, 2015, a *MarketWatch* story by Francine McKenna, February 1, 2016, provides more context about the impact on the pricing of stocks: "There were big gaps between the value of underlying indexes and the exchange-traded funds that track them, and many of the largest-cap stocks experienced brief swoons that were 10% or more below their previous close." See full story, SEC, industry to dig into Aug. 24 volatility that hit ETFs, big-cap stocks. https://www.marketwatch.com/story/sec-industry-to-dig-into-aug-24-volatility-that-hit-etfs-big-cap-stocks-2016-01-19

[30] See, footnote 6.

markets. But today you still have the SIP.[31] That also is faster, and you get better prices.

GIRA: You're exactly right, those are issues that need to be looked at. And the commission has said they are all looking at those issues as well.

SCHWARTZ: Are you focusing more attention on areas such as liquidity, which I mentioned in my opening remarks today, and also on price discovery? Because those are complex things to get your arms around. In part it's extremely hard to measure them. If you can't measure them how do you study them? But is there more attention being paid to them? Because that is where my focus turns to the question of what is market quality now, compared to the past?

GIRA: From a FINRA perspective, market quality issues are important to us, but they are a little different for us because we don't operate an exchange, only the over-the-counter market where FINRA is not part of the trade execution process.[32] However, our focus increasingly is on best execution, which is sort of related to price discovery and liquidity.[33] We want to make sure that investors are getting the best prices possible. It used to be that you could tell when a trade was done outside the inside, and that was an obvious best execution concern. Now we are dealing with whether an order would have been handled better if it was routed to a different venue from a price improvement standpoint, or from a liquidity standpoint.

I think that best execution is getting more nuanced. The focus is on the quality of prices customers receive, which is impacted by market liquidity and price discovery.

BILL HARTS [Modern Markets Initiative]: You spoke about regulatory efforts to rain in spoofing, which we wholeheartedly agree with.[34] We're wondering if FINRA intends to issue more guidance, or will it try to make clearer what spoofing is? What is the exact behavior you are looking for and targeting?

GIRA: We are in the process of developing monthly report cards for firms that will tell them when they, or their customers, are engaging in conduct that is setting off red flags in our market manipulation program. We will never reveal our secret sauce for detecting things like layering and spoofing, but we will explain in general terms what we think is layering and spoofing and other manipulative conduct.[35] We're hoping that the report cards will educate firms in a richer way, because they

---

[31] The "consolidated tape" is a high-speed, electronic system that reports the latest price and volume data on sales of exchange-listed stocks. The data reflected on the consolidated tape are generated by various market centers, including all securities exchanges, electronic communications networks (ECNs), and third-market broker-dealers. Internet sites that provide updated market information and financial news programs on television often include trade reports from the consolidated tape. Source: SEC.

[32] See, FINRA Market Regulation. http://www.finra.org/industry/market-regulation

[33] See, Best Execution/www.sec.gov/answers/bestex.htm

[34] Spoofing is defined under the 2010 Dodd-Frank Act as, "the illegal practice of bidding or offering with intent to cancel before execution." Some regulators use the terms "spoofing" and "layering" interchangeably.

[35] Ibid.

will actually be able to see the conduct that emanated from them that we flagged as suspicious.

BERNARD DONOFER [Baruch College]: We all talk about the fragmented markets in the US today, and everybody is pretty clear on that. I'm wondering about the fragmentation of the regulatory environment. We have the SEC, the CFTC, and FINRA; and we have the Fed. There's a whole list. And look at the number of regulations coming out of Dodd-Frank, hundreds of thousands of pages have come out of this.[36] Have we overly fragmented the regulatory environment? And as a regulator, how do you reconcile your regulations with everybody else?

GIRA: Excellent question. You know, from like an SEC/CFTC perspective, we definitely are the outlier around the world. Regulation of equities, and all related derivatives, tend to be combined in one organization in other jurisdictions, and that is one obvious thing to think about. Is it likely to happen? Probably not.

In a perfect world, regulators should not overlap, and they each should have their own respective expertise and strengths. The strength of FINRA is that we are the boots on the ground. We are very focused on investor protection and customer-oriented issues. The exchanges have their own strengths too—real-time surveillance, innovative trading systems, and a focus on market structure.

Going back to the cross-market surveillance program that we operate for FINRA and our client exchanges, I think that program reflects how regulators can best cooperate and coordinate in a way that does not duplicate efforts.

We also spend much more time with the SEC coordinating on cases. Sometimes we have stood down, and sometimes they have stood down. From the industry's perspective, we cannot have an environment where you've got multiple regulators looking at the same activity.

DONOFER: I can also see it on the other side as a firm being regulated, having to go through similar information with regulator after regulator. I have talked to friends and they have compliance departments that employ 40, 50, 100 people, who do nothing else except deal with regulators. It becomes very, very expensive and very complex.

GIRA: It has been a focus of FINRA to try to be more efficient in our outreach to firms, and to not ask for the same material two or three times. In fact, we recently launched a system called Gateway, a centralized platform for firms to receive and respond to regulatory inquiries.[37] It also lets FINRA staff see if there are duplicate requests to a firm, or if two areas within FINRA are focusing on the same issue. Admittedly, increasing the efficiency of our processes is still a work in progress though.

---

[36] Formally known as The Dodd–Frank Wall Street Reform and Consumer Protection Act Dodd-Frank was enacted on July 21, 2010, in response to the Great Recession of 2007 to 2009. The law impacts all federal financial regulatory agencies and almost every aspect of the US financial services industry.

[37] See, FINRA Gateway. http://www.finra.org/industry/firm-gateway

LARRY TABB [Tabb Group]: You mentioned two interesting things. One, the whole microwave and the latency race; and second, best execution.[38] The way I perceive things (and I could be wrong), I'm not measured and I'm not as regulated. But folks mostly look at best execution in terms of SIP because that's the regulated data feed. Increasingly, however, folks speed up and use direct feeds and low latency.[39] What is your view on how you will start governing best execution? Will it be more on direct feeds; and what's actually happening in the market? Or the couple of millisecond delay SIP?[40]

GIRA: There are a lot of efforts underway to improve the latency of the SIP level data, and to monitor the relative latency of the SIP feeds at the exchange's direct feeds. We are still using SIP level information. However, we do have direct feeds from the exchanges. It would be very troubling for us to see a firm using the proprietary feeds for its own trading, while using the SIP feeds for its customers' trading—where it was clear that the use of the direct feed was advantageous to the firm. And on that note, let me conclude by thanking you all for listening.

---

[38] See, footnote 28.

[39] For an extensive study on the debate between SIP versus Direct Feeds, see, SIP vs. Direct Feeds Latency—What are the Rules?Bloomberg Tradebook, May 15, 2014 https://www.bloomberg.com/professional/blog/sip-vs-direct-feeds-latency-rules/

[40] Ibid.

Chapter 2
Technology's Challenge to Regulators

Larry Tabb, John Adam, Gregg Berman, Anthony Fortunato, Greg Wood, and John Zecca

LARRY TABB: If we look closely enough at some of the issues that arise with regulation—from technology and the markets, to Reg NMS and the automation of these markets—we realize how our market structure was supposed to work much better.[1] There wasn't supposed to be much concern about who matched with whom electronically because of the processes we developed. Everything was supposed to become much simpler, with no trade tickets and desks in sight.

Yet people are now saying the automated markets today are much more opaque than the old markets, where people actually did business on a manual basis.

On that note, we've a great panel to discuss the challenges of regulating markets in a technology-oriented environment. The premise is NMS, the National Market

[1] Reg NMS (Regulation National Market System) was adopted by the Securities and Exchange Commission in 2005 and introduced two years later to further advance the ideals of a national market system. The regulation includes the order protection, or trade-through rule; access rule (fair access) to market data including quotations; rules on sub-penny trading and on market data.

L. Tabb (✉)
TABB Group, New York, NY, USA

J. Adam
Portware, New York, NY, USA

G. Berman
Ernst & Young, New York, NY, USA

A. Fortunato
Instinet, New York, NY, USA

G. Wood
Deutsche Bank, New York, NY, USA

J. Zecca
NASDAQ, New York, NY, USA

R. A. Schwartz et al. (eds.), *40 Years of Experience with the National Market System (NMS)*, Zicklin School of Business Financial Markets Series,
https://doi.org/10.1007/978-3-030-91912-2_2

System, turning 40.[2] Anthony, like it or not, you're one of the older, more experienced guys on the panel.

ANTHONY FORTUNATO: More experienced, thank you![laughter]

TABB: I should stay away from the word older! The question is how has the National Market System changed the markets from your perspective at Instinet, itself a very original electronic broker.[3] Are the markets better now than before?

FORTUNATO: No question, the markets are better now than ever before. Everybody agrees with that. Spreads are tighter; more volume can go through the pipes, all the exchanges compete. Indeed, there are many ways to execute a stock, and there are dark pools, and exchanges. That said, it's complicated.

If somebody wanted to start a broker dealer today, he or she would have to decide whether to use somebody else's technology, or to build their own instead. And building their own would be an onerous, expensive matter. Connectivity alone to all the protected quotes, understanding what exactly the bid and offers are, and making sure you're doing the appropriate routing for your clients' orders, is very complicated. Reg NMS made it that way.[4]

When this market was being planned, I don't think the planners thought about the speeds we would eventually achieve today in the marketplace. People talk about Moore's Law, about how things become bigger, better, faster, and stronger over time.[5] I don't think they ever envisaged us getting to where we are discussing transactions and trades that are handled in microseconds and nanoseconds.

That said, arguably, we're in a market where one of the largest players can shut down for four hours.[6] I'm going to argue that nobody really saw it coming. There was no blip on a chart to indicate it was on the horizon. No one knew the shutdown was coming.

Still, we're very resilient as an industy. If a customer goes into their E*Trade, or Schwab accounts and enters and sends a market order, the customer is guaranteed to get the best price, the most available price at the time—with all the information, all

[2] Federal legislation launched on June 4, 1975, to amend the Securities Exchange Act of 1934. The 1975 amendments instructed the Securities and Exchange Commission to cooperate with the industry in creating a National Market System along with an ambitious system for the clearance and settlement of securities transactions nationwide. The amendments also provided for the prohibition of fixed-commission rates, promulgated earlier by the SEC in its Rule 19b-3.

[3] History of Instinet. https://www.instinet.com/about-instinet/history.html

[4] The Order Protection Rule requires that each exchange establishes and enforces policies to ensure consistent price quotation for all NMS stocks, which include those on the major stock exchanges as well as many over-the-counter (OTC) stocks. The Order Protection Rule rule is also known as "Rule 611," or the "trade-through rule." Investopedia Protected quotes refers to each exchanges best bid and offer being protected under the regulations.

[5] Moore's Law refers to Moore's perception that the number of transistors on a microchip doubles every two years, though the cost of computers is halved. Moore's Law states that we can expect the speed and capability of our computers to increase every couple of years, and we will pay less for them. Source: Investopedia.

[6] Referring to an incident that saw the New York Stock Exchange's operation shut down for operation for four hours during the trading day.

the derivative information available. And the customer is going to get a fair price.[7] In this regard, Reg NMS has been successful.

TABB: John, that's the view of a self-interested broker, of course. Let's hear from a self-interested exchange. How has the National Market System changed you? Certainly you're not a monopoly anymore.

JOHN ZECCA: Well that's true. First of all, we should probably look at it from the macro level. If Bob Schwartz's point is correct, you've got to look at a ship, at its stability in a storm. The financial crisis showed that the system had a lot of resilience.[8] We did not have clearing issues in the way some industry products had problems. There was still price discovery. It was still a very liquid market.

So, from that very high level, I thought, it has been a success. Here are the two areas I'd like to focus on. The obvious one is the fragmentation and the complexity in the market. Self-interested exchange aside, if you have 40 dark pools, and off-exchange trading, at what point is price discovery impacted? And that is the question people a lot smarter than I are trying to assess. Are we there, are we close?

In Europe there's talk about trying to bring some of that back with limits on dark pools.[9] What happens here is a separate question. But there is definitely room for experimentation on that piece.

The second area that sometimes gets lost is that the National Market System plan did create the concept of pushing us as self-regulatory organizations and exchanges, to work together in the context of plans. These plans could be the likes of the consolidated data plans, the limit up/limit down plan, or the tick pilot that is pending.[10] In the old days, we didn't coordinate like this as an industry. Now when there is a question to be assessed, we are collectively reaching a common conclusion. Hopefully, we are reaching that conclusion with a lot of input from the industry, from people like you, and obviously with input from the SEC.

---

[7] Referring to market participants being able to get all the information to conduct a trade, from options to ETFs, and at the "correct" price.

[8] Referring to the well-documented global financial crisis of 2007 and 2008, tied in the US to subprime mortgage lending. As a reminder, the fall of Lehman Brothers, a global banking behemoth, in September 2008, almost brought the world's financial system, to its knees. The worst recession in 80 years followed, but it took massive amounts of fiscal stimulus in the US to avoid a downward economic spiral, according to financial historians.

[9] Europe is about to make most of its stock market off-limits to secretive "dark pools." John Detrixhe. Quartz. June 27, 2017. https://qz.com/1014472/europe-is-about-to-make-most-of-its-stock-market-off-limits-to-secretive-dark-pools/

[10] The Order Audit Trail System (OATS) is an automated computer system owned by the National Association of Security Dealers (NASD) used to record information relating to orders, quotes, and other related trade data from all equities traded on the NASDAQ, including over-the-counter (OTC) stocks. This system simplifies an order's progression from the initial receipt of the order to its eventual execution or cancellation, for easy tracking for auditing purposes. In early 2017, FINRA proposed the phase out of OATS as a new system, the Consolidate Audit Trail (CAT), comes on line. Source: Investopedia Limit Up/Limit Down. NASDAQ Frequently Asked Questions: https://www.nasdaqtrader.com/content/MarketRegulation/LULD_FAQ.pdf. See, SEC Approves Pilot Program to Assess Tick Size Impact for Smaller Companies. Center for Financial Stability, May 7, 2015. http://centerforfinancialstability.org/wp/?p=5987.

How we have developed market structure is, in some ways, different than it is in other countries. In most of those countries you have a single market. We have created a National Market System in the US because we have preserved competition, which I think we all believe has brought positives to the market.

TABB: Gregg, how has this impacted the regulator's view? Certainly, the regulators kind of brought together the national market structure, pushed NMS, and tried to create a competitive environment. From a regulatory standpoint, have they succeeded? Can they handle this automated market they have now created?

GREGG BERMAN: To help put that into context, I'd like to start with your original question, comparing how it was in the past to what it is today. Because that really informs how regulators have to think about the market.

One of the challenges is this: If we go back in time and ask how have things progressed, where are we at today in comparison, the baseline itself always ends up changing in every single industry. Think about it. About 25 years ago, it probably took the average person about an hour to write a one page memo on a typewriter. How long does it take the average person to write a memo today, using Microsoft Word? The same exact hour! You can't write something in three seconds. Suppose you wanted to produce something of the same quality, and the same style today with the same typos. Well the fonts are still all the same, so you can still do that in about three minutes. But it's going to get kicked back to you! Hey, where's your embedded graph? How come you don't have special fonts, where are your headers and footers?

In other words, the product itself has changed, as I just illustrated in my example. People have not been content, saying we can do the same thing we used to do, but that we can do it better. They say we will do something completely different today.

When we look at Reg NMS and the markets, what's missing from the dialog is that the markets today are doing a lot of things that the markets didn't do in the past. There are, in fact, an enormous number of things the market didn't do in the past. For example, it was not possible 20 years ago for a retail investor to buy anything on a computer like we do today. That construct didn't exist.

Today, it is possible for a retail investor to buy practically anything on a computer. But that creates new challenges for regulators. That's not just from the technology point of view, like saying here's the same kind of order flow today as we had in the past, or here's the latest technology, so how do we stay on top of it? It's not that simple. It's actually new service needs we have created; and this exists in a way that didn't exist in the past.

That really hits home in the combination of new products and services. Instead of having a manual market, or human-driven markets—where humans can only absorb so much information at once—you have a new situation. When you've adapted today's advanced technologies, you can have trading strategies that rely on multiple inputs, indeed thousands of inputs at the same time. We're trading across the board. This is not really talking about, say, fragmentation of different venues, which is certainly one aspect of this. But today you're able to trade many, many different products at the same time. Exchange-traded products embody that entire construct. Understanding how all of that fits together poses some of the greatest challenges for regulators. That's new. This phenomena just did not exist in any way, shape or form, say, even 15 years ago.

TABB: I assume the SEC is looking at some of these issues more closely now than before?

BERMAN: When I was at the SEC, we looked at a lot of these issues. The SEC looked at these issues before I went there too. I'm sure the agency is continuing to look at them since I've left. There's a very, very deep bench today at the agency. In fact, there is a very deep bench at more than just the SEC, but at a lot of other agencies. And a lot of that came from the need to bring a lot more people into those different agencies.

The key is to spend as much time as possible on the empirical side of the equation. There's always the rush to say, hmm, this is a practice, this actually is a conflict, it must be bad. If you don't have any data and there's no way of knowing, then that might be the right answer. But certainly it behooves everybody to make sure that, if there is data, there's something to look at.

TABB: Greg Wood, you work closely with the CFTC, and the futures regulators.[11] Are the issues kind of the same over there? Are they able to deal with the data and the analytics? They don't have the kind of fragmentation you have on the equity side. But there's still a lot of volume.

GREG WOOD: That's very true. I've been involved in the Futures Industry Association for the last five years.[12] I've spent a lot of time working with the CFTC with regards to the electronic trading of futures. As Larry Tabb said, he and I worked together on the CFTC's Technology Advisory Committee that set up a subcommittee on automated and high-frequency trading. As much as there was a lot of focus on the definition of high-frequency trading that Larry and I worked on, we really wanted to make it clear to the CFTC that automated trading is a major part of their markets. It's pervasive, which is a big mind-shift for the regulators to adjust to.

Futures' market structure does not have the same fragmentation as US equities markets. But it does have correlation with many other markets. Futures prices have many inputs, many parameters that come from across the underlying markets and other derivatives markets, including other expiries across the maturity curve of the futures instrument. Traders will price in different factors based on whatever affects those markets. For example, whether they are crops, whether it's interest rates, or whether they are a forward look on the S&P, or the Dow Jones indices.

FIA has spent a lot of time preparing papers to help the regulators understand what has happened as these markets have evolved. The Chicago futures markets finally closed almost all of their trading pits in Chicago, back in July of this year, 2015. The last remaining open outcry futures market in the US is, at the time of this panel, the S&P 500 pit. So, we have now seen pretty much a 99.9 percent transition from floor trading to electronical trading here in the US. This has been a challenge for the regulators, as they adapt to new trading practices, and to the increased

[11] See, Commodity Futures Trading Commission (CFTC) https://www.cftc.gov/.

[12] See, Futures Industry Association (FIA). https://fia.org/

automation of trading. Historically, there were certain challenges around regulating energy, and the bustle of the floor. But as markets have become more automated, regulators now have to deal with far more participants interacting in the electronic futures markets, compared to a relatively small number of traders on the floor in Chicago. This is where the industry has to partner with the regulators to help them understand these new challenges, due to the evolution that has gone on. And also to help the regulator to be better tooled to monitor activity in these fast-paced markets. They must be able to ensure that they're making the right decisions concerning their oversight of how those markets now function.

TABB: Yes, it's a little different as you migrate from a pit where you can punch some guy in the face. It's hard to see somebody punching somebody else in an electronic market!

WOOD: Metaphorically.

TABB: Metaphorically, exactly. What does that actually look like? John, let's bring it back to you. As we transition to a more electronic market, what are some of the gaps, and what are the things you think of that the regulators could do a little bit better job on? What are the glaring gaps? Do you think you're kind of on the right track?

ZECCA: It was a completely different world for surveillance and regulation in the past compared with today. One of the major changes—and I think it's true of all markets, not just in ours—is that the trading platform has taken on the first line of defense in surveillance and regulation that it didn't have in the past. The system, itself, is programmed not to allow certain types of prohibited activity, whether it's trade-throughs, or whether it's certain order types performed in a certain way.[13] The record, of course, is a lot clearer, as far as what happened and when. In some ways, it's easier to deconstruct than it would have been back in the old days, when you had people on the floor.

That said, there are tremendous challenges. One, of course, is the market fragmentation. There is no getting around that in terms of the source of information and the ability to hide, and mask activity across various markets. We've moved in the direction of more consolidated surveillance to try to look across markets and attack activity.[14] I think those are some early steps. But the people doing the surveillance must be more technologically savvy than ever before.

---

[13] The SEC explained it in their final rule on Reg NMS, adapted in 2005:

> A trade-through occurs when one trading center executes an order at a price that is inferior to the price of a protected quotation, often representing an investor limit order, displayed by another trading center.

[14] See, the Consolidated Audit Plan (CAT) https://www.catnmsplan.com/index.html.

> On July 11, 2012, the US Securities and Exchange Commission (SEC) voted to adopt Rule 613 under Regulation NMS requiring the national securities exchanges and national securities associations listed below (collectively, the SROs) to submit an NMS plan (Plan) to the SEC to create, implement, and maintain a consolidated audit trail (CAT).

On my side, we've hired programmers. I think other markets have done the same. And these programmers are not just involved in assessing whether our systems operate correctly, because that is the first line now in the regulation. They are also involved in other analyses of activity. I don't think we've seen new activity, in particular, whether it's a result of high-frequency trading or other things. But I do think we are seeing an acceleration in the ability to do certain types of activity, particularly activity that benefits from speeds. So it has changed the complexion. Perhaps we can get more detail on what some of those are. That has focused our attention in different ways than it might have in the old days, when we were trying to see if people posted the orders quickly enough, or things like that.

TABB: John Adam, from a technology perspective and from an EMS perspective, how do you guys see your clients interfacing with regulators? What are some of the gaps and issues?[15]

JOHN ADAM: As noted by others, we have solved some of this, certainly from an EMS perspective for institutional investors. The OMSs and EMSs are much, much better now at enforcing the firm's policy, right? What a firm can or cannot do with an order is pretty well understood to be based on a set of trading rules that you can put into a trading system. By programming these rules into your system, you can, in effect, protect your traders from getting on the wrong side of these rules and violating securities laws. There are still challenges in the sheer volume of data we're looking at. The sheer volume of data that needs to be consolidated. If something does go wrong in the market,it is enormous. If you look at the objectives of the Consolidated Audit Trail, there are lots of headlines about the petabytes of data to be put together in this regard.[16] Having spent the majority of my career in product management, I am concerned about the SLA in this.[17]

You have all this data, and it's big data. But big data, in and of itself, is never the answer. So it's a lot more important to understand what we are going to ask this massive pile of data. More importantly, how are the regulators going to use it, and what techniques are they going to use? We can't just have a human look at all of that data in three days, and then expect a definitive picture of what's going on.

What sort of techniques, analysis or artificial intelligence from machine learning can be used to reconstruct this, at the speed to which the markets perform? Because

[15] An Order Management System (OMS) is a software application for facilitating and managing the order and trade flow between the (buy-side) client and different execution venues. In contrast to an OMS, an Execution Management System (EMS), is focused on real-time trading, real-time market data, and analytics. Source ITIVITI.

[16] See, The Consolidated Audit Trail (CAT) https://www.catnmsplan.com/. A petabyte (PB) is a measure of memory or data storage capacity that is equal to 2 to the 50th power of bytes. There are 1024 terabytes (TB) in a petabyte—or 1 million gigabytes (GB)—and approximately 1024 PB make up one exabyte. Source: techtarget.com.

[17] A service-level agreement (SLA) is a contract between a service provider and its customers that documents what services the provider will furnish and defines the service standards the provider is obligated to meet. Source: techtarget.com. The speaker further elaborated in a follow up that his broad-based concern was with the rules governing data collection and management, and the parameters of trade execution, and in how this would manifest itself in so-called SLAs.

there is a fundamental mismatch between how fast the systems that are creating the markets, that are quoting and are executing the orders work, and how quickly a human can analyze what all of those machines did in the aggregate. That's probably the biggest gap I see, and the biggest concern.

TABB: Given that a lot of your clients are buy-side institutional investors, are they able to keep up and manage this? I guess to a certain extent their execution quality is impacted by this?

ADAM: A lot of our customers right now are looking at data warehousing initiatives, in order to have all that information electronically available in one place. So if one of the SROs, or the regulatory bodies, come knocking, they have the data available to present to them.[18] That piece is well understood. From the buy-side perspective, an EMS can write a pretty impressive transaction file. However, reading that transaction file is not the way I'd want to spend a Friday night, I must add!

TABB: Anthony, you guys are very involved with electronic trading, as well, on the agency side. How are you seeing and supporting your clients on this regulatory side? Is the buy-side being serviced well here?

FORTUNATO: I would say that 80 percent of all broker-dealers are at a point where transparency is paramount for all of their clients. That's become front and center for everybody over the past three or four years. Any buy-side trader today can ask and expect their broker to explain where the buy-side trader's order is executed. The buy-side can ask their broker: Did the broker provide or remove liquidity; what instruction caused the broker to trade on behalf of the buy-side at that time, at that price? So in and of itself, the buy-side has more information than they've ever had in their lives.

I started my career at Morgan Stanley in the IT department. Then I moved out to the derivatives desk. When I was in the derivatives desk, people would give me orders at 3:00 p.m. on a Wednesday to trade a spread in Hong Kong, and they would give me a one percent limit.[19] Invariably, they'd get a fill somewhere around the one percent on that spread. But they had no market data. They would not know what the prices were at any given point in time. They wouldn't know if they lined up. Invariably, they might get a better price than the one percent, and it would be because the high and low of the day didn't allow a worse price to happen. Now, they can go on their Bloomberg machine for information. They can go on their Reuters machine. They can get any amount of information they want at any time from multiple places.

Sometimes it leads to analysis paralysis. We had a client ask us to look at how many of their trades transacted outside the NBBO.[20] Off the top of my head, I'm

[18] SROs, or Self-Regulatory Organizations, are non-governmental organization empowered to create and enforce their own industry and professional regulations and standards.

[19] As Anthony Fortunato explained in a follow up, he would get, for example, a "stub" order, say to trade in Hong Kong, with a one percent limit, which is the difference between the two prices involved. So in this example, he would be satisfied to sell at 10 and buy at say 9.99, a "one percent differential," otherwise known as the spread.

[20] National Best Bid and Offer (NBBO). "National best bid and national best offer means, with respect to quotations for an NMS Security, the best bid and best offer for such security that are

guessing very few, if any. But when you try to match up all the time stamps that you get, my time stamp versus NASDAQ's time stamp, versus my data provider's time stamp, there's as many as 75 quote changes say in a millisecond transaction time. In that time frame, the stock could be quoted that many times—multiple times—in a range from 25.06 to 25.14.It's very had to match that up, right?[21]

But as I stated in the beginning, you should know that when you send your order, you are getting the best price at that time for that security, relative to any other derivative market, any ETF, any future. You are getting the correct price. And people should be very comfortable with that.

TABB: We'll talk about regulations and markets, technology and infrastructure, and things like that. Let's bring it back to Gregg Berman and John Zecca. We've seen a couple of pretty high-profile prosecutions on spoofing.[22] This idea of let me put in a large order that I'm not going to actually get filled on, push it in my direction, and then make a profit that way. Certainly the exchanges and the regulators are getting better at catching these things. But how do you think this is going to change behavior?

BERMAN: I can speak more generally on the constructs around spoofing and layering.[23] Some of the biggest challenges the regulators have faced are in a market where it was much more like one person, or even one machine, trading a few things at once. In this scenario, there was little reason to put a quote in and then take that quote out, and then put the quote back in and take that quote out again.

You can imagine a person who's just manually trading nothing. Pick whatever stock you want, if that person says order, cancel, order, cancel, order, cancel, you say well there can't possibly be a reason for that. There could be something manipulative happening.

But in today's environment there are an incredible number of economically-driven reasons to place orders and to cancel them very quickly, that are completely legitimate. A lot of it has to do with the fact that not only are there multiple markets, but you are trying to keep prices in line between different stocks and derivatives, and different types of ETFs.

When regulators look at the construct of someone sending an order, it is very difficult to look at that in the abstract, or just in that one instance, and to say this person sends an order and then cancels it. Is that spoofing? Is that layering if it is done on both sides of the market? The answer is always you don't know. You have to see what else that person is doing. What's the strategy employed? What's the

---

calculated and disseminated on a current and continuing basis by a plan processor pursuant to an effective national market system plan." Source: Code of Federal Regulations/C.F.R. § 600(b)(42).

[21] As he explained in a follow-up, he was referring to the fact that a stock can have multiple prices in a transaction, so then the questions become, which one of those prices are you supposed to be analyzing?

[22] Spoofing is defined under the 2010 Dodd-Frank Act as, "the illegal practice of bidding or offering with intent to cancel before execution." Some regulators use the terms "spoofing" and "layering" interchangeably.

[23] Ibid.

economic reason for doing that? Most of the time you'll find that not only is that okay, but if the activity wasn't happening there would be direct harm to retail investors. Because the retail investors would be getting really bad prices when they try to line up a certain product.

That means there is some percentage of time that someone is actually doing something bad. Perhaps they're doing it for the sole purpose of trying to manipulate the market. The big challenge is being able to filter out those types of things, especially echoing some of the comments that Tom Gira made this morning.[24] A lot of the things involve multiple markets. And that compounds the issue, making it even worse.

John, you had talked about how, when we have the consolidated audit trail, what would we do with the data?[25] If it takes 25 hours to do a day of surveillance, that doesn't work because that means by the end of the week you've practically lost a full day's work and, by the end of the year, you're two months behind. The regulators and the industry, itself, has to go to a more disbursed model. That's where the SROs of the world are doing first line defense. Market participants are doing the zero line defense by saying, 'Hey, I'm on the buy-side, I see something I don't like.' In this way these same market participants can talk directly to their broker if they suspect some odd, or improper trading activity. Then you have the bigger giant surveillance systems that try to piece everything together when it is needed.[26]

TABB: Isn't that mostly automated? I would assume that with the millions of quotes and trades that is kind of automated.

ADAM: The first line of defense, I think is this. None of the heads of desks I work with are waiting for the regulators to call them and say, wait, "I think you might have got gamed here." They are having, as I'm sure Anthony can attest to, vigorous conversations with their brokers about the price they got if they feel that something has gone wrong, or that something untoward has happened.

The challenge at the SROs is context, right? Big data without a context, or a sense of what you're asking it, or what else is happening in the backdrop, is pretty impressive, particularly among the largest asset managers and investment banks who advertise during major golf tournaments. But it's really useless if you don't know what you want to ask it, and if you don't have a sense of what your model of the context is.

If it's looking at who's got both sides of the order, we need some definition, or at least a good enough definition of what was the intent. Were these orders a pair? Was somebody on both sides of the market? What else was this firm doing? What body is ultimately responsible for it? And if you don't have that, then, yeah, you are going to get into these gigantic market data collection projects where it's going to take 25 or more hours to analyze a day's worth of data. That's where you get into trouble.

---

[24] Tom (Thomas)Gira was a keynote speaker at the 2015 conference, as referenced elsewhere in this book. https://www.finra.org/about/governance/finra-executives#market

[25] See, footnote 14.

[26] Referring to the Consolidated Audit Trail.

TABB: Anthony, you're smiling and nodding, do you want to add something?

FORTUNATO: We are scrutinized a lot by the regulators and clients, by the media, and by the industry in general. We welcome it. Our clients should be very comfortable in knowing that we will provide them with all the information we can possibly provide them within our limitations. They should also know that as an agency only broker-dealer, they don't have to trade with me. We do our best to execute at the best price at all times on their behalf. But then the latest round of public headlines came out on various allegations and scandals in the markets—and I am confused. Who is at fault in all of this? I don't know if it is the trader who is actually being fingered and asked the question at the center of the allegations, or whether it is the trader's boss, the trader's boss's PM, or the PM's investor's consultant who is getting the question.[27]

TABB: Somewhere up the line.

FORTUNATO: But eventually it comes down to us. Where why did this happen? You have to respond to client questionnaires and client requests. If you can't respond, then you're in a lot of trouble.

TABB: John, on the exchange side and the regulatory arm, how does an exchange look at this? Let's get back to the spoofing issues. How will it impact you guys, and how do you look at the markets and at the order flow that goes through it?

ZECCA: It's a timely question. The *New York Times* had an article asking whether the Panther case will change the complexion of spoofing, and sort of how traders trade.[28]

The first question is how do you define it? Of course, that is the hard part. On some levels, like on the futures side, with Dodd-Frank the government stepped in and sort of said, all right, this is now the official definition.[29] That's how the criminal indictment against Panther Trading moved forward.

What we've recognized is that there's two words, two phrases, that are usually used—one is you didn't have the intent to actually execute the trade; and the second

---

[27] In a follow-up, Anthony Fortunato said he was asking where this deep probing was really coming from. Was it coming from the trader, or his PM; or did some consultant ask the PM what their processes it; or did the people who gave the PM the money ask the question? "You answer it differently depending on where the question is coming from," Fortunato noted. At time of conference, several firms, such as Barclays and ITG, brushed up against the regulators on questionable trading practices, triggering much industry reflection by customers and trading firms. "It was basically a whack a mole kind of reaction to the events," said Fortunato.

[28] High-Frequency Trader Charged With Manipulating Commodity Prices. William Alden. October 2, 2014. *New York Times*. Dealbook. https://dealbook.nytimes.com/2014/10/02/high-frequency-trader-charged-with-manipulating-commodity-prices/

[29] The Dodd-Frank Wall Street Reform and Consumer Protection Act is a massive piece of financial reform legislation passed during the Obama administration in 2010 as a response to the financial crisis of 2008. Named after sponsors Sen. Christopher J. Dodd (D-Conn.) and Rep. Barney Frank (D-Mass.), the act contains numerous provisions, spelled out over roughly 2,300 pages, that were to be implemented over a period of several years. Dodd-Frank established a number of new government agencies tasked with overseeing the various components of the act and, by extension, various aspects of the financial system. President Donald Trump pledged to repeal Dodd-Frank and, in May 2018, signed a new law rolling back significant portions of it. Source: Investopedia.

which appears from time to time, is that, the trades were not correlated to the market. They were essentially outside the market.

Neither, by itself, is a full definition of the conduct. It certainly would not be the sole criteria we would use to bring a case. Which is why we issued some guidance earlier this year, as I think some other markets have, by saying, look, it's a pattern. I'm not going to speak to the facts of the Panther case directly. But with some of these cases that we've brought, or have seen develop, the pattern does tend to be obvious. You can watch their activities switch sides, in a very rhythmic pattern across the market that does not bear a direct relationship to market making or other functions.

TABB: So you can see some of this stuff going on?

ZECCA: It's generally a huge build-up on one side of the market, with small trades on the other side trying to see where the market is. As the market moves to the other side, you sort of move to try to get the best price. Then, with all your volume, you're trying to push the market on the other side up. Then you execute and quickly switch sides. It doesn't correlate necessarily to activity in the market generally with the pattern of trading of the stock, or it doesn't vary by stock. It is that pattern that comes through.

For Chief Compliance Officers and others who have to figure where is the line, there is never going to be a number. If we said, it's 59 orders, everyone would do 58. I think the question really comes down to, are you pulling the market towards you, not in correlation with the size of your order or other normal factors? And is this happening over time, and in a consistent pattern on both sides?

Do I think there is room for improvement in definitions? Yes, but it is always going to be a hard one to define. But whether it's us, whether it's FINRA, whether it's the SEC, it is definitely something that's getting a lot of focus right now.

TABB: Do you think we'll be seeing more of these cases?

ZECCA: I do.

TABB: So now they're going to gang up on spoofers I guess?

BERMAN: I would like to echo something John said about the CCOs (Chief Compliance Officers). There is a fine line between activity that involves orders and cancellations that would be considered spoofing; and perhaps activity that would be considered more economic. If I was a CCO, I would not sleep because of this. Here's the reason. If you have oversight of a group of traders who began trading in a certain fashion, a lot of the algos, whether they're liquidity taking or liquidity providing, are seeking to pick up on economic patterns. But when the price action is dictating the economic pattern, those same algos begin to pick up on the price action, itself. It is very conceivable that a market participant would say that it looks like completely legitimate activity when an algo does something in this scenario. As the algo is then tweaked and programmed across a bunch of stocks with back testing, someone might observe, "Hey, this algo is doing fairly well, but actually the activity it is triggering is spoofing." In this kind of scenario, it may not be clear to someone how this transition occurred from one activity to the other activity that looked like spoofing. It is very possible that that can happen.

If I was a CCO, I would be paranoid that, even with the best intentions, you could have traders who end up having inadvertently stepped into this. Clearly there are some who have probably advertently done it. But in some of these cases, I think market participants will have to start looking at how algos are operated to avoid these kind of situations. Then they will have to ask themselves, do we even do anything like that? And if we do, how would we even know as a firm?

TABB: That brings me to some thoughts that I had had years ago. In terms of AI, or Artificial Intelligence, and markets, let's just turn these machine learning engines on. With a bunch of back testing data, let's find economic patterns. I'm not even sure what this thing is doing but I know it makes money. That makes that kind of thing kind of really, really dangerous. So you have to know what your machine is doing so that you don't run afoul of the rules.

Let's bring Greg into this. CME Rule 575 was one of the first codified rules out there around spoofing.[30] How has that impacted the futures side? Clearly, Panther was more on the energy side. That's I guess where they caught them.

WOOD: Energy futures, yes. I was in Chicago last week for an industry conference when the news broke about the criminal case and the prosecution.[31] The case has generated a lot of mixed feelings, mostly concern as to what this means for the futures markets and their participants. The CFTC, and the self-regulatory organizations in the futures space, such as the CME, have been very proactive in market surveillance over several years. The Panther situation was a prosecution first by the CME, and then by the CFTC. Now it's gone through a criminal prosecution with the Department of Justice, so it's gone one step further.

What does this mean in terms of the futures markets? You have an exchange like the CME that issues Rule 575, which refers to *disruptive trading prohibited*. It says very clearly that you cannot place orders unless you have the intent to trade. As a very simple example, this means that at the time of this panel, test orders are now not allowed on the CME's Globex platform.[32]

TABB: One trading player recently got nailed in relation to spoofing. Their first trade was like a test trade.

WOOD: The FIA immediately went back to the CME and said, look, we use test orders for legitimate reasons, as well. It's called *production connectivity testing*.[33]

---

[30] CME Rule 575, Disruptive Practices Prohibited, prohibits the entering of an order or causing the entry of an order with the intent to cancel the order before execution or to modify the order to avoid execution. This practice is commonly known as spoofing. https://www.cmegroup.com/rulebook/files/cme-group-Rule-575.pdf. CME adopts new Rule 575 prohibiting certain disruptive trading practices. *Norton Rose Fulbright*. September 8, 2014. https://www.regulationtomorrow.com/us/cme-adopts-new-rule-575-prohibiting-certain-disruptive-trading-practices/

[31] US trader found guilty in landmark 'spoofing' case. Philip Stafford. Lindsay Whipp and Gregory Meyer. *Financial Times*. November 3, 2015. https://www.ft.com/content/d7197620-8287-11e5-8095-ed1a37d1e096

[32] See, Globex. https://www.cmegroup.com/globex.html

[33] Since 2015 there have been several modifications to CME Rule 575, which have slowly allowed certain types of test orders. Its primary purpose is to prevent orders being placed on the exchange without any intent to trade. For example, by creating a false sense of depth in a market to facilitate

We're not testing algos. We're testing basically every Sunday night when futures systems restart for trading 24 hours a day, 5.5 days a week, to make sure the systems are up and functioning correctly.[34] Brokers usually place an order through to the market before our clients do. Historically, that's not something that has been considered disruptive, but under the rules of 575 it now is.

We have asked the CME to implement a test symbol for the purpose of placing test orders as explained previously. In equities, everyone has been using the test ticker ZVZZT for many years, but to finally get a futures test symbol is a relatively amazing thing. However, under the current CME implementation, it is only available during the pre-open, so I can place an order and cancel it without intent to trade, since I am using the test symbol, and am placing the order when the matching engine is not matching orders and generating trades.

At present, we don't believe it will be offered during the trading session because of the concern that market participants will use it for more and more production tests, leading to potential concerns regarding the capacity of the matching engine.[35]

The Panther case has raised a very interesting point about the ability of market participants to place orders *without* the intent to trade, but *with* the intent to avoid potential disruption to the market through a faulty system.

But it now has many people in the futures space concerned about what is *intent* to trade. The word *intent* has always been used to mean that you *meant* to do something. Indeed, the word intent has always been used within the futures space to mean that you *meant* to do something. For example, a self-match is only considered a wash trade if there was intent to trade with yourself for a manipulative reason. Self-matches can happen in automated markets without intent.[36]

Previous definitions for spoofing in the futures world haven't mentioned intent. When we get to Dodd-Frank and some of the language used in the Panther case, we

disruptive practices such as layering or spoofing. Greg Wood added in a follow-up: "It's basically a 'pipe clean' test to make sure that all of the systems that are used by a broker to route orders to the market are up and running correctly. The broker will place a small order—without the intent to trade—to make sure that the order reaches the market. Once the order has been accepted, it is then cancelled. This gives the broker the confidence that the systems are working before their clients start placing orders when live trading starts in earnest."

[34] "Futures markets are open nearly 24 h a day, starting on Sunday evening and finally closing on Friday afternoon," explained Wood in a follow-up note. "This means that there is very limited time to recycle systems, unlike equities markets where they are closed overnight. The ability to place a test order for futures markets is very important to make sure that the broker and client systems are working correctly in a 24 × 5.5 environment."

[35] As of writing, this is still the case. See, CME Global Test Products. https://www.cmegroup.com/confluence/display/EPICSANDBOX/CME+Globex+Test+Products

[36] Refers to, "the matching of orders for accounts with common ownership, within and across different Globex Firm IDs and within and across clearing firms," according to the CME, in a description of the CME Globex Self-Match Prevention Functionality.

now get into the concept of *deception*.[37] Now this is where it gets very scary from a real world point of view.

If I use an iceberg order in any market, which is the simplest execution algo you could find, is that *deceit*?[38] I can use an iceberg order to show only 100 contracts out of the thousand that I want to trade, because I know I could potentially have an impact on price discovery, by showing my full size in the order book. My intent is to trade all 1000 contracts out of it. But I'm doing what I would naturally do as a trader. I'm trying to be smart about how I trade. There is no deceit, just normal practice.

Similarly, if I'm a momentum trader, which is very common in the Commodity Trader Advisor space in futures, and I'm chasing the market, and trying to place orders as the market moves away from me, then I'm having to cancel out stale orders as I continually chase that market. There is intent to trade, but the orders are not getting to the market fast enough. With regard to potential spoofing, I'm not on both sides of the market. I'm following it as it's going up, and I'm following it as it's going down. I'm not switching constantly. But again, what's my intent there? Is it the fact that I'm placing orders, and then rapidly canceling? Is there a concept of deception behind that?

We would argue not. And this is what has made us very scared in the futures market. We need to have further conversations with the regulators about what are the legitimate practices, and what are clearly manipulative practices.

TABB: Are there answers? Do we have answers to these questions, or are they still questions?

WOOD: They are still questions. These are still items where it comes back to cooperation with the regulators, and the industry, to work through these points. Where something may have seemed closed, it is wide open. It has a lot of people very nervous now, and not just in utilizing algos to *preserve* alpha, for which execution algos are prevalent in just about every asset class. These algos generate and cancel orders as markets move, based on a selected execution strategy.

TABB: Gregg, do you want to step in?

BERMAN: Greg Wood brought up something that has puzzled me for a few years. We talk about price discovery in the market, and the importance of price discovery. But it's like be careful what you wish for. Today it is very, very common, almost ubiquitous, that if you are a buy-side firm, and you want to buy a lot of

---

[37] Section 747 of the Dodd-Frank Wall Street Reform and Consumer Protection Act amended the Commodity Exchange Act to expressly prohibit certain disruptive trading practices. Specifically, CEA section 4c(a)(5) states that it shall be unlawful for any person to engage in any trading, practice, or conduct on or subject to the rules of a registered entity that:

(a) Violates bids or offers;
(b) Demonstrates intentional or reckless disregard for the orderly execution of transactions during the closing period; or
(c) Is, is of the character of, or is commonly known to the trade as, 'spoofing' (bidding or offering with the intent to cancel the bid or offer before execution).

[38] See, Iceberg Order. https://www.investopedia.com/terms/i/icebergorder.asp

something, you're not going to signal that to anybody. You're going to put it through an execution algo. Why? Because there is definitely a price for liquidity.

If you want to buy 50,000 shares of even a large-cap stock, you are not going to get the inside bid, you're going to have to move that price. There's an economic number. Whether or not that economic number is say 3 cents or 5 cents doesn't matter; you're going to try to pay less than what that is.[39]

WOOD: That's called market impact, that's a well-qualified term.

BERMAN: So there's an impact. Now some people think that the impact, the natural impact, is zero, so any impact is negative. Some people think the natural impact should be zero, that any impact is problematic. Yet a lot of studies show otherwise, that there will always an impact. It can't be zero. The idea of no market impact does not add up. Certainly, if I want to buy 10 million shares of something, to say I have a right to do that and not move the price at all, seems a bit unrealistic.

There has to be an impact. The question is whether or not you are paying greater than the impact, in which case the market is not efficient for price discovery. Or, if you are paying less than the impact, in that case the market is not efficient in price discovery. It works both ways. I'm not quite sure how prepared the industry is to go down the path, Greg, that you had mentioned, about what's deception and what is not deception. It would be quite crazy to get to a place where you said if I wanted to trade 5000 shares, and I knew that, but I only put 100 shares in the market at a time, am I somehow deceiving the market because I am not allowing it to do full price discovery? I If you're an academic, the answer I think is yes. It's the exact same thing as cancelling an order. I'm just not showing all of my interest.

TABB: That would be bad.

BERMAN: That would be a bizarre outcome to get to.

TABB: Right.

BERMAN: The wording used when talking about different types of spoofing is important, especially as the industry grapples with what is and is not spoofing behavior and activity. These are very, very big issues. I don't see that the industry has really started grappling with them yet.

ADAM: I think that this is one of the biggest regulatory gaps, that we don't have a good means of systematically determining intent. You can't look at these actions. It's not just with equities or futures. If you look at the headlines, there's the same exact problem happening in the FX markets right now.[40]

Then there is all of the debate around last look.[41] Did my bank pull that price because Switzerland accidentally announced in the middle of the day that they're

---

[39] Referring to how much the market is moved to buy the stock, for example, 3 or 5 cents.

[40] FX is for Foreign Exchange.

[41] Trading practice that was once more common in the FX markets when someone puts out a request for a quote, and where the last look gives the dealer an opportunity to adjust their price. The concept of "last look" was indeed once prevalent in FX trading, where a dealer could decide whether to accept or reject a client's order depending on whether it was in the dealer's best interest to do so. See, Principle 17 of the FX Global Code of Conduct. https://www.globalfxc.org/docs/fx_global.pdf

depegging from the euro, and it saved me from a problem? Or, were they gaming my order by cancelling it? But now they know that I'm a buyer of Swiss francs.

Until we can get to a regulatory model that says here's the amount of time, and factors we'll consider when determining intent,—and here's the data that we will look at, it's pretty challenging. It is challenging to have a 72-hour deadline, or goal of determining what occurred when something systematically happens in the market

TABB: I don't know what the right word is. But really the buy-side's intent is pretty quantified because the PM gives the trader an order, the order is sitting on the guy's blotter, and it's the trader's job to get that order done.

ADAM: I would agree with that. The buy-side already has controls. They're even stronger over in Europe under MiFID 2.[42] If I'm sitting in Europe on a trading desk, I have to say why this particular order is going to this particular broker, and what do I expect to get out of that? Do I want them to go stealth?[43] Do I want them to start in a dark pool? Do I want them to pace the VWAP? I have to say, and then I can give all of that over to the regulators to do it.[44]

Here's where I think the buy-side has the biggest challenge. Who's on the other side of that order, and what are they doing? Why should I have to explain that I'm trading a million shares of a stock to someone who is trading in lots of 100? What benefit do they get out of the information? I know what I lose; I don't know what they gain.

WOOD: Here's a perspective from the broker-dealer side. Institutional buy-side investors have a lot of compliance checks that they must go through. As a broker-dealer providing access to equity markets, or as a Futures Commission Merchant (FCM), providing access to the futures markets, I have a responsibility from the regulators to oversee the access to the marketplace. That makes me very cautious in terms of who I give access to.

If I give direct access to the market where a client is not going through my pipes, instead it's going direct to the Chicago Mercantile Exchange, then I need to make sure I know that client very well.[45] I need to at least understand their trading strategies. There is a concern due to the scrutiny that's now going on around spoofing and other disruptive trading practices. There may be instances where market participants are engaged in practices that may be deemed disruptive, and since they are coming through your access to the exchange, whether it is through your pipes, or your membership on the exchange, then you as the FCM are on the hook for their activity. If the regulators pick up on that before you as the FCM notices, there is the potential for *failure to supervise* a client's trading activity as their FCM. This potential regulatory view will not just scare the buy-side, it will also scare the broker-dealers, or FCMs from providing certain types of market access.

---

[42] What is Mifid II and how will it affect EU's financial industry? Far-reaching rules will have a big impact on everything from banks to brokers. *Financial Times*. September 15, 2017 https://www.ft.com/content/ae935520-96ff-11e7-b83c-9588e51488a0

[43] "Stealth" is a trading term to describe the search for non-displayed liquidity, typically in an algorithmic driven trading program.

[44] VWAP is the Volume Weighted Average Price.

[45] Referring to sponsored access.

TABB: That was an issue maybe eight or ten years ago on the clearing side. That was when, all of a sudden, there were all these lawsuits around corresponding clearing. Anthony, you're dealing with a lot of clients you provide access to.[46] Is this something you're worried about?

FORTUNATO: There's a lot more to trading than just buy this, or sell at this price. There's buy this but don't be more than this percent of the volume, don't interact with these venues, don't go to this dark pool. I'm prohibited by my client from trading at this broker. It's a lot more than just buy or sell this.

The August 24th Flash Crash offered a really interesting glimpse into the market.[47] People were pounding the table, saying we should get rid of market orders![48] And I am sitting there and saying, why are we getting rid of market orders? I think a market order is one of the most elegant orders available. It forces people to make a decision immediately with all the information they have available. Who am I to say anything if a client sends a market order in? I know you sent the market order in, so will I put a 3 percent limit on it, because I don't think you really mean a market order?[49] Really? My client's instructions are a market order. So let's just say I did put a 3 percent limit on the order, and then all of a sudden the stock falls out of bed, and I didn't trade anything? I then go back to the client, saying yeah, I was working in your best interest to make sure that you don't disrupt the market![50] A regulator might look at me two and a half years later and say, why did you send this order down and disrupt the market?[51]

It's very difficult, right? You can put all the controls around that as you want. I think limit up/limit down, is excellent.[52] The fact that they codified it across all

[46] As background, many of the issues arising from clearing, result from the inability to meet margin requirements due to deliberate or overtrading, analysts say.

[47] Aug. 24, 2015 Flash Crash Part Of Wall St. History. Sumit Roy. http://etf.com. August 22, 2016. https://www.etf.com/sections/features-and-news/aug-24-2015-flash-crash-part-wall-st-history?nopaging=1. What happened during the Aug 24 'flash crash.' Bob Pisani. *CNBC*. September 25, 2015. https://www.cnbc.com/2015/09/25/what-happened-during-the-aug-24-flash-crash.html

[48] Referring to the Flash Crash of August 24, 2015.

[49] Anthony Fortunato explained in a follow-up how some market observers had reacted to the aforementioned ETF crash, in the manner of Monday morning quarter backers, touting ideas like a 3 percent limit, in an effort by their reckoning to offset the worse impact of that crash. Regardless of the potential risks or rewards of how that might have played out, Fortunato noted how he is obliged tofollow the clients' instruction.

[50] Referring to an example here of a 3 percent limit on the price of a stock order. Thus, if the stock is trading currently at 20 when a market order is received, this trader would stop trading at 19.40, or 3 percent down from 20. It is, therefore, referring to a 3 percent deviation from the last traded price.

[51] Anthony Fortunato explained in a follow-up that he was referring to the fact that industry regulators typically don't get around to questioning any suspicious, or unusual order, until years after it is transacted. Thus, if the marketplace wants to introduce a new trading rule, he is fine with it. But it is a different matter if a client wants to change the legal parameters of an order type. He can't accept that demand since regulators would not condone it to begin with.

[52] See, NASDAQ Frequently Asked Questions: https://www.nasdaqtrader.com/content/MarketRegulation/LULD_FAQ.pdf

exchanges, instead of letting different exchanges have disparate rules is excellent. People really have to step back, and say one or two problems are going to happen. It's just the nature of the complexity in these situations. There will be a problem, and you have to have a little bit of patience. If it's a problem that happens today, two months from now, four months from now, six months from now, then that's a bigger problem and a different matter.[53] If it's a problem that happens today, you realize it, you fix it, and it never happens again. That's a good solution. But you shouldn't be penalized for having that problem in the first place.

TABB: I'll open it up for questions.

JACK FRANCIS [Professor of Finance, Baruch College]: I'm curious about this new Reg SCI.[54] Can anybody help me resolve my uncertainty? Is the hardware in place? Is the software in place? Is it implemented at your office? Is it implemented at your competitors' office? When can we expect it to go public?

TABB: It's supposed to be live now, right?

ZECCA: It went live. We're probably the most directly affected, although some of you may have ATSs that are impacted. So it's exchanges, high-volume ATSs that are impacted, and it's sort of about resiliency. You've got to have testing. I will say though, when you speak to the Commission, invariably it comes back to cyber security. I think from their perspective that is one of the key issues.

We've put a lot of our time into Reg SCI. There are a lot of players that we talk about in this fragmented market. I agree with my colleagues. One of my main fears is the brittle market concept that we have to have this perfect market, or else we stop. That is a problem. You know, we should be able to handle significant outages, other issues, and keep the markets going, unless it's an extreme emergency.

In this context, for the parties that are covered it is live, the testing part, which I think will help bring in the industry. You're supposed to choose your firms that you believe need to test with you. Some of that doesn't go live until the industry testing next year. So the first piece is in place now, the second piece in 2016. But there are gaps. The SEC has recognized this. The SEC asked if it should be broader. And as an industry we will have to decide whether that's necessary.

TABB: SCI is a rule basically that came out of the Flash Crash, and some of the issues around SIP outages.[55] Some of the folks that are not covered are the

[53] That is, if the problem is recurring, versus a one-off problem.

[54] Regulation Systems Compliance and Integrity (Regulation SCI) is a set of rules created by the United States Securities and Exchange Commission to monitor the security and capabilities of US securities markets' technological infrastructure. The Commission adopted Regulation SCI and Form SCI ("Form") in November 2014.

[55] Flash Crash of May 6, 2010 lasted about 36 min, erasing 998.5 points in the Dow Jones Industrial Average and then quickly recouped much of the losses as the various indexes rapidly rebounded in this high-speed, electronic trading phenomena. SIP is the acronym for Securities Industry Processor. https://www.nasdaq.com/articles/nasdaq-sets-record-straight-about-sip-2016-10-25. SEC PRESS RELEASE: SEC Proposes to Modernize Key Market Infrastructure Responsible for Collecting, Consolidating, and Disseminating Securities Market Data. Seeks to Introduce Competitive Forces to Core Components of the System for the First Time. February 14, 2020.

internalizers and the smaller ATSs.[56] Do you think we'll get to a point where those guys are included?

ZECCA: There has to be some level of proportionality for the cost involved, particularly if we're asking about the broker community. The trouble is that some of the bigger problems can come from a failure at a smaller firm. You don't have to be a huge firm to pump a lot of erroneous orders into the market.

Let's make the tweaks, talk about expansion, but at some point the whole market has to be covered by some level of protection. Now the Market Access Rule, and some other rules that apply to broker-dealers, have tried to help with some of that by having this gatekeeper concept (as was mentioned earlier).[57]

You're responsible for the flow that comes to you. If you're the one sitting at the exchange, you've got to make sure you have controls in place to prevent duplicative orders, and other problems. But standardizing that system will be a positive.

FORTUNATO: We certainly would be partnering with the exchanges for their testing if we're a significant enough share of their trading volume. To that end, our ATS is not actually covered because it's not large enough in terms of volume. But it's an interesting rule.

As regards Reg SCI and what can happen, let me mention something separate that happened a while back in the market. In this case, I'm pretty sure Knight Capital Group did not suddenly wake up and say let's just throw a code change in here, and see what happens. The market took all of their trades, and executed them very smoothly. But the New York Stock Exchange realized something was off because Knight was an outlier in this scenario versus their normal trading patterns The NYSE called Knight up and let them know. But Reg SCI couldn't stop that.[58] In any event, I don't think anybody at the SEC is going to come into my shop, and tell one of my algo developers how best to code our algo changes. It's just patting you on the head, saying do a good job. Make sure you don't make a mistake.

TABB: And if you lose $400 million we'll fine you another $10 million on top of it?

WOOD: Reg SCI is obviously an equities-only initiative, it doesn't cover the futures markets. But it's an example of what we're talking about here. The challenge for the regulators is to understand the markets and their systems, and how they work

[56] Internalizers refers to internalization. A trade is internalized for an investor when it is handled and executed by their "internalizing" brokerage firm using securities held by this investor's brokerage. Brokerage firms that internalize orders, can sometimes benefit from the spread, in this case, the difference between what they pay for the shares and what they sell them for.

[57] The Securities and Exchange Commission adopted the final version of Rule 15c3-5 on November 3, 2010. See, Risk Management Controls for Brokers or Dealers with Market Access. Securities and Exchange Commission. https://www.sec.gov/rules/final/2010/34-63241.pdf

[58] Knight reportedly had a problem in the incident described, and it didn't realize it, explained the speaker in a follow up. The New York Stock Exchange, on the other hand, was monitoring Knight and did realize it had a problem, because Knight was trading at levels much different than it would normally trade. NYSE cancels traders after algo glitch. *Financial Times*. Michael Mackenzie and Arash Massoudi. August 1. 2012. https://www.ft.com/content/bd5f2af8-dbe7-11e1-8d78-00144feab49a

in an increasingly automated environment. A large part of that understanding is how a trading venue itself works. At the same time, a venue, whether an exchange, an ECN, or an ATS, should meet certain regulatory standards. Reg SCI looks to address that.

Other concerns are about the technology of the market participants. We have the example of Knight Capital Group.[59] When you look at the details of cases like that, you find a lapse in quality control, and a lapse in risk control, as well. We're talking about bad coding procedures, no risk controls in place, failure to comply with Rule 15c35, and so on.[60]

To the *brittle* market point, yes, we're only as good as the weakest link. My view always has been for the regulators to understand the challenges, and to strive to get market practices up to a standard. Not necessarily by mandating how one thing should be done, or another thing should be done, but by saying that these are the best practices that market participants should follow. These are the practices that you should follow, if you have access to the markets, and if you fail to maintain quality of risk controls, then that is where the regulator should take action to address shortfalls.

STEVEN SACHS[Chief Compliance Officer, FBN Securities]: We're a sell-side firm. Our customers are institutional customers, and most of these institutional customers just don't deal with my firm. Nobody has heard of our firm, but that said they have multiple accounts. So if a market participant wants to do market manipulation, and there's a whole host of it, from the regulator's point of view, it shouldn't really be just looking at the broker-dealer or the sell-side firm. So I want to know what your thoughts and comments are.

TABB: That ties into this: We never really got around to the CAT discussion, that was a question we had talked a little bit about.[61] But how do we work across all this fragmented infrastructure to find all these guys across accounts, across exchanges, across dark pools?

ZECCA: The consolidated audit trail, or CAT, will help. In theory, it would offer a full list of the order: Where it moves, so we can trace the order, and whether it is split between firms. In other words, is it routed to different destinations? Right now, it is a complex matter, and it does lead particularly to false positives where you have situations where something seems like it could be manipulative conduct. CAT is promising that we'll be in a different world for that level of information.

---

[59] See, Administrative Proceeding. SEC. October 16, 2013. https://www.sec.gov/litigation/admin/2013/34-70694.pdf

[60] See, SECURITIES AND EXCHANGE COMMISSION 17 CFR PART 240 [Release No. 34-63241; File No. S7-03-10] RIN 3235-AK53 Risk Management Controls for Brokers or Dealers with Market Access https://www.sec.gov/rules/final/2010/34-63241.pdf. Otherwise known as the Market Access Rule, part of which requires a broker/dealer to have risk controls in place—which Knight Capital did not. The Securities and Exchange Commission adopted the final version of Rule 15c3-5 on November 3, 2010. See, Risk Management Controls for Brokers or Dealers with Market Access. Securities and Exchange Commission. https://www.sec.gov/rules/final/2010/34-63241.pdf. See, Key Topics, FINRA. https://www.finra.org/rules-guidance/key-topics/market-access

[61] See, footnote 14.

ADAM: One essential thing is that the monitoring enforcement, such as the SEC and FINRA, has to move to a model where a human trader, or staff at broker dealers, are getting notified of exceptions, of something that fits into either a certain pattern, or doesn't fit into a certain pattern.

To illustrate my point: Last Saturday, my bank did a really good job of this. Let me explain. I never buy shoes on anything except on Amazon. But the one time I went to Paragon, they declined my credit card because they knew that I didn't buy these brand of shoes at Paragon very often. So this matter of monitoring and enforcement has been solved, in this particular sense, in my example. On a much broader scale, the federal government has been working with both Medicare and defense contractors to find suppliers that just don't fit the pattern. For example, there was the case in Des Moines, Iowa, where some 5000 magnetic resonance imaging (MRI) scans, were reported, and that's just weird, right?[62] We need to move to a similar model where across all participants in the market, you have something sitting over CAT that is telling you this is normal, or that this is not normal, or somehow this doesn't fit right. Whenever you roll out a system like the CAT, you get a ton of false positives.

It's the job of the system designers, and it's a full-time job, to figure out how you lower those false positives over time so that somebody who is in a position to handle this—say somebody who is at a trading firm—can determine that something doesn't feel right. In other words, they are in a position to look and flag something to either an SRO, or to a regulator.

CHRIS RODRIGUEZ [Baruch College Student]: With an ever changing line between egregious, suspicious activity, is this regulatory oversight just costly overkill, or do regulators need a tighter specific regulation? Then again, legislation takes time, so do you feel like that is fundamentally impossible?

TABB: That's a really good question. Should the regulators just get the hell out of the way, and let the market sort it out?

WOOD: I don't think the regulators can get out of the way, because obviously they're tasked with overseeing the markets. I think it's a very fine line between being too prescriptive and finding the appropriate balance between principles that actually works for the marketplace.

The challenge for the regulator, as you allude to, is the fact that you can set certain standards. Unfortunately, human nature will always find ways to game that. What may have been fine one minute, suddenly becomes wrong the next. And that's a challenge. It comes back to the earlier point that the regulators need to learn as the market evolves, understand the evolution, and keep track of developments in how trading occurs, especially as it becomes more automated.

ZECCA: I won't personalize it by speaking for myself. I'll say more the SEC, or just regulation generally. One of the difficult issues they face, is that when something goes wrong, they're almost viewed as an insurer of good markets. So it's very hard for them not to react to each problem and come up with a solution.

[62] Referring to the detection of a suspected federal government fraud case, using new technology and data analysis that counted an inflated number of MRIs. This inflated number was hugely out of proportion to the typical demand in the community.

As I mentioned earlier, part of that has been to try to get the SROs and, hopefully, the industry to come up themselves with answers to some of these problems. That can ground it a little more in reality.

ANDY BROOKS [T. Rowe Price]: I'm not sure this is the result of 40 years of NMS. One of the outcomes of what's happening today is keeping up with market data. You guys are technologists, and there is just a flood of market data. (By the way, the cost is growing exponentially). Can somebody tell me what's happening? Why that's good? Who's in charge of setting these prices? Can someone tell me whether it's out of control, and we generate the data? And yet we have to buy it for ourselves?[63]

TABB: Have you been looking at my laptop? I'm in the process of writing something just about that.

BROOKS: Well, good, because there is no connection to inflation, or anything else anywhere close.

ZECCA: Again, it's a system where things are regulated. We have to get approval from the Commission, we do have industry advisory involvement. We certainly have heard the concerns. Frankly, there's been litigation involved with SIFMA, so I can't go into all the details.

I will say that, overall, for most firms the data costs are a comparatively small percentage of their overall costs. We have the richest data in the world. There are a lot of countries where there is a very limited amount of data. In an advisory report back in the early 2000s, the idea was that there should be the ability to compete with your data, and for more rich data. That's the environment that we're in now.

TABB: Gregg Berman, I'll put you on the spot. Is there any thought that the pricing of SIP data is scrutinized a lot more than pricing of direct feeds at the SEC? Is there any view of trying to put a little bit more scrutiny on direct feeds, or that's a whole different area that you were involved in?

BERMAN: Correct.[64]

TABB: Thank you.

---

[63] See, footnote 55.

[64] Speaker's use of the singular "correct" per his instructions in a follow-up, does not, of course, address Larry Tabb's final questions in any detail. It remains in place to confirm the substance of the questions.

Chapter 3
The Global View

Nandini Sukumar

ROBERT SCHWARTZ: It is my great pleasure to introduce Nandini Sukumar. Nandini will present the international dimension, a topic of paramount importance for properly understanding market structure.

It is very difficult to find someone more knowledgeable and international on this topic than Nandini. You get up in the morning, Nandini, and speak to market practitioners by phone, first in Asia. Then you move with the sun a bit closer to the Americas, and finally you're tuned to Europe and the US. Then you catch a little sleep, and start all over again. In this whirlwind manner, you travel the globe, with great energy and speed, east to west, north to south.

It's very interesting how market structure issues are perceived differently, in different regions and at different exchanges. How you keep up with it all that, and navigate your way through it all, simply amazes me. Nandini is a remarkable professional. I welcome you.

NANDINI SUKUMAR: It's good to be here at Baruch, thinking aloud about, "40 Years of Experience with NMS: Who are the Winners and What have we Learned?"

When Bob Schwartz asked me to speak on the topic, I smiled wryly because all the SEC-regulated North American exchanges are members of the World Federation of Exchanges (WFE).[1] Then I smiled wryly again because all the exchanges that

[1] The World Federation of Exchanges: https://www.world-exchanges.org/

N. Sukumar (✉)
World Federation of Exchanges, London, UK

R. A. Schwartz et al. (eds.), *40 Years of Experience with the National Market System (NMS)*, Zicklin School of Business Financial Markets Series,
https://doi.org/10.1007/978-3-030-91912-2_3

might have perspectives on NMS, or on Reg NMS, in Asia or EMEA, are also members of the WFE.[2]

The World Federation of Exchanges is the global industry association for exchanges and clearing houses. We represent about 150 public markets and CCPs around the world.[3] We were founded in 1961 and like many venerable institutions, the date of our inception requires us to put a pin in a calendar on a wall. NYSE, NASDAQ, BATS, TMX, are all WFE members, as is the Chicago Board Options Exchange. Bill Brodsky who, as all of you know, has lived market structure for the last 50 years, is associated with the WFE for the last 20 at least, and was our chairman in 2009.[4]

Our members span every geography and time zone. In the Americas region, as we call it, in addition to all the US exchanges, we have the Latin American markets including, for example, BOVESPA in Brazil, and in Colombia and Santiago.[5] In EMEA, Euronext and the Swiss exchange, were founding members.[6]

Also, in that region, we include the Johannesburg Stock Exchange, the Saudi Stock Exchange, and the Casablanca Stock Exchange. In Asia, in addition to SGX and Hong Kong, we have six Chinese exchanges, both the Indian exchanges and Japan. So, as you can see, we cover most public markets around the world.

I will take this opportunity to reflect on how our members, exchanges and clearing houses, as well as our regulators and policy makers, both internationally and in other markets, and not just in Europe, are thinking about markets and approaching financial market regulation in the wake of Reg NMS.[7]

In Europe, we have just had 1500 pages of technical standards on MiFID 2. We were all reading them swiftly because we were expecting to implement them in

---

[2] The National Market System (NMS)was launched by the US government on June 4, 1975, to amend the Securities Exchange Act of 1934. These 1975 amendments instructed the Securities and Exchange Commission to cooperate with the industry in creating a National Market System with an ambitious system for the clearance and settlement of securities transactions nationwide. The amendments also provided for the prohibition of fixed-commission rates, promulgated earlier by the SEC in its Rule 19b-3. Reg NMS (Regulation National Market System) was adopted by the Securities and Exchange Commission in 2005 and introduced two years later to further advance the ideals of a national market system. The regulation includes the order protection, or trade-through rule; access rule (fair access) to market data including quotations; rules on sub-penny trading and on market data. EMEA is shorthand for Europe, the Middle East and Africa.

[3] Central Counterparties, or CCPs, refers here to exchanges.

[4] Bill (William) J. Brodsky, a panelist at this conference, is the former Chairman & CEO, of the Chicago Board Options Exchange.

[5] For current members of the WFE, see website: https://www.world-exchanges.org/membership-events

[6] EMEA is shorthand for Europe, the Middle East and Africa.

[7] Reg NMS (Regulation National Market System) was adopted by the Securities and Exchange Commission in 2005 and introduced two years later to further advance the ideals of a national market system. The regulation includes the order protection, or trade-through rule; access rule (fair access) to market data including quotations; rules on sub-penny trading and on market data.

2017. However, the day before yesterday, we discovered we had a year more to implement them, so MiFID 2 is extended now to 2018.[8]

In Asia, where each individual country regulator is sovereign, we have individualized and evolutionary regulation in the context of technology, High Frequency Trading (HFT), market quality, and market fragmentation.[9]

In the many other markets and regions, such as Africa, the Middle East, Southeast Asia and Central Asia where WFE members operate, regulators, exchanges and clearing houses have looked to the US as a role model, even as they grapple with issues that are removed from all that we have spoken of here today so far.

Let me first reflect briefly on the National Market System, on MiFID 2, and then finally offer you an international perspective on some of the issues that we, as an industry, ponder, as we sit outside these shores. The good news is that I won't take 30 min to do it!

Before turning to the international perspective, it's perhaps wise for us to have a look at the original reasons for the introduction of the NMS in the US. In 1975, as you all know, Congress directed the SEC to enable the establishment of a National Market System to link together the various markets that traded securities.[10] The intention was to utilize opportunities created by new data processing and communication technologies to achieve the objectives of efficient, competitive, fair and orderly markets that are in the public interest and that protect investors. The subtext was meeting the investment needs of the public, and reducing the cost of capital for listed companies. This, as a vision and mandate, is still with us today as a template for what effective markets should look like.

Now, without commenting on the current state of play in US markets, it's fair to say that all regulation everywhere has unintended consequences. And that is why regulators review legislation to assess the impact, and determine whether changes need to be made.

Moreover, conditions do change. New technologies emerge that enable new types of trading behavior. As we've heard today, economic conditions change as the recent financial crisis so aptly demonstrated.[11] So, these necessitate a continuing assessment of the regulatory framework. We must ensure that it is still fit for the purpose it was designed.

---

[8] Europe's revised Markets in Financial Instruments Directive, or MiFID 2, created to improve transparency and eliminate conflicts of interest across the financial services industry, took effect at the start of 2018.

[9] The US and European markets share common regulations though Asia does not, the speaker noted in a follow-up.

[10] Federal legislation launched on June 4, 1975, to amend the Securities Exchange Act of 1934. The 1975 amendments instructed the Securities and Exchange Commission to cooperate with the industry in creating a National Market System along with an ambitious system for the clearance and settlement of securities transactions nationwide. The amendments also provided for the prohibition of fixed-commission rates, promulgated earlier by the SEC in its Rule 19b-3.

[11] Referring to the Financial Crisis of 2007 and 2008 and the subsequent "Crash" on September 16, 2008, with the failures of major financial institutions in the US, including, most famously, Lehman Brothers. This occurred as a result of a chain of event blamed by analysts on toxic subprime loans.

And that's one of the things that both the US and Europe have in common at the moment. In Asia, there are multiple regulatory jurisdictions, and several individual country regulators, and most WFE members are looking at different aspects of the market. Technology, both from an investor protection market stability perspective, and from a disruptive innovation perspective—HFT stands out on the latter—is under the microscope. Competition, liquidity, and efficient price discovery are also being examined. Broadly speaking, in Asia, there is very little rhetoric around harmonization, and there is a consequent focus on what is best for each individual market structure.

Reg NMS was introduced in the US in 2005 after a five-year review period, to ensure that the NMS system was compatible with the needs of today's markets. In setting out the principles underpinning it, the SEC highlighted the need to first ensure competition among markets and competition among orders.

The rationale was that competition among markets would promote more efficient and innovative trading services; and that competition among orders in an integrated market structure would promote more efficient pricing for individual stocks. This notion of competition amongst markets with different trading structures and approaches was a central tenet of the US approach to equity market structure. Until fairly recently, that was somewhat unique to the US.

The SEC also cared about a National Market System that would serve the interests of long-term investors in listed companies. One of the most important goals of the equity markets, and for WFE members today, still is to minimize the transaction costs for long-term investors, and thereby reduce the cost of capital for listed companies. We will touch on that a little later when I talk about the sustainability debate that our members encounter.

Reg NMS has been a template for transparency and competition, and a model that has been widely used, obviously with regional specificity, around the world. Much of the innovation that has emerged, BATS, for example, has grown out of Reg NMS and the climate it created.[12] So, the regulatory structure that has come out of Reg NMS has been like an incubation space that any scientist would be proud of.

After that period of incubation, we have seen how MTFs or ATSs seemed to want to become exchanges.[13] BATS, for example, became a full member of WFE last

[12] See, CBOE Holdings Announces Close of Acquisition of Bats Global Markets. Press Release. March 1, 2017. http://ir.cboe.com/press-releases/2017/03-01-2017.aspx

[13] An MTF, or multilateral trading facility, is a European term for a trading system that facilitates the exchange of financial instruments between multiple parties. Multilateral trading facilities allow eligible contract participants to gather and transfer a variety of securities, especially instruments that may not have an official market. These facilities are often electronic systems controlled by approved market operators or larger investment banks. Traders will usually submit orders electronically, where a matching software engine is used to pair buyers with sellers. Source: Investopedia. An ATS, or Alternative Trading System, is the US regulatory term for a non-exchange trading venue, such as ECNS, call markets and dark pools, that matches buyers and sellers in transactions.

year, since it was now regulated the same as their national market, both in London and in the US.[14]

Everyone here this morning has spoken a lot about spreads coming down, the impact on shares, and how, broadly speaking, this has been widely good for investors. The numbers back that up.

Turning to Europe, we need to go back a bit to the Markets and Financial Instruments Directive, or MiFID, as it is commonly known. MiFID was introduced in 2007 as part of the European Commission's Financial Services Action Plan, itself part of an ambitious regulatory reform agenda aimed at creating a single market for investment services in Europe. It sought, not unlike NMS in the US, to foster greater competition among service providers including trading platforms, thereby creating deeper, more integrated and liquid markets. That would drive down the cost of capital for issuers, and deliver better and cheaper services for investors. This ultimately contributes to economic growth and job creation. Like the US, it has produced a radical change in the equity markets of the region.

In the 2010 review of MiFID, the Commission identified a number of benefits because of the introduction of the new regulatory framework. These included greater competition between the trading venues, lower trading costs per transaction, reduced bid-ask spreads, and faster trading times. Investors also had more choice, and greater opportunities for pan-European trading.

MiFID focused on competition. It was designed to foster competition between equity trading venues by abolishing the concentration rule, and by creating new classes of venues.[15] Many of the new classes of venues, such as Chi-X Europe and Bats Europe, have been very successful.

However, there was also market fragmentation, carrying with it the risks of lower liquidity and the impact on price formation, in addition to making it harder to have a holistic view of the markets. It also led to a situation where there was, to put it simply, an uneven playing field between exchanges and other alternative venues.

European regulators concluded that, while MiFID created competition between these services and brought more choice and lower prices for investors, shortcomings were exposed in the wake of the financial crisis.[16] This, coupled with significant changes in the financial markets in the proceeding years, arguably a direct consequence of the introduction of MiFID, resulted in the proposed reform of MiFID, or in MiFID 2.

In 2011, the European Commission tabled proposals to revise MiFID with a focus on :1. More robust and efficient market structures, essentially leveling the playing fields between different types of trading platforms, and ensuring all relevant platforms fell under the regulatory net; 2. Recognition of technological innovation

[14] WFE members are all regulated exchanges. There are also "non-membership" categories at the WFE for "Affiliates" and "Long Term Partners."

[15] The concentration rule had required that stocks be traded via local markets.

[16] Referring to the Financial Crisis of 2007 and 2008 and the subsequent "Crash" on September 16, 2008, with the failures of major financial institutions in the US, including, most famously, Lehman Brothers. This occurred as a result of a chain of event blamed by analysts on toxic subprime loans.

and management of any potential risks associated with them; and 3. Improved transparency, both in equity markets and non-equity markets.

The directive giving effect to MiFID 2 was adopted in May, 2014. The draft regulatory technical standards were released for comment in September of this year. As I said, up until two days ago, we were expecting to start implementing it in early 2017, but now we have until 2018.

MiFID 2, and the corresponding regulations on the MiFID, introduced significant changes in a number of areas. These changes included the introduction of OTFs, or Organized Trading Facilities, and SIs, or Systematic Internalizers, and trading obligations; organizational requirements which include governance and enumeration; trade reporting, including extending consolidated tape providers (Europe does not have a consolidated tape); publication arrangements, transaction reporting, extending the scope and requirements for reporting; and high-frequency trading, including provisions to ensure HFT does not adversely affect market integrity.[17]

It was also broader in many ways than some of the US regulations were. There is a transparency requirement, which includes the extension of scope for equity and non-equity instruments. The requirement swept in commodities, and it introduces position reporting (for example) and [position] limits regime.

MiFID 2 is now moving forward. Also, that was how it was in 2004, when US exchange leaders, such as Bill Brodsky, who is here with us today, testified on the impact and consequences of Reg NMS, and the evolution they saw it bringing into the US marketplace. In the years ahead, we will see MiFID 2 play out in Europe.

MiFID is a slightly different creature to Reg NMS, however. It speaks to many of the same themes, competition among trading venues, best execution, a consolidated tape, and a desire to update regulation so it reflects technological and market developments. The two also stem from the same bedrock idea of a common market, and a will to ensure that there is some degree of harmonization and consistency across the respective regions.

But clearly the detail between MiFID and Reg NMS is different. If you look at some of the regulation in Europe around high-frequency trading, and the measures that MiFID 2 prescribes, MiFID 2 is also broader in scope. That reflects a desire to bring non-equity markets into a world where competition, best execution, regulated innovation and investor protection, remain at the heart of the regulated market.

Additionally, the differences in market structure will mean that the end product will be different in Europe than in the US. But there are large parts of the world where neither MiFID, nor NMS or Reg NMS, prevail, particularly on daily life. In Asia, we have several significant financial centers with broad, deep, liquid stock markets, among them Hong Kong, Singapore, Tokyo, India, China and Australia, to name a few.

---

[17] "Systematic internalisers (SIs) are investment firms which, on an organised, frequent, systematic and substantial basis, deal on own account by executing client orders outside a regulated market, MTF or OTF without operating a multilateral system." Emissions-EUETS.com. European Union Emissions Trading Scheme—legal point of view.

The WFE board has 17 members. I typically use it as a good sounding board for the strength of any particular region, so it's a good reflection and snapshot of a region. A third of our board is from Asia Pacific, and is represented by Taiwan, China, Korea, Japan, Hong Kong and India. Here is what is common to all of them: A desire for strong and efficient market structure, and for transparent markets, trading with good quality information available to investors. There is also a desire to improve speed and efficiency. And there is a desire among members to promote, and to be seen to promote, fair trading to ensure that investors get the best price, and to ensure that those who trade on the markets have adequate protection.

These values are widely espoused across the world. Forty years beyond NMS, these values remain fresh. But what these markets don't have is a common regulator. They are also in different stages of development, they operate in different market structures, and they are in economies with very different investor cultures.

By the end of the third quarter of 2014, the value of shared trading (I'm quoting our WFE statistics) increased by 56 percent worldwide). And that was only a 12 percent increase if you excluded mainland China. The Asian region accounts for 48 percent of the total value of share trading, and 34 percent of total market capitalization, according to our statistics. That's in the third quarter of 2015.

Let's now turn explicitly to the issues that we're grappling with today. When Bob Schwartz asked me to speak, he asked that I offer the international perspective. The WFE, as you can tell, has a fairly unique perspective. We thought it might be useful to dive into the themes of this conference briefly, that is, the themes of technology and the challenge to regulators. I'm in the enviable position of following Larry Tabb's panel at this conference today: Competition, fair and level playing fields, what have we learned; and to give you the varied perspective of exchanges around the world, many of whom inhabit different ecosystems of the US. Many grapple with the same issues.

Let's take the first perspective, which is technology and the challenge to regulators. As Bob said in his introductory remarks, the role of technology in the exchange world is clearly the single biggest change, both beneficial and with complexity, that has occurred in the industry since NMS.

Fifteen years ago OM, then trying to buy the London Stock Exchange, and now part of NASDAQ, was considered radical for saying they were in a technology business which happened to operate an exchange. [18] Not every exchange runs a technology business. But it's fair to say there isn't an exchange in the world whose fortunes aren't tied to its technology. And as the significance of technology has grown, so, too, has regulatory scrutiny. And this is true around the world.

Whenever I think about technology and the role of the regulator, I feel compelled to start with the story of the Nigerian Stock Exchange.[19] Last year, we admitted the

[18] In October 2000, the proposed merger collapsed after Swedish group OM, which had owned the Stockholm exchange OMX, made an ultimately failed bid for the London Stock Exchange. For more, see, https://en.wikipedia.org/wiki/Stockholm_Stock_Exchange, For more, see also, http://www.nasdaqomxnordic.com/

[19] The Nigerian Stock Exchange. http://www.nse.com.ng/

Nigerian Stock Exchange to membership of the WFE. Many of you will know the CEO of the Nigerian Stock Exchange, Oscar Onyema, from his time at the American Stock Exchange.[20] He now leads an exchange headquartered in Lagos that's a poster child for any startup trading platform. They're nimble; they're hungry; they're technology-focused.

We visited them in Lagos last year and discovered that the exchange's company cars were armored SUVs. The exchange security guards, both outside the building and outside the data center, wore camouflage and carried guns. So, a theme that's emerged from the cyber security debate that we have now is the link between operational risk and physical security, and we have a working group for both.

DTCC, for example, which is very active in this space, has the heads of both work streams reporting into their Chief Information Security Office, or CISO.[21] As the world has grown increasingly uncertain, the physical security of technology is something that many exchanges and regulators consider. So I want you to hold the image of the Nigerian Stock Exchange, as we turn to cyber security or resilience, as it's increasingly referred to.

Cyber is a single, universal, unifying theme between exchanges as diverse as NASDAQ's and Santiago's, for example. Regardless of an exchange's size, from the CEO onwards there is awareness, and that awareness is only partly driven by the potential impact on the market.

Sunday we start our biannual WFE MIT conference in Boston. Five years ago the majority of the delegates were CTOs, or chief technology Officers. Now it's a pretty evenly split between the CTOs, and the chief information security officers.

Cyber is also a practitioner issue. Exchanges contend with it at the coalface of technology. But it's one they are increasingly being asked to provide a policy or regulatory response to. We have a cyber security practitioner group at the WFE, founded by NASDAQ and ICE, as you would expect. And at the WFE we also have a policy committee where we respond to consultations and public policy.

We spend a significant amount of our time being the central counterparty, if you like, between the cyber group, whose work is closed to the world—it's a practitioner group, where they speak to each other—and between the policy committee. I give that to you as one point in the conversation about technology.

On the second, blockchain and bitcoin, I was surprised that there wasn't more conversation around it in the earlier panel. It's a big exchange subject for the moment, and a lot of exchanges are looking at the enabling power of the technology. Is this the next big bang? Certainly, a lot of industry people say it is, Larry Tabb being one of them. I think he's predicting 2016 as an advent period for this. We'll know in the next couple of years whether it is or not.[22]

---

[20] Oscar Onyema was senior vice president and Chief Administrative Officer of the American Stock Exchange (Amex), which is now part of NYSE Amex Equities.

[21] Depository Trust & Clearing Corporation (DTCC): http://www.dtcc.com/

[22] Nandini Sukurmar noted in a follow-up in late 2018 that Larry Tabb's prediction for 2016 hadn't come to pass.

There are many other things we could consider in this particular space—speed, for example. FINRA was talking earlier at this conference of picoseconds, even as the industry debates whether the speed race is over.[23]

As a final topic on technology, I will talk about linkage models. NMS and Reg NMS mean markets are more interconnected than ever before. Internationally, linkage models include Mercado Integrado Latinoamericano (MILA), started in 2011 and linking Chile, Colombia, Peru and Mexico. Then there is the Shanghai-Hong Kong Connect Model, being hailed as potentially the new paradigm for doing business in China; and the ASEAN, or the Association of Southeast Asian Nations link, which are all attempting to open the door.[24]

Globally, and not just in the US anymore, here's a question many regulators and stakeholders are trying to answer: What is the appropriate regulatory model to ensure that the benefits of an interconnected system are celebrated?

I'll turn now to competition and equality. This debate is synonymous with liquidity and investor protection. Other markets still look to the US as a benchmark for liquid stock markets. Those who operate in the US markets live with the ongoing debate on the impact of regulation on liquidity.

Amid a quest for transparency, which protects investors and reinforces confidence in markets, dark pools are proliferating.[25] It's important that market structures focus on ensuring consistent liquidity, displayed liquidity, in the highest levels of order competition possible.

In many WFE member markets, ensuring liquidity for investors so that they can execute efficiently, is something an exchange thinks about constantly. Many national exchanges don't take stock market liquidity for granted at all. It's something they have to work on every day.

One of the debates we're having within the WFE is this: How do exchanges promote an appropriate market structure that guarantees liquidity? To reflect on an issue that flanks the liquidity debate internationally, let's think about the SME debate.

For exchanges, the responsibility for sourcing and ensuring liquidity in your markets doesn't end with the big companies on your markets. As the world seeks to put the financial crisis behind it, the capital markets union in Europe has shifted firmly to the growth agenda.[26] Regulators and stakeholders talk a lot about SMEs, or

---

[23] FINRA, or Financial Industry Regulatory Authority. https://www.finra.org/

[24] Latin American Integrated Market: https://perureports.com/latin-american-integrated-market-mila/. Shenzhen-Hong Kong Stock Connect connects the Shenzhen Stock Exchange and the Hong Kong Stock Exchange.

[25] For a comprehensive account of dark pools and their opposite in lit markets, see Dark Pools: Fear of the Dark. Third Way. Lauren Oppenheimer, John Vahey. August 28, 2013. http://www.thirdway.org/report/dark-pools-fear-of-the-dark. As the authors explain: "Dark pools are private, electronic stock trading venues that allow buyers and sellers of a stock to be matched anonymously. In a dark pool, prices are not displayed to investors—stock prices are dark. Dark trading is an alternative to trading on a "lit" exchange, like the New York Stock Exchange (NYSE), where traders benefit from visible prices."

[26] See, Capital markets union. https://ec.europa.eu/info/business-economy-euro/growth-and-investment/capital-markets-union_en

small and medium-sized enterprises; and how can exchanges and regulators find ways that markets-based financing can serve the real economy, and plug the gap that bank leverage leaving the system has taken out.

The US has always been a leader in markets-based financing, and has fostered very successful SME markets. Around the world, exchanges are looking to the US to reference the right market structure for SMEs. This is a debate complicated by the fact that there seems to be no magic formula.

At a technical committee of the WFE recently, we had a workshop about SMEs with two different member exchanges present. One was the Johannesburg Stock Exchange, the other was the Moscow exchange, both of whom had very different experiences, and both had very different results. But they had very similar market structures in the way they approached their SME markets.

Accordingly, this is absolutely an ongoing debate within exchanges: how do you find the right formula to promote SME markets and markets-based financing?

The second issue, again reflecting on competition and the level-playing field, is sustainability, or how companies are approaching environmental, social and governance issues (that is, ESG for short) and what information they are disclosing. Exchanges are the link between investors and issuers. Investors are seeking better ESG data from issuers, and they are increasingly asking exchanges to provide that data. While exchanges who operate fair, liquid transparent, and orderly markets are prepared and do take ESG data from issuers, one of the questions that all big equity exchanges and small equity exchanges are asking is this: How do you facilitate a market structure in which there is equality between the listed companies, and between the exchanges? How do you find the balance between investor needs and issuer needs?

Before I conclude, let me reflect on what exchanges and stakeholders, at the international level, are looking to learn.

On one front is demutualization.[27] We're in the second wave of demutualization in the industry. Only 22 WFE members are demutualized. In the US pretty much every market is demutualized. And if you look at the second wave, it's a balance between large exchanges and small exchanges, so there isn't a particular trend. On the one hand, you have Korea, which is going to be a big exchange demutualization in Asia when it happens. You have Israel which lists many high-growth stocks. You have Colombo in Sri Lanka, Nigeria, and Amman in Jordan.

What is the right model? Is demutualization the right model for exchanges? Should they be private, should they be public? This is something I leave with you all to think about.

On a second front is the role of international financial centers. Right now, if you want to open an international financial center, you're in a competitive business. We estimate that there are at least 12 regions, or 12 countries around the world, many with big, liquid stock markets, looking at opening international financial centers.

---

[27] See, Demutualization of Securities Exchange: A Regulatory Perspective. JA Elliott. International Monetary Fund. July 1, 2002. https://www.imf.org/en/Publications/WP/Issues/2016/12/30/Demutualization-of-Securities-Exchanges-A-Regulatory-Perspective-15889

Kazakhstan in Central Asia, for example, is now moving its exchange from Almaty to Astana, building this remarkable new city to house the financial center. Many countries in Africa, Morocco, South Africa and Mauritius, want to have a financial center; almost every market in the Middle East wants to be the hub, the financial center. The Saudi Stock Exchange is running a road show at the moment. It went to Singapore, to London and then to New York, to talk about how they would like to be the international finance hub for their region.

What is the appropriate model to become an international financial center? NMS is a good way for markets around the world to reflect on that.

And to conclude, I want to leave you with a thought about markets opening up. The US has always been a pioneer here. Across the world, we have markets that are opening up quickly to international participation. For example, China, the Middle East and Saudi Arabia, are all opening to qualified financial investors.

What is the most appropriate model, the most appropriate market structure when you open a market that's been closed for decades to the international world? I leave you with this thought—that all exchanges look to the US because of the liquidity that has existed and remains here. Everyone in the world wants that kind of liquidity. Everybody globally worries about investor protection. Everybody worries about how to facilitate capital formation, especially on SME markets.

So we come here talking about NMS 40 years on. Who are the winners? What have we learned? I give you these questions because I think the world is looking often to the US markets for some of the answers.

SCHWARTZ: When I talked to Nandini over the Atlantic by phone, she said that a half an hour would be a long time for her presentation. Fifteen minutes into our telephone talk, I said you've now used up 45 minutes! [laughter] I wish we had had more time for this global view because it is so important.

Chapter 4
Has NMS-Induced Competition Delivered?

Tim Mahoney, Nazli Sila Alan, Stephen Cavoli, Bryan Christian, Joe Gawronski, and Dave Weisberger

ROBERT SCHWARTZ: Soon after last year's conference, Sila Alan and I had a productive and most enjoyable lunch with Tim Mahoney. It was a fruitful lunch. The lunch was so productive, in fact, that we were inspired to write a paper that was subsequently published in *The Journal of Portfolio Management*. Please welcome our co-author, Tim Mahoney.[1]

TIM MAHONEY: Our topic on this panel is competition in the NMS, or National Market System.[2] I'll start by framing the issue. I was in London last week. You cannot be in London without thinking about Winston Churchill. One of my favorite

[1] Combatting Turbulence in the Equity Market: Get the Listed Companies on Board. *The Journal of Portfolio Management*. Summer 2015. Alan, Nazli Sila, Mahoney, Timothy, Schwartz, Robert A. https://jpm.pm-research.com/content/41/4/8

[2] The National Market System was launched with Federal legislation on June 4, 1975, to amend the Securities Exchange Act of 1934. The 1975 amendments instructed the Securities and Exchange Commission to cooperate with the industry in creating this National Market System along with an ambitious system for the clearance and settlement of securities transactions nationwide. The amendments also provided for the prohibition of fixed-commission rates, promulgated earlier by the SEC in its Rule 19b-3.

T. Mahoney (✉)
BIDS Trading, LLC, New York, NY, USA

N. S. Alan
Fairfield University, Fairfield, CT, USA

S. Cavoli
Virtu Financial, New York, NY, USA

B. Christian
BATS, New York, NY, USA

J. Gawronski
Rosenblatt Securities, New York, NY, USA

D. Weisberger
Markit, New York, NY, USA

R. A. Schwartz et al. (eds.), *40 Years of Experience with the National Market System (NMS)*, Zicklin School of Business Financial Markets Series,
https://doi.org/10.1007/978-3-030-91912-2_4

Winston Churchill quotes is, "Democracy is the worst form of government except for all those other forms that have been tried from time to time."[3] And that makes me think a lot about the equity markets in the United States.

We're highly critical of our own marketplace here in the US. But if you look back 40 years, to 1975, and the Amendments, I'm astonished, particularly having just been in London. I'm astonished at how perfectly orchestrated we are here in the US.[4] We basically separated key parts in the art form of trading, which is price discovery and size discovery. And now with that approach to trading, we have fostered competition among venues. But we also very cleverly created the plumbing, the science part of it, and standardized it very much, effectively nationalizing clearing and the CTA (the Consolidated Tape Association). There is still nothing similar in Europe.[5] It was really fascinating seeing how market structure works in London.

I will start by talking about competition. In honor of Veterans Day, I'm going to first select my friend, Steve Cavoli, a West Point, and a Ranger School graduate.[6] Steve, has competition made the US markets better?

STEPHEN CAVOLI: Yes!

MAHONEY: Next! Joe [laughter].

JOE GAWRONSKI: Hey, do not give me an opportunity, I'll take it!

CAVOLI: I served during a very peaceful time in our nation's history. If you're thanking people for their service, thank the kids who served during a different period in recent US history, starting from 2001.[7] They have achieved some absolutely remarkable things over a sustained period of time.

We have talked about competition today. We talk about it all the time. And when we talk about it, we tend to dive right into the weeds. We really beat ourselves up through a kind of self-criticism of how these things function, and how the markets function. The reality is that the structure of the equity markets is in good shape.

I look at this in two basic ways. The first is a framework. Forty years ago, with the introduction of the National Market System, we decided that we're looking for fair, transparent, and largely stable markets.[8] On the fair side, we're talking about things like fair access that exists for participants today. We're not talking about

---

[3] "Many forms of Government have been tried and will be tried in this world of sin and woe. No one pretends that democracy is perfect or all-wise. Indeed, it has been said that democracy is the worst form of Government except for all those other forms that have been tried from time to time...." Winston S. Churchill, 11 November 1947.

[4] See, footnote 2.

[5] Prior to the introduction of the National Market System in 1975, there was no consolidated tape and each exchange in the US had its own clearing license. After 1975 clearing was effectively nationalized with the creation of the consolidated tape. The Consolidated Tape Association (CTA) in the US oversees the distribution of real-time trade information on securities listed on the New York Stock Exchange, Bats and other markets.

[6] Stephen (Steve) Cavoli graduated from the US Military Academy at West Point in 1977, and later from the US Army Airborne, Infantry and Ranger Schools. He served in the 101st Airborne Division.

[7] 2001 was the year the US military invaded Afghanistan.

[8] See, footnote 2.

equal markets, in the sense that the outcome for each participant and investor is always the same. There's a difference between fairness of access, and the equality of outcome. They are very distinct. Yet we conflate them all the time.

Then you look at the framework, or the architecture of a market. By and large, we all agree that the market itself, the broad tenets, are good. The broad tenets have largely been provided, albeit over time. From 1975 until about the mid-1990s, you really didn't have a lot of progress.[9] Then, starting in the mid-1990s, you had the introduction of Reg ATS, the Order Handling Rules, and other regulations.[10] Rule 390 was also repealed. [11]

MAHONEY: Which is a crazy big deal?

CAVOLI: If you do not know, 390 was a specific New York Stock Exchange rule that disallowed member organizations from trading off exchange, as late as 2001.

MAHONEY: In the beginning, the NYSE was truly the roach motel. You couldn't get out.[12]

CAVOLI: When Rule 391 was repealed, stocks listed prior to 1979 were grandfathered in, while stocks listed after that date were permitted to be traded off-exchange. And that's where industry leaders like Don Weeden really came in and did a lot of great work.[13]

Anyway, we beat ourselves up. Now we're into the details, the practical application of it. I'll let other people talk about the likes of access fees and fragmentation.[14] But we need to largely agree that this is a great marketplace in the US. At the end of the day, we're really talking about the last mile, refining a very good self-correcting market over a long period of time.

[9] See, footnote 2.

[10] See, Reg ATS. https://www.sec.gov/rules/final/34-40760.txt. The SEC's Order Handling Rules of 1997 and Beyond: Perspective and Outcomes of the Landmark Regulation RICHARD LINDSEY, JOHN AIDAN BYRNE, AND ROBERT A. SCHWARTZ. The Journal of Portfolio Management. Spring 2016 http://www.iijournals.com/doi/pdfplus/10.3905/jpm.2016.42.3.056

[11] Reg ATS: https://www.sec.gov/rules/final/34-40760.txt. Rule 390, repealed in 2000 by the New York Stock Exchange, required members to receive permissions before trading an exchange-listed security off the exchange floor. https://www.sec.gov/rules/sro/ny9948o.htm

[12] The late Professor Junius Peake coined the colorful term "roach motel" to describe the New York Stock Exchange during this period in its history. Peake pointed this out to reporter Carolyn Said in 2005, right after Charles Schwab had decided to move its listing from the NYSE to NASDAQ, that until the NYSE had made the rule change, neither Schwab nor any other company could have easily transferred from the Big Board. "I called it the Roach Motel rule," Professor Peake said of the old rule. "You could get in, but you couldn't get out."

[13] For history on Don Weeden, his family, and their contribution to Wall Street, see, Weeden & Co. The New York Stock Exchange and The Struggle Over a National Securities Market. Donald E Weeden (2002).

[14] See, Bloomberg is taking a shot at the New York Stock Exchange (again). Matt Turner. *Business Insider*, April 19, 2017. https://www.businessinsider.com/bloomberg-letter-targets-nyse-trading-fee-changes-2017-4

MAHONEY: We will turn to Sila, the academic on the panel who will stabilize us! Because left to our own devices, the rest of this panel would diverge into who knows what. Sila is also our co-author.[15]

NAZLI SILA ALAN: What is better? That is the first thing you need to define when we ask has NMS- induced competition been delivered? Has competition made the markets better? When we say better market quality, what do we mean by that?

Clearly, we are talking in terms of speed of execution; and trading costs such as spreads, the fees, and so on. These have come down tremendously, everybody agrees on that. So, from a liquidity perspective, market quality is better. But another way to assess the quality of markets, is to look at volatility. Volatility is like the sister, or the brother of liquidity. In that regard, Bob and I have done a lot of work, especially on the intraday volatility of the markets. We have assessed the stability aspect of the markets.[16]

Here is what we have observed. Looking at it over a long period, starting from the early '90s through 2012, we see that, in the US markets, intraday volatility has increased tremendously. When we compare the NYSE list of stocks with the NASDAQ list of stocks, we see the increase has specifically been for the NYSE list, which we all know has taken the brunt of fragmentation. The NYSE had over a 90 percent market share before Reg NMS was enacted.[17] Once the competition was triggered, NYSE's market share went below 30 percent. In our study, we see that the NYSE stocks were the ones that fragmented the most, we observe that their volatility has increased the most.

On the NASDAQ market, it was always sort of fragmented to begin with, since NASDAQ historically comprised multiple dealers. In our observations, we do not see the NASDAQ stocks being affected that much in the way the NYSE stocks were affected.

As a result, my view on whether competition has made the markets better is this. From a stability perspective, which is one of the points that Stephen Cavoli above was mentioning, I don't think so.

MAHONEY: Bryan, when I consider competition, I certainly think about the ETF space. But the remarkable story is about Direct Edge and BATS becoming exchanges.[18] And, of course, we have IEX becoming an exchange.[19] You guys have been a real driver of competition; and have made the markets better. Talk a little bit about your journey. How do you view competition?

---

[15] See, footnote 1.

[16] Price Discovery: The Economic Function of a Stock Exchange. Nazli Sila Alan and Robert A. Schwartz. *The Journal of Portfolio Management*, Fall 2013, Vol. 40, No.1, pp. 124–132.

[17] Reg NMS (Regulation National Market System) was adopted by the Securities and Exchange Commission in 2005 and introduced two years later to further advance the ideals of a national market system. The regulation includes the order protection, or trade-through rule; access rule (fair access) to market data including quotations; rules on sub-penny trading and on market data.

[18] Direct Edge and BATS are now part of the CBOE, see https://markets.cboe.com/us/equities/

[19] See, IEX Group. https://iextrading.com/

BRYAN CHRISTIAN: It depends on which one of my business cards you look at. I have had the pleasure of working at pretty much all exchanges, so it's been good for my career. All joking aside, I've had the pleasure of working at the startup organizations, whether it be BRUT, or at NASDAQ when they were taking on the New York Stock Exchange, whether it be Direct Edge, and now BATS.

You get a different perspective any time a technology-type firm is bringing competition. You create a different perspective that ultimately is driven, not necessarily by the company itself, but by our members.[20] So, competition is driven by the customers, the membership. At the same time, the marketplace continues to seek out more markets, and more models.

Industry models that are not effective will disappear and no longer do business, because in this business the strongest survive. What makes competition work is ultimately an organization, whether it be an ATS, (Alternative Trading System) or an exchange that will make something different and provide a unique value to the marketplace.

BATS just launched another options exchange, BZX Exchange.[21] We'd all argue that the market doesn't need another exchange. But we had great participation by customers. We bring a value proposition which is a lower-cost proposition. So, the market would have responded. I am thinking of the participation by customers who were attracted by a competitive model.

Competition continues to grow because of the demands by customers with their order flow, which moves around seeking the best models available for their business. In the final analysis, exchanges that are providing value will win in the way they do business, and gain market share. You also see exchanges go out of business when they are not providing value. An entity like IEX is providing a value to the Street. That's a value that the Street has responded to and wants to support. In this way, competition is generating more innovation.

MAHONEY: Dave, you and I actually traded in a non-competitive market. That dates back to the '80s when we had the Don Johnson look, rocking our way coming into work every day.[22]

DAVE WEISBERGER: No, I'm too much of a geek.

MAHONEY: Give me your views on competition since you have been on both sides of the coin. Literally, you could tell stories of Dick Grasso on one side, and Bobby Moore on the other.[23]

---

[20] In this context, Bryan Christian was referring to BATS' customers as "members," a term itself which has a specific meaning at US exchanges.

[21] For history of BATS, see, What Is BATS? *the balance*. Kimberly Amadeo. April 24, 2019. https://www.thebalance.com/what-is-bats-3306185

[22] Reference to character in popular Miami Vice television series of the 1980's.

[23] Dave Weisberger worked on "both" sides of the Street, on the buy-side and sell-side, including a stint at technology disrupter, Lava Trading. On one side, Dick Grasso was the former CEO of the New York Stock Exchange. On the other, Bobby Moore, who worked in senior management at Smith Barney, was a mutual friend of Mahoney and Weisberger.

WEISBERGER: My favorite story on competition is from the Crash of 1987.[24] It's funny. There are plenty of people here in this room who were on trading desks back in 1987. In my own case, I physically witnessed something interesting on the day of the '87 Crash.

As a side note, let me explain something about the Flash Crash of 2010, or any of the other market crashes after 1987 that, like the crash in 2010, had significantly more volume traded than during the '87 Crash.[25] In these subsequent crashes, there was typically much less upheaval and more technology. The 2010 Flash Crash was essentially a 10-minute blip on market radars and the impact was miniscule compared to 1987. In fact, people talk more about the Flash Crash of May 2010, which had significantly more volume, yet had far smaller negative implications in terms of market structure.

Let me pick up my story. To this day, I wonder if Seth MacFarlane knew somebody on the Morgan Stanley desk during the Crash of 1987.[26] In the afternoon on that day, when the phone rang on the OTC trading desk at Morgan Stanley, I heard a couple of OTC traders on that desk say how they couldn't answer the phone because they'd be made to buy stock and couldn't. One said, "Well, I'm not going to answer the phone." And as it kept ringing, the other one finally picks up the phone and says, "I clean, I clean," to the person on the other end, and added, "No, no, no trade, I clean," and then he suddenly hung up. You know, that was allowed back in the day. Whoever was looking to sell had to look somewhere else. The fact that Morgan Stanley was displaying a quote at the time didn't matter.

Talking about events from the past, things like this happened, and you had 'backing away' complaints.[27] But little of consequence occurred as a result of those complaints. There was a sort of handshake agreement between the NASDAQ market makers to keep the market under control. But it did result in a bit of trouble for them in 1996, with the billion dollar collusion settlement.[28] On the NYSE floor, if you

---

[24] "The first contemporary global financial crisis unfolded in the autumn of 1987 on a day known infamously as Black Monday. A chain reaction of market distress sent global stock exchanges plummeting in a matter of hours. In the United States, the Dow Jones Industrial Average (DJIA) dropped 22.6 percent in a single trading session, a loss that remains the largest one-day stock market decline in history. At the time, it also marked the sharpest market downturn in the United States since the Great Depression." Source: Stock Market Crash of 1987. Federal Reserve History. Donald Bernhardt and Marshall Eckblad, Federal Reserve Bank of Chicago. https://www.federalreservehistory.org/essays/stock_market_crash_of_1987

[25] The Flash Crash of May 6, 2010, lasted about 36 minutes, erasing 998.5 points, or about 9 percent in the Dow Jones Industrial Average, and then quickly recouping the losses as the various indexes rapidly rebounded in this high-speed, electronic trading phenomena. At the time, it was a record one-day point decline on an intraday basis in the history of Dow Jones Industrial Average.

[26] Seth MacFarlane is the creator of the TV series, Family Guy. There is a running gag in the series where one of the characters shows up for room service, uttering, "I clean, I clean."

[27] Backing away is an industry term to describe when traders don't honor quotes they have made in the marketplace.

[28] See, Justice Department Charges 24 Major NASDAQ securities firms with Fixing Transaction Costs for Investors. https://www.justice.gov/archive/opa/pr/1996/July96/343-at.html.

were in pretty good terms with the floor governors, you could get away with a lot of questionable stuff, too.[29]

It's often said that sunlight is the best disinfectant. The reality is that when you have competition and transparency, a lot of these things can't happen. I'd asked you if we were going to talk about IEX. But since Bryan Christian mentioned it, I will now add that I find the IEX exchange brouhaha amusing.[30]

The Citadel letter on IEX approval talks about a bunch of things and makes some very good points.[31] In fact, there are two important things with IEX that everyone is talking about. One makes absolute sense. We should revisit this. That is, should a speed bump be allowed? I'll explain why.

The other thing is whether the IEX should have any possible advantage from that speed bump for IEX's router, or from their pegging?[32] Here's my answer: That particular advantage for the IEX router, created by the speed bump, should not be allowed. There's just no two ways about it, it's black and white. Frankly, Reg NMS developed the way it did because people were objecting to the NYSE, and to the way the Exchange treated the regional exchanges via ITS (the Intermarket Trading System).[33] Back in the day, the NYSE would only honor a quote from a regional exchange if it was a bad quote, if you will, that would lose money for the trader on that regional exchange. Otherwise, the NYSE specialists would just step in front of those quotes, and trade with the inbound order themselves.

That's a little harsh. But various and sundry presidents of regional exchanges, whether Sandy Frucher from the Philadelphia Stock Exchange (Philly), or others, would tell me this, and the data kind of showed that was sort of true. It was a problem. What did we do? Let me first tell you a story.

I was once at a meeting at the Boston Options Exchange with Annette Nazareth. Annette was handling trading and markets at the Securities and Exchange

[29] Opinions expressed by the speaker are the speaker's own opinions and do not necessarily reflect the views and opinions of the editors.

[30] For further insights on "speed bumps, see, Speed Bumps Are the Hot New Thing for Exchanges Stock markets are customizing delays for executing trades. That's going to make things pretty messy. Matt Levine. *Bloomberg*. August 31, 2016. https://www.bloomberg.com/opinion/articles/2016-08-31 /speed-bumps-are-the-hot-new-thing-for-exchanges

[31] Citadel SEC Comment Letter, April 14, 2016, which contains the key arguments outlined. https://www.sec.gov/comments/10-222/10222-470.pdf

[32] See, footnote 29. Pegging allows clients to price orders relative to the current market price for a security. Source: Nasdaqtrader.com.

[33] See, footnote 17. The Intermarket Trading System (ITS)is an electronic communications network linking the trading floors of seven registered exchanges to permit trading among them in stocks listed on either the NYSE or AMEX and one or more regional exchanges. Through ITS, any broker or market maker on the floor of any participating exchange can reach other participants for an execution whenever the nationwide quote shows a better price available. A floor broker on the exchange can enter an ITS order to assure execution of all of an offering or bid, instead of splitting it with competing brokers. Source: NASDAQ definition.

Committee.[34] Thomas Peterffy, who was also present, remarked, what really should be done is this: Only allow equities quotes to be protected if they're electronically accessible.[35] Then over the course of several years, when Reg NMS was codified, it became the law. The point of Reg NMS, however, was not to allow the person on the other end of the quote to have an option.[36] Because the quote is either firm or not. The fact that it was translated into speed is one of those historical oddities. But it wasn't the reason behind Reg NMS rulemaking, it was never about speed. It was always about a quote being firm. That's why the IEX speed bump is so interesting.

I understand the SEC denied speed bumps from other exchanges in the past. So, in order to allow the exchange application, the SEC should probably codify some speed threshold for this speed bump. Rather than doing what they normally do, which is to come up with, say, 500 microseconds or some other number, make the speed threshold some version of some standard deviation of how the routers and everything interacts with it. But the key is no option. That is, don't give anybody an advantage to back away from a quote.

The IEX speed bump wasn't supposed to give market participants an option. But, as Jamil Nazarali from Citadel told an STA gathering, "Hey, you know, the IEX router gets an option–IEX get to see quotes before everybody else." And that was our "ah-ha" wake-up moment, when we were told and reminded about this option!

When you look at it in terms of competition, what are we really saying? We're saying, here's IEX coming in; it's great for competition, but don't allow the IEX to have an unfair advantage because a level playing field is the bedrock of Reg NMS.[37]

---

[34] Annette Nazareth, former SEC Commissioners from 2005 to 2008, joined the SEC in 1998 as senior counsel to former SEC Chairman Arthur Levitt. She later served as SEC Director of the Division of Market Regulation from 1999 to August 2005. She left the SEC in 2008 to pursue a career in the private sector. As of writing, Nazareth is a partner at Davis Polk & Wardwell based in the firm's Washington, D.C. office. See, SEC bio. https://www.sec.gov/about/commissioner/nazareth.htm

[35] Thomas Peterffy is the Founder and Chairman of Interactive Brokers. The meeting was on the sidelines of the separate Boston Options Exchange meeting, in the period prior to Reg NMS as the outlines of the regulation were coming together. Weisberger was on the board of directors of the Boston Options Exchange.

[36] See, footnote 17.

[37] In a follow-up, referring to the "advantage" for IEX he described on the panel, Dave Weisberger noted that "as a matter of historical record, IEX eliminated that advantage in a subsequent filing." At the time of the conference, many firms criticized IEX's proposed order routing mechanism in SEC Comment letters. Under directions from the SEC, IEX subsequently modified its router to eliminate the advantage over other participants, that was said to be inherent in the router. See, Citadel Letter on IEX to Brent J. Fields, Secretary, Securities and Exchange Commission. November 30, 2015 https://www.sec.gov/comments/10-222/10222-28.pdf. See, Citadel's subsequent SEC Comment to Fields, April 14, 2016. Citadel states: "We applaud the Securities and Exchange Commission ("SEC" or "Commission") for apparently requiring IEX to remove the speed advantage that IEX initially proposed to give its affiliated router over all other market participants." https://www.sec.gov/comments/10-222/10222-470.pdf. In an analysis of the issues surrounding the IEX router, Bill Harts, an industry veteran and consultant, wrote this extensive note:

MAHONEY: Here's what is interesting about Rosenblatt. A floor broker being successful in this marketplace is pretty amazing. Dick Rosenblatt at Rosenblatt has done a wonderful job in transforming his firm, which really is constantly ahead of change. Give us some perspective, Joe, from your history at Rosenblatt. What do you think of competition? The floor historically was the great monopoly of all time. You've transformed yourself so much that people probably don't even think about you as being a NYSE guy. How is your firm able to succeed and remain relevant?

GAWRONSKI: Dick Rosenblatt always had the foresight.[38]

MAHONEY: You were one of the first direct guys?[39]

GAWRONSKI: Yes, definitely. But we were also the first to offer DOT to customers, as previously it existed just for members.[40] We came up with the way that someone could enter an order, and then it would hit our book, and be a DOT order. We were the first guys to offer DOT to the buy-side. We always embraced

---

In the old, pre-Reg NMS days, this is exactly what the old NYSE specialists used to do. Let's say the New York York Exchange was bidding $20 for 500 shares of XYZ, and $19 for 10,000 shares of XYZ, when they received an order to sell 5,000 shares market. At the same time, let's say the Philly [Philadelphia Stock] Exchange was bidding $20 for 100 shares: Chicago Stock Exchange $20 for 100 shares, and Boston Stock Exchange $20 for 100 shares. Upon receipt, the specialist would know that he could execute 500 shares of the 5,000-share order at $20. But the remainder would have to be executed at the next higher price in the order book - $19. So, the specialist would execute the 500 shares and tell his clerk to "Hold the print!" They would then immediately send orders to the three regional exchanges to sell 100 shares each, via the Intermarket Trading System. (ITS) The regional specialists were obliged to fill the NYSE orders, but as soon as they did, the NYSE would report the 500 shares at $20, immediately followed by 4,200 shares at $19. So, in essence, the regional specialists were "tricked" into selling at a bad price. If they had known about the first 500 shares, they might have moved out of the way first.

The Securites and Exchange Commission "hated" this behavior, which is why they shut down ITS, and replaced it with the Reg NMS routing rules between exchanges. But then along comes IEX who had a router that effectively did the same thing! Because of how their system was set up, they would execute a partial order (say, 500 shares), but because of their speed bump, the trade would not get reported to the Consolidated Tape until 300 microseconds later. Before it was reported, IEX would route out the remainder of the order to the other exchanges, thereby picking off limit orders at their competitor exchanges. Thus, orders sent to IEX had a "free option" to see what other markets were trading at. Eventually the SEC forced IEX to change this behavior, prior to granting it exchange approval. In effect, the SEC told IEX they had to report the trade immediately without a speedbump delay.

[38] Dick Rosenblatt, founder and CEO of Rosenblatt Securities.

[39] Referring to "direct access" trading systems that allows traders to trade stock and other financial instrument directly with a market maker or specialist on the floor of the exchange, for immediate order execution.

[40] SuperDot was the electronic system used by the New York Stock Exchange to route market orders and limit orders from investors or their agents to a specialist located on the floor of the exchange. SuperDot was the upgraded form of the previous electronic system used to route orders, known as the Designated Order Turnaround (DOT) system.

automation. I say we because Dick is my business partner, and before I was there, he embraced DOT and automation.

When Dick started on the floor in 1969, the year I was born—and I like to tease Dick [Rosenblatt] about that—people told him to run the other way, the computers are taking over.

MAHONEY: Really, back then?

GAWRONSKI: Even back then. So, it took a long time. But eventually, they were right at some point. Look, we've always embraced automation, and we believe in competing. At the time it was competing with the specialist. In other words, we were the counterpoint to the specialist representing the public.[41]

But to take it back to the larger point about competition, I believe that this competition is good. I even say that, despite the fact that the NYSE's market share was decimated, and that's where we made our living. But we are the largest floor broker on the NYSE today. We actually do better today than we did when New York had an 80–85 percent market share.

MAHONEY: Why do you think that is? What has made you successful when a vast majority of the floor guys have lost market share and business?

GAWRONSKI: Part of it is diversity. For a few years we lost money on the floor. But Dick Rosenblatt was insistent on keeping the floor, as he thought there was value added for customers. Certain things like parity are an advantage to institutional customers.[42] He thought that, if we stuck with it, and gave the NYSE time to develop the technology, we could eventually have a tool set that would be of great advantage to institutional investors. He wanted to stick with it. Frankly, I was wrong. I wanted to cut the floor, not entirely. But I wanted to reduce our floor exposure because we were losing money there. Luckily, the rest of the business was making some money, so we could withstand it.

Looking at competition overall, I'll make a couple of points. The first is Reg NMS really made competition among venues a primary goal. And the regulators have probably gone a little far in that. I'll talk about that in a second. But it's not just the competition among venues; it's among intermediaries. Before it was the specialist at a post, trading IBM, for example. That was the only place you could go, practically speaking. It was a half-dozen market makers that had retail flow that could take advantage of things in the NASDAQ markets.[43]

When you open it up, and not just to Virtu, for example, but to many dozens of firms that can now make markets and that do make markets, some may fade, some

[41] The NYSE specialists at the time, traded as principals while Rosenblatt Securities represented the public, that is the buy-side, as agents.

[42] Instead of simply "price-time priority," in the case of "parity" a certain class of market participant, such as a floor broker, can be on an equal plane with other orders even if those orders were placed earlier. See, https://www.nyse.com/publicdocs/nyse/markets/nyse/Parity_and_Priority_Fact_Sheet.pdf

[43] In a follow-up, Gawronski explained that in both cases, the dynamics were the same. Specialists on the NYSE "had close to a monopoly" while NASDAQ market makers, "had close to a monopoly" so that both groups "had informational advantages from the order flow they were seeing."

may have different opinions on things. Certainly, if the market data out there is not good, let's say because of a market glitch, maybe a lot of market participants will temporarily shut down. But I still think, at least on a day to day basis, that a bunch of people beating the hell out of each other to be the NBBO, is a better market in theory. [44] That's for sure on the NBBO.[45]

Now if we get to the point about what's the reality, I'd say, yes, investors now have better outcomes. I love the way Sila put it, we're talking about liquidity in this instance. If we talk about that, it's really undeniable. Look at ITG industry figures, and at data from such firms as Elkins McSherry and Abel Noser. You'll notice a significant reduction in transaction costs over a period of 20 years or so in market structure transformation.

Now there are some negatives that come along with this increase in market making competition, or maybe it's just coincidental. For instance, perhaps we have more intraday volatility as has been suggested. I'd also add the resilience issues. When we have a more complex market, we have risks that we didn't anticipate. When New York suffers a technology problem and the exchange shuts down, it's great that everyone can still trade NYSE-listed stocks given the many alternatives as a result of venue competition. And the fact that today's market makers make markets across those venues. When everyone is like, darn, what about the close? What are we going to do? How are we going to close the NYSE-listed stocks? The indexers, ETFs, mutual funds and so on rely on the NYSE's closing price for their own end of day processes and accounting. Luckily, the NYSE was able to resolve its technology issues and get back online in the most recent incident on July 7.[46] The SROs, self-regulatory organizations, and the regulators, have to sit down with the market participants and figure out how we are going to deal with this in the future, because we might not be so lucky next time.

We're always playing a little catch up on that resilience front, I feel. Whether it's floods, or it's something else. We're trying to figure out how this complexity can work. That complexity is a risk. But besides that risk, what the TCA doesn't measure are other things like data costs, connectivity costs that are borne directly by the users, and are not embedded in a commission, or price paid for a stock.[47] As another example, Rosenblatt has a six-person market structure group, and our clients are paying for that. So, someone has to spend money to analyze the complexity, as well as to connect to all the venues, and to take in all the different market data feeds, and so on.

---

[44] "Bunch of people" is referring to trading participants.

[45] In simple terms, the National Best Bid and Offer, NBBO, requires brokers under US regulation, to guarantee customers receive the best prevailing ask price when they buy securities, and the best prevailing bid price when they sell.

[46] See, Trading resumes on NYSE after nearly 4-hour outage. Patrick Gillespie, Matt Egan and Heather Long. *CNNMoney*. July 8, 2015. https://money.cnn.com/2015/07/08/investing/nyse-suspends-trading/

[47] TCA, or Transaction Cost Analysis is a method of determining the efficiency of a company's portfolio transactions. Source: ft.com/lexicon.

MAHONEY: We know, and I know Joe.[48]

GAWRONSKI: Someone has to spend money on understanding market structure. Before, it was basically taken for granted. People basically understood the simplicity of it. It doesn't mean it was better, but people have to pay for it today.

MAHONEY: Overall, the other thing you can't deny is that there are less people in our business. This market structure has a lot fewer human beings involved than in the past.

GAWRONSKI: Look, the floor is still an allure, especially to foreigners. Foreigners love to come over and see the floor. But I only really want to take them to the floor at the open at 9:30 A.M., the most active time, with the most people there, the news channels are buzzing, the bell is ringing. There are people who come down for that bell, at the open or the close. In the middle of the day, the floor can be like watching paint dry.

Even our floor guys, their time is not spent in the trading crowds, *per se*. Sure, on an IPO, or an M&A announcement, there may be some people at a post. But, for the most part, even though there's a human involved, they're doing it via the handheld.[49] So they're getting an electronic order, and they're posting it to the book, using a D-quote, or some order type that way.[50] And the people element is significantly reduced. With any of the big off floor market makers, you see the same thing, the people element has been reduced. That's a big savings on personnel costs. That's a fair counterpoint to my earlier comment about extra costs for dealing with a more complex market structure that we incur today. In fact, you also have a lot less people in general.

CAVOLI: We're a product of that, the ability to compete, over time. Simply put, we do nothing more sophisticated than what Vinnie Viola did when he was a market maker local on the NYMEX.[51] It's no different. And much like your boss, he saw electronification coming. Vinny was a strategic visionary who founded Virtu Financial.

GAWRONSKI: He made a lot more money, I'm sorry to say.

CAVOLI: He went to West Point! But Vinny knew that he could take this basic function of transferring natural liquidity, in an electronic form. And with really tight, discreet and disciplined lockdowns, he was able to carve out a business.[52] And that wouldn't have been possible without the fairness, the transparency, and the stability that we tried to achieve in 1975. I'm not arguing that over time we didn't sometimes stumble and trip. It's like my big Italian family. We love each other. We

---

[48] As Mahoney noted in a follow-up, his point is that it is "expensive" to run a brokerage.

[49] Handheld devices used by traders on the floor of the New York Stock Exchange to facilitate customer orders and their business.

[50] A D-Quote is regarded as a discretionary quote, a special-order type used by brokers, particularly popular at the close.

[51] Vincent "Vinnie" Viola is the former chairman of the New York Mercantile Exchange (NYMEX), and the founder and chairman of Virtu Financial.

[52] "Disciplined lockdowns" refers to the internal risk parameters built into the Virtu Financial trading systems.

have the best intentions. And we move forward all the time, even after we might have a minor dust up.

So, we've done that. We've self-corrected over the years. It's this competition, between what I always call imperfect competition and imperfect regulation. The two can never be perfect. Some would argue that Rule 611, the Order Protection Rule, is really about promoting unfettered competition.[53] This was, in a sense, the government getting involved, once again, in the dynamics of pricing which it had removed itself from in 1975 with the launch of the National Market System by federal legislation. But this time it was not exactly as a mandate like in 1975, when the NMS required an end to fixed-commission rates. And this fragmentation exists because the NBBO is a bit subsidized, isn't it, by the government? I don't mean to sound like a libertarian here.

MAHONEY: Dave, is the NBBO subsidized?[54]

WEISBERGER: Oh, yes, no doubt. I was in Europe last week and I'm going back there next week. One thing is absolutely true: the European market structure has less subsidization. I mean there's a lot that the US does better. The US certainly has substantially more liquidity as a percent of market capital, a much freer, more competitive market; and trading costs in the US are lower to the extent that you're looking at agency trading costs. But Europe does one thing that we don't do. It is something I've talked a lot about to many of you. I'm looking back at Frank Hathaway since we both talked about this recently.[55] What happens in Europe has to do with tick size. And for everyone in the US who has tick pilot fatigue, this tick size pilot doesn't even address what happens in Europe.[56]

---

[53] Rule 611 of Reg NMS, enacted in 2007, was introduced to protect against trade-throughs. Order Protection Rule is part of Reg NMS (Regulation National Market System) adopted by the Securities and Exchange Commission in 2005 and introduced two years later to further advance the ideals of a national market system. The regulation includes the order protection, or trade-through rule; access rule (fair access) to market data including quotations; rules on sub-penny trading and on market data. See, Securities and Exchange Commission , Memo, Rule 611: www.sec.gov/spotlight/emsac/memo-rule-611-regulation-nms.pdf. Order Protection Rule. https://www.investopedia.com/terms/o/order-protection-rule.asp. Source: Investopedia.

[54] In follow-ups, these speakers, referring to this "subsidy" said they were talking in an abstract sense also. The trade-through rule has indirectly helped foster the growth of multiple exchanges, these analysts say. As Weisberger has noted, speaking more directly about this so-called subsidy, market makers have often traded a large universe of stocks, from small-caps to large-caps, sometimes profiting on one group of stocks, say small-caps with their wider spreads than large-caps. That, in effect, then "subsidizes" their trading in these large caps with much narrower spreads, and potentially less scope for dealer profits.

[55] Frank Hathaway, NASDAQ chief economist, at the time of the conference.

[56] As of writing, a tick-size pilot program in the US was scheduled to take effect in October 2016, the goal being to stimulate more trading in small companies via wider trading increments. US exchanges started quoting stocks in pennies in 2001, ending the practice for over 200 years of pricing equities in fractions.

In Europe, the tick and the spread are very correlated, because they actually adjust the tick size to relate to the spread.[57] By contrast, the US has a one size fits all. So, all the hullaballoo about market structure and competition basically falls prey to what Stephen Cavoli was talking about. The reality is this. The stuff that everyone talks about on rebates, focuses on the top couple of hundred names, where a one penny tick size is simply way, way too wide.[58]

Consequently, in those liquid names the top couple of hundred—there is subsidization happening for the more thinly-traded stocks, which have the same tick size as larger cap stocks in the US. That's why you have inverted venues.[59] If you cap rebates, you're actually going to be increasing effective spreads and driving up trading costs in all the stocks where the tick size is not too wide.

That is simple economics, as market makers widen their quotes to adjust. You know, the obvious answer is probably to go to sub-pennies for many of the liquid stocks, if you're looking at this from an academic perspective. That would allow quote competition to re-emerge. But here is the reality: You have a lot of cross subsidization in our market. Stocks that trade with tick sizes wider than they probably should, are extremely profitable for market makers with the current level of rebates, which subsidizes other stocks. There are some stocks where it's essentially, you know, Goldilocks—that is, the tick size is just perfect!

Maybe the rebate structure is fine in terms of incenting liquidity. But then you have stocks where the rebate structure is too low to offset the cost of providing liquidity. As a result, you have a lot more volatility of the actual spread, as market makers are not involved.

There's a lot of that sort of thing in our market because it's nowhere near as monolithic, or as black and white, as aggregate statistical data show. The aggregate data disproportionately weighs the most active stocks that trade with high liquidity.

MAHONEY: You mentioned Europe. When I think about Europe, I'm struck most by the fact that Europe doesn't have a consolidated tape, and it doesn't have central clearing. It's stunning how complicated clearing is there. And then there's

---

[57] As David Weisberger explained in a follow up, the tick size was adjusted to the spread in European markets so that, for example, if the spread was 10 pence, then the corresponding tick size was five pence. In US, by contrast, if stock traded at a 10-cent spread the tick size was a penny; and if stock traded at dollar spread, the tick size is still a penny.

[58] The Clock for Market Structure Change Is Ticking. Capital Markets Outlook 2015. Ivy Schmerken, January 07, 2015. The SEC is conducting a broad review of US equity market structure, but the most important proposals are the tick-size pilot, maker-taker rebates, dark pools, and order routing transparency. http://www.wallstreetandtech.com/trading-technology/the-clock-for-market-structure-change-is-ticking/d/d-id/131813

[59] As noted by one trading executive, traders use "inverted venues to 'cut the queue' because cost-sensitive smart order routers target inverted venues first." As he further elaborated, to trade passively in stocks with large queues at the primary exchange, "the only way to do so is by posting on a different exchange." An inverted venue refers to an exchange that offers two models to lure more equity trading volume, the conventional maker taker model and a taker-maker model, or inverted rebate system where the liquidity taker is paid for handling a trade. Examples of exchanges offering inverted rebates have included Nasdaq BX, Bats BYX and Bats EDGA.

the EBBO, the European Best Bid and Offer.[60] Yet it's difficult, it's astounding, to think that in 1975 the SEC got this absolutely right. You have competition and price discovery, but in terms of the SIP, the SEC centralized it.[61] So let's talk about the SIP, which is one of your favorite topics, Dave. What is the problem with the SIP? Is it that we didn't have competition there?

WEISBERGER: It's governance. I mean its governance, and lack of competition. The fact of the matter is that there isn't just one SIP. There are, in effect, three SIPs because the speed of light can't be repealed.[62] Let me explain. It takes 180 microseconds each way to travel between the three data centers that handle US equities, so where the SIP is located creates material differences. I know there are people, and politicians, who like to try to repeal natural laws, supply and demand, and to take on the speed of light. The reality is that the SIP, at any point in time, in each of the three main data centers, is somewhat different, as the sequencing will be different. It takes a couple of hundred microseconds to get from the farthest one to the exchange where you might have your systems—and there is no way around that.

The biggest issue with the SIP isn't so much that there is one, because that's probably a pretty good idea. Actually, it's that the two exchanges, the NYSE and NASDAQ, who are not represented on this dais except by past history, both sell competing products—that is, data products.[63] There's no transparency in the governance model of the SIP.

I won't continue like my friend, Brett Redfearn, beating the drum on this, for those who watched the webcast of the Market Structure Advisory Committee will be reminded.[64] The truth is that it probably should be open. We probably should not have industry participants with vested interests having a product better than the SIP being the ones who administer and run the SIP. It would just be bad optics. Even if they did the right thing, the conflict of interest looks bad.

GAWRONSKI: I'd say governance is the problem. I wouldn't solve it by injecting competition. That's because I think there are things like the SIP that are meant to be a utility. It's valuable in this country that we have centralized clearing. There are advantages.

[60] European Best Bid and Offer (EBBO) is a regulatory mandate that brokers provide current best prices available for buying or selling financial instruments. EBBO is the European equivalent of the National Best Bid and Offer (NBBO) in the U.S. Source: Investopedia.

[61] More about the SIP, or Securities Industry Processor. https://www.nasdaq.com/articles/nasdaq-sets-record-straight-about-sip-2016-10-25

[62] Ibid.

[63] Refers to the private consolidated data products built from "direct market data feeds offered by NASDAQ and the parent company of the NYSE.

[64] *Brett Redfearn* was named the US Securities and Exchange Commission's Director of the Division of Trading and Markets in October 2017. *Redfearn* joined the SEC from JP Morgan, where he was Global Head of Market Structure for the Corporate and Investment Bank. Source: sec.gov. Redfearn had frequently raised his concerns about what he saw as the lack of competition in the governance of SIP.

WEISBERGER: When I say competition, I'm not saying that we need competitive SIPS. I'm saying we should have competition, real competition in bidding for that central utility—the SIP—and with SLAs (Service Level Agreements) around it.

GAWRONSKI: I agree.

WEISBERGER: I haven't a firm opinion.

GAWRONSKI: Europe doesn't have a consolidated tape. When market participants in the US assemble their own data from all the exchanges, it's based on when they're getting it; and how fast they assemble it. That's the market as they interpret it at the time. But it's useful to have one thing like a SIP.

I do think the governance is messed up. There's resilience problems which have been discussed. What NASDAQ and the New York Stock Exchange proposed, to have some type of backup to each other, makes sense in the context of what we have now.[65] But I would agree that some type of more open, transparent process makes sense too, especially when you talk to people involved in these various bidding situations. There's suggestions of horse trading and different things that happen for different votes. That's problematic.

MAHONEY: Steve, would you like to have competing SIPS and competing clearing?

CAVOLI: If there is no competition for the SIP, it will be like rent control where most people don't pay attention to it—yet rent control causes economic harm. So, if you have competition for the SIP maybe that will result in something more reliable for the SIP.[66]

I think of the SIP and direct feeds, as competing with each other, albeit in different products. The ecosystem of participants is not monolithic. There are a variety of different, objective purposes for consuming market data.

I'm not too sure about the fairness of direct feeds versus the SIP. I don't know if I have too much religion around that. But I go back to the notion of fairness and equality. If you're a long-term investor holding stock for five years, or you're a retail investor, you're needs around market data, trading tools, and access, are completely different.

There should be a symbiosis among all of these participants—that is, investors with a short term and long term time horizons—with respect to, in this case, liquidity provisioning, or in how they all work together. Frankly, I don't know how a SIP committee of industry people who come together to sprinkle fairness fairy dust all over the marketplace, will work. I'm skeptical. My reasoning is this: Who will come up with something that is fair for the entire market?

MAHONEY: Bryan, you're the only guy here who is on the SIP committee, so you tell us. Think about competition in that sense. Do you think that would be better with competition, is it a governance issue? I'm struck by Europe, in particular,

---

[65] In a note, Gawronski explained that they proposed "backing each other up on the competitive SIPs."

[66] Cavoli notes in a follow up that Virtu used "direct feeds" but did not depend on a SIP for the purpose of trading. However, it used the SIP for gleaning some information, he also notes.

where the clearing process seems so complex. We got it right here in the US by nationalizing clearing, for all intents and purposes.

CHRISTIAN: Ultimately, from a governance standpoint it's important to know that we've got all the exchanges sitting around the table discussing this and taking the responsibility.

BATS has essentially advanced the idea that we should have a buy-side and a sell-side presence on the SIP committee. That type of transparency will help us as an industry; it will give more people the opportunity to understand the process that goes into it. The SIP, itself, continues to provide a value to the Street; and an improved SIP would help everybody here.

Having more industry representation on the SIP committee that represents the community at large is something we at BATS support. In this way, a larger cross section of the community is represented.

MAHONEY: Sila, how do you look at competition in this part of the world, the clearing, SIP and price discovery?

ALAN: Europe is definitely trying to catch up with the US to create its own consolidated tape.[67] Europe would benefit from that. But since it is just not one big country with many exchanges, but actually a number of different countries within Europe, it's harder to implement the same thing in Europe.

Another place that I want to give an example from is the Turkish Stock Exchange where we have done some work.[68] It is a completely consolidated market. One hundred percent, and Turkey doesn't need a separate SIP. In Turkey, the data are completely consolidated. Once again, when I look at it from the liquidity and volatility perspectives, and at the time series data in Turkey, on how market quality has changed—and how these things have changed in Turkey compared to the US market—we have seen this: The market in Turkey has not been affected as much, in terms of the intraday volatility.

Having that consolidated aspect of the market has benefitted the market in Turkey, even throughout the worst heat of the financial crisis (around 2007 and 2008). The Turkish stock market was not affected much by this. The liquidity did not dry up as much as we've seen around here in the US.

Here is the concern I have about fragmentation in the US. Yes, it improves liquidity in terms of the costs; and it has increased volumes tremendously. We've been talking about big data a lot today. But all these additional market participants providing all this additional liquidity do not have the responsibility to stay in the market when they are needed the most. That's why we end up having all these mini-like flash crashes in the US, such as the August 24th crash this year when the Dow dropped about 1100 points in the first five minutes of trading. It seems that whenever these market participants are needed to provide liquidity, they are not there. That's why I was saying earlier that, from a liquidity perspective, the US markets

[67] Alan noted in a follow-up that Europe did not have a consolidated tape at the time of the conference.

[68] Alan, N.S. and R. Schwartz, 2013, "Research Report for the Istanbul Stock Exchange: Analysis of Market Quality at the ISE."

seems to be better. But from a volatility perspective, not so much. But even on the liquidity side, I feel like it's not at an optimal level in that sense.

WEISBERGER: I wrote a paper a few years ago on this subject when I was at Two Sigma.[69] As the paper notes, we did not see anything close to the level of volatility, the intraday increase you're talking about.[70] I'd love to actually dig in with you in terms of potential other correlations.

But there are a few things that we did see. Arguably, the single thing that Reg NMS did that was anticompetitive, which Stephen Cavoli kind of was alluding to, is directly relevant here.

One of our hypotheses in the paper I wrote was that the rules decreased capital provision, and made the market more susceptible to flash events.[71] Essentially, the argument is this: Reg NMS, in addition to creating massive competition at the exchange small order level, and decreasing transaction costs, at the same time dramatically decreased competition in terms of capital provision by the large broker dealers.

Now the reason for this is incredibly clear to anyone who has ever committed capital. Under Reg NMS, instead of being able to buy at some point below the bid, or sell above the offer, without anyone really knowing what you've done, you have to advertise exactly what you've done in the market.[72] By the way, the capital committer has no cushion in terms of where this capital committer, or market maker, is buying or selling.[73]

Worse than that, when you use the stop exemption of Rule 611, you give a free option to your client.[74] This means that in a scenario where there's hidden liquidity, and you are actually getting a really great deal providing liquidity, the client gets

---

[69] Two Sigma. https://www.twosigma.com/

[70] Automated trading and the evolution of market structure and its effect on volatility and liquidity. *David Weisberger. Paul Rosa.* Two Sigma. 2013. https://www.scribd.com/document/156988602/Automated-equity-trading-The-evolution-of-market-structure-and-its-effect-on-volatility-and-liquidity

[71] David Weisberger ran the broker dealer arm of Two Sigma.

[72] In this context, advertise means showing the trade to the market despite having taken a position. In effect, this means that if the market maker bought stock, the market is being told the market maker did so and are now long that stock.

[73] Cushion, in this case, means decreasing the market impact that would occur if the order was executed against the bids and offers that are displayed to the public.

[74] See, Rule 611 of the adopting release. https://www.sec.gov/rules/final/34-51808fr.pdf. The "stop" exemption means that brokers are allowed to offer clients a conditional fill. Dave Weisberger offered this example in a follow up. A stock is trading at $100, with the lowest offer at $100.01. A client asks where they could buy 25,000 shares from the broker. The broker can not sell to the client above $100.01, unless they buy from the seller on whatever exchange posts that price, but could, as an example, offer to "stop" the client at $100.25. If the broker was able to buy all 25,000 shares at less than or equal to an average of $100.25subsequently, the client would get that fill. If, however, they couldn't because the price rose above $100.25, then the client would get filled at that price.

that—instead of the market maker.[75] And in a scenario where there isn't hidden liquidity, and committing capital would be profitable, that is when the market maker is allowed to commit capital. So capital commission decreased dramatically, as more market makers sought to profit from this available liquidity, which in turn put downward pressure on commissions.[76]

The second thing that happened: We decided as an industry that it was really bad to have a high cancel to order ratio. This is one of the dumbest things that people talk about, when they talk about high-frequency trading.[77] What that directly does is this: It stops brokers and traders from putting their marginal utility curves into action.[78]

Think about the way an actual trader approaches the market. Consider what happens if another participant asks you how much you would bid for 250,000; for 500,000; and for a million. You will bid lower for a million. And so, as you move farther from the bid, you would find far more liquidity. Similarly, as you move farther from the offer, you would find much more liquidity.

In our market, we've essentially told people don't do that, because when you do that you have to cancel, and we don't like that canceling. The actual liquidity available gets far lower as you move farther away from the best bid and offer. People use the words mini flash crashes. That's a little overly dramatic for me. But the reality is it creates air pockets of liquidity in the market because we have told people not to quote away from the bid or the offer.

Those are the two things Reg NMS did. It essentially says don't commit capital; and don't quote away from the bid or the offer. So, of course, you will get these air pockets of liquidity when large orders are entered.

The one thing we can't legislate is people doing dumb things. When someone trades dumb by putting in an order that's too big and pushes a button, bad things will happen. I would suspect that's a large part of what the industry has seen.

---

[75] Hidden liquidity means bids and offers that are not displayed. They could, for example, be at the NBBO, or outside the NBBO.

[76] As Dave Weisberger stressed in a follow-up: "When there is hidden liquidity the client gets the benefit. And when there is not, that is when the market maker is allowed to commit capital."

[77] Weisberger noted in a follow-up that a high cancel to trade (or order) ratio was deemed within the industry to be indicative of "spoofing," so it was considered questionable. "Obviously, it can exist in legitimate circumstances, but considering the compliance headache, most avoid such strategies," he added, referring to the cancel to trade strategy.

[78] Dave Weisberger explained this further in a follow-up example. He explained: "A trader may be willing to buy as much as one million shares at 49.50 when the stock is trading at 50. When the stock price goes down to 49.54, he will not be as willing to buy even a half a million shares at 49.50, so he will typically adjust his price down, say to buy the half a million shares. Constantly, this trader is cancelling in this fashion, as prices change. So, a trader could trigger a great number of price changes as a result, each showing prices at which he is willing to place orders in response to the market moves. Every time it does this, the trader cancels and adjusts. So, in this sense, you don't have liquidity away from the book anymore, which is what the marginal utility curve reference is about."

Now that does not mean the markets aren't more efficient. But it does mean broker dealers cannot commit as much capital. And so, this one anti-competitive part of Reg NMS is actually causing what you've seen.

CAVOLI: That is exactly the point. The regulators through Rule 611 defined best execution, as what is available at the NBBO.[79] Not to be melodramatic, the competition that was unleashed involved a tradeoff. The NYSE had to evolve with the opening up of competition, and the electronification of markets. The NYSE basically told the regulators that, if you are going to do this to the exchange, you must give the exchange order protection, and that led to Rule 611. In other words, the NYSE got order protection (in the trade-through rule) so that its market was protected on it, the primary exchange, and that was horse trading.

Order protection never existed at NASDAQ. It existed though at the New York Stock Exchange for the NYSE's own benefit, which is an oversimplification. But it was then extended at the NYSE, with the introduction of the Reg NMS Order Protection Rule.[80]That opened competition for New York's flow. But it didn't allow other venues who wanted to provide alternatives and real best execution to investors—like OptiMark back in the late 1990s—to compete on size and price outside of the NBBO.[81] In a way the Order Protection Rule Rule of Reg NMS unleashed competition. But in another way, it inhibited it. It said you can do whatever you want in this room when you are trading; but this room is just a subset of a much larger building.[82] It wasn't unfettered competition that Reg NMS unleashed on the market. That's another thing people fail to properly remember or understand.

[79] Brokers are legally required to seek the best execution reasonably available for their customers' orders. To comply with this requirement, brokers evaluate the orders they receive from all customers in the aggregate and periodically assess which competing markets, market makers, or electronic communications networks (ECNs) offer the most favorable terms of execution. Some of the factors a broker must consider when seeking best execution of customers' orders include: the opportunity to get a better price than what is currently quoted, the speed of execution, and the likelihood that the trade will be executed. SEC rules require broker-dealers to provide quarterly reports on routing of customer orders and require markets to supply monthly reports on execution quality. More information, including links to the monthly market reports, is available here: http://www.sec.gov/investor/pubs/exquality.htm. Source: SEC.gov. Details on the basics of trade execution—including order routing, payment-for-order-flow, and internalization—are found in Trade Execution: What Every Investor Should Know. www.sec.gov/answers/bestex.htm.

> National best bid and national best offer (NBBO) means, with respect to quotations for an NMS Security, the best bid and best offer for such security that are calculated and disseminated on a current and continuing basis by a plan processor pursuant to an effective national market system plan. (Source: Code of Federal Regulations/C.F.R. § 600(b)(42))

[80] See, footnote 53.

[81] Founded by William Lupien, OptiMark enabled traders to electronically submit highly customized orders, and have them anonymously matched with other OptiMark clients.

[82] In a follow-up, Stephen Cavoli elaborated thusly on his view of the Order Protection Rule of Reg NMS: "My point on it is this. It said, now you can trade away from the NYSE—its fast—but the compromise is you have to trade at the NBBO, and the NYSE is protected." Added Cavoli, referring to the New York Stock Exchange: "So is that really competition? You can go anywhere you

GAWRONSKI: Dave, earlier you used the term subsidy. If you think about it, again, in very simple terms, let's say the specialists on the NYSE, always subsidized the less liquid stocks. If they wanted the good listings, the big listings that trade a lot where they just made money, every day, then they needed to subsidize the smaller caps. The same thing on the NASDAQ desks, there were loss ratios in this sense. You knew you were making a market for Fidelity; you knew you were going to lose at times.

I had mentioned maybe we'd get back to small caps. That's why the less liquid stocks in some ways probably haven't fared as well, and where capital commitment is actually needed. It's not there the same way as it was before. Now we have this HFT, or high-frequency trading, where there's a lot of liquidity provision, or a lot of volume, depending on which side of the debate you're on. But it is not lasting for a long time, and it is not in size. It is very different because there is no subsidy that allows small-cap liquidity provision to happen anymore.

There may be a lot of studies on this topic. Back in 2009 we studied and wrote about high-frequency trading at our firm.[83] At the time, there was an NYSE study on quoted spreads. It looked at pre-Reg NMS and post-Reg NMS. It broke it down into the NASDAQ 100 and NYSE 100, and everything else. At any given level of volatility, pre- and post-Reg NMS, quoted spreads declined significantly in the NYSE and NASDAQ 100s in the most liquid names.

It was only at a VIX level of 15 or lower, that stocks outside of the 200 most liquid actually fared better from a quoted spread perspective.[84] That was the NYSE's own study as I just mentioned. I don't know exactly why the NYSE conducted the study because at that point it was a *fait accompli*, since decimalization was adapted in the 1999–2001 period. Therefore, it wasn't likely to change anything.

But in the research on small caps, I have not seen any convincing evidence that changes in market structure have benefitted their liquidity. Trading them remains a challenge. It is due to historical reasons, like some of the one's you guys were citing. I offer another kind of example within that, which is subsidies.

CAVOLI: I agree 100 percent. But here's one little benefit for all of us who used to watch this. The market linkages that occurred because of Rule 611, for example, did help. I remember this vividly when I worked at Morgan Stanley because I was corrected about it when a buy-side trader was coming through Morgan. We couldn't access it, and we didn't access it, because the cost trade off wasn't worth it to connect all the venues.[85]

---

want, but you can only trade at, let's call them the physical prices, basically? You can compete all you want within these prison grounds."

[83] The report was published internally for clients of Rosenblatt Securities, explaining the dynamics of high-frequency trading (HFT), noting the major players in HFT.

[84] See, VIX is the CBOE Volatility Index, known by its ticker symbol VIX. https://www.investopedia.com/ask/answers/021015/what-cboe-volatility-index-vix.asp

[85] There was no regulatory obligation for Morgan Stanley to connect to an ECN, since the market was less linked on an electronic and regulatory basis during this period of market history, according to Stephen Cavoli in a follow-up.

MAHONEY: Let's just jump to small caps for a second. Let me frame it, and we'll have a general small-cap discussion. My own sense is that it's unfair that we blame market structure on lack of liquidity in small caps. Ultimately, the small cap was always illiquid. When you had bigger spreads and paid higher, the average commission rate was 7 cents back then, and you were paying huge commission. You had quarter spreads in over the counter stocks. Somehow, it masked the lack of liquidity. And the other thing, Reg FD, or Fair Disclosure was a killer.[86] So you lose your edge in it. The Research Settlement was an enormous part of it.[87]

So, I guess I am skeptical.

GAWRONSKI: There was a lot happening. But to be clear, when I'm saying that about small caps, I'm not saying that market structure made it worse. I'm just saying, yes, small caps were always difficult to trade. Market structure didn't improve anything. Whereas with liquid stocks it really did improve that, because it just collapsed spreads so much.

WEISBERGER: Tim, I've gone on quite poetically.

MAHONEY: You can do it again now.

WEISBERGER: There is this whole notion on the research settlement.[88] Let me say this. Yes, there were things happening that were unsavory. Anyone who knows the firms where I was working, and which had employed the analyst, Jack Grubman—back in the day, understands these things were happening, and probably think they shouldn't have been happening.[89]

But the reality is that traders were essentially paid by the investment bank to maintain markets in small caps, because the investment bank wanted to get those deals. Yes, traders used to lose a little bit of money and maintain liquidity, but they couldn't do so any longer after we broke that linkage.

Much more basic than that is the point I was making before, about capital commitment, and how Reg NMS made it much less profitable. I've been asked on multiple panels whether, if there was one thing I would change about Reg NMS, what would it be? Believe it or not, it isn't about rebates, it's not about access fees.[90] It's not any of that stuff, which I think frankly is a lot of noise about not very much. What would make a big difference is a block exemption from the Order Protection Rule of Reg NMS for securities, defined based not on 10,000 shares and $200,000, but defined based on a percent of Average Daily Volume (ADV).[91]

Here's how that would work. In small-cap securities, if institutions want to participate, the institutions would want to buy a substantial amount of a day's volume

---

[86] Regulation Fair Disclosure (Reg FD) eancted by the Securities and Exchange Commission to help prevent certain selective disclosure by public companies to market professionals and certain shareholders. Source: Investopedia.

[87] See, Research Settlement https://www.sec.gov/news/press/2003-55.htm

[88] Ibid.

[89] Ibid.

[90] See, footnote 60.

[91] As Dave Weisberger explained in a follow-up, the idea of this exemption was floated privately by many industry participants, but never formally proposed as an industry rule.

when they want to buy these small-caps. But the broker dealer community today is not equipped to do so efficiently due to Reg NMS. So, they have to get incredibly patient.

In large caps, it's true that institutional investors want to buy a lot of stock. But because of the dynamics of the market, where liquidity is very good for large-cap stocks, it's not that important to get capital unless you are buying a really large position. So, my argument is to allow dealers to compete via a block exemption, and to let the buy-side and the dealers prove that it was best execution after the fact, instead of banning the activity. That would be done based on aggregated data, which ameliorates a lot of the concerns with the exemption.

MAHONEY: Is part of all this the fact that technology has made us better, or was it the regulatory competition? What's our advantage in the US if we're the best market in the world? What's that number you quote, Dave, is it the turnover?

WEISBERGER: In percentage terms, the US equity markets basically trade three times as much as the combined market cap of all the other G7.

MAHONEY: Is that a structural advantage because we have competition? Is it that we use technology better? If we hadn't had Reg NMS, could technology, in and of itself, have made us more efficient? Or is it the linkage of those two things? Why did it work out this way?

WEISBERGER: I was trading in Europe in the early '90s. For those in France and Canada who are familiar with history, the CATS was the first order-based system that really was dominant.[92] Here's my point: Europe was automated long before the U.S. was automated. In the U.S. there was an oligopoly at NASDAQ, for instance, which didn't get shattered until the Order Handling Rules.[93] We also had an ATS called Instinet.[94]

GAWRONSKI: Yes, the basic order book stuff existed, electronic trading, and that's nothing unique.

WEISBERGER: People should understand that Instinet existed. Yet only the dealers were able to see what was going on in Instinet, and they profited from the difference in that spread. I always find it amusing when ex-Instinet people start acting like they have halos on their heads. Shining big lights on things because Instinet was, literally, one of the largest crimes in terms of what it was.[95] It was a market that allowed you to trade in a quarter widespread.

MAHONEY: I should have stopped the panel debate here!

---

[92] CATS (Computer Assisted Trading System) was an automated exchange system developed by the Toronto Stock Exchange, activated on November 18, 1977, with 90 stocks[1] The Paris Bourse purchased the system in the early 1980s and implemented it as CAC (Cotation Assistée en Continu).

[93] The SEC's Order Handling Rules of 1997 and Beyond: Perspective and Outcomes of the Landmark Regulation RICHARD LINDSEY, JOHN AIDAN BYRNE, AND ROBERT A. SCHWARTZ. The Journal of Portfolio Management. Spring 2016 http://www.iijournals.com/doi/pdfplus/10.3905/jpm.2016.42.3.056

[94] History of Instinet. https://www.instinet.com/about-instinet/history.html

[95] This speaker on this panel, like many other panelists at this Baruch conference series, is expressing his own views here, and not necessarily the views of the editors.

WEISBERGER: The broker-dealers made that money on a riskless basis. And it happened constantly all day long; and everyone who knows about it understands it.

So, we had the technology to show the real spread, but not everyone got to see the spread.

GAWRONSKI: The first question is from Instinet! (laughter).

CAVOLI: Are you talking about the fact there was a private Instinet book, and then there was the public book? Before 1996, there was I-Only for institutions only on Instinet and it was legal. Then there was a public book that the market saw. So, all day long market makers on the institutional side knew exactly where the book was and were able to profit in a way that was not possible for the public.[96]

WEISBERGER: I'm not talking about now. I'm talking about pre-'96.[97] No, this is before the subsequent Order Handling Rules which fixed the situation![98]

CAVOLI: But it's more of a cocktail effect, in that you needed several conditions to exist prior to this happening. Both the technological and regulatory changes were necessary for the various market structure changes that have occurred.

MAHONEY: Right.

CAVOLI: You can't just isolate one thing, since one is necessary but insufficient. You need more than the technological.

MAHONEY: So, you also need regulation?

CAVOLI: You also need regulation. Here's the historian in me. If I get this a bit wrong, humor me. When the spreads went from an eighth to a sixteenth, nothing really happened. But the Order Handling Rules told the market maker you had to do one of three things: either you (1) took the client order and you traded it; or (2)you routed it or you posted the limit order; or (3) you could route it to another market maker.

Once limit order competition entered the market, you saw spreads narrow quickly. I don't think it's an either/or. The conversation about market structure and things we wrestle with are always so difficult. That's because we don't live in a world of black or white in market structure. Too often we want a nice little answer, a tight little formula that says that's good, and this is bad.

You just can't do that. We make a series of trade-offs every day. I really believe that it's always this cocktail effect, as I just mentioned. That's why we, as an entity, the market, take incremental steps, not big steps. The good news is (and I've said it about 800 times) we have been on a constant march since 1975, continually

[96] History of Instinet. https://www.instinet.com/about-instinet/history.html

[97] Referring to the allegations of NASDAQ market maker collusion among firms that resulted in a settlement in a $900 million civil suit in 1997.

[98] The SEC's Order Handling Rules of 1997 and Beyond: Perspective and Outcomes of the Landmark Regulation RICHARD LINDSEY, JOHN AIDAN BYRNE, AND ROBERT A. SCHWARTZ. The Journal of Portfolio Management. Spring 2016 http://www.iijournals.com/doi/pdfplus/10.3905/jpm.2016.42.3.056

self-correcting, making the market structure better and better and better, via regulation and technology innovation.[99] By and large, we've done a pretty good job of it.

MAHONEY: I'll open it up to questions.

JIM TOES [Security Traders Association]: Question for Bryan. The second options exchange that BATS just started deals with priority on the book, versus time/price priority. What are your general thoughts about the priority on the book, and the definition of professional customers?

CHRISTIAN: One of the points made up here is that technology and the barriers to entry now in the exchange space are low, but the markets continue to be complex. We, as the Street, continue to educate people on the complexities of these markets.

On the options side, which I'm alluding to, you have the more differentiated model when it comes to professional customers versus retail customers; and how you prioritize that in the marketplace is what you are currently dealing with.

On the equity side, we're sort of evolving into that a little bit with some of the retail price improvement mechanisms among the various exchanges, and with the definition for these price improvement programs. But it's an evolving discussion. The discussion continues to be fruitful. How the industry evolves is more around the complexity of the market structure, and the technology that supports it.

I don't have a simple answer. But from my perspective, a unified approach is really important. The complexity and unintended consequences in this market structure is further magnified by how the exchanges define retail participation for equity and other customers. From my perspective, I'm more in the camp of a unified approach. The options side has taken a unified approach. But it is a bit more complicated as exchanges tweak their definitions for the likes of retail participation.

STEVEN SACHS [FTN Securities]: I want to focus on the August 24th mentioned on the panel today. Morgan Stanley published a piece about how much money was actually lost on that day.[100]

CAVOLI: I'm going to be very careful about how I approach it. But specifically, as to the ETF question, it's not too difficult. You come in, and you price an ETF. So, we make markets in ETFs, and there is this ETF, XLF, involving 71 or 72 constituent parts. You kind of add them up by weighting, throwing in some cash, the management fee, whatever it is, and it gives you the right value to trade that.

Now I'm going to circle back because it speaks to stability. So, all of a sudden, there's this cognitive dissonance, you price this ETF at X, it's trading at Y, regardless of whether it's rich or cheap; and then we suddenly have a series of lockdowns. I've heard people say they didn't want to catch a falling knife in the market, as we

---

[99] Referring to the National Market System launched with Federal legislation on June 4, 1975. See, footnote 2.

[100] SEC report sheds light on the August flash crash. Jennelle Marle. *Washington Post.* December 30, 2015. https://www.washingtonpost.com/news/get-there/wp/2015/12/30/sec-report-sheds-light-on-the-august-flash-crash/?noredirect=on

talk about what happened in this case. But it's not so much that as much as that there wasn't a market there. We didn't have a market![101]

MAHONEY: Because everything wasn't open, right?

CAVOLI: We had this disharmony in the way NASDAQ names traded before the open, in the way New York Stock Exchange names traded after the open. And there wasn't good information for us on this particular day. When that happens, we think we're the dope, right? So, we had to lock down, and step back to figure it out.

MAHONEY: To me that was a technical issue, it's about how we open stocks.

CAVOLI: We could go on about Rule 48, which governs the opening of stocks on the NYSE—and about harmony among exchanges. These are the tactical, or very nuanced issues that we could discuss in the market structure debate. But NASDAQ generally opens up fine. So, when things get more and more volatile, do we need people stepping in? Frankly, the electronic mechanism in our market structure is actually pretty effective as it is.

WEISBERGER: The one thing, Steve, that's important to understand are ETFs like EWJ, an ETF that trades in Japan. Market makers have built the logic to understand how to trade that based on correlated instruments, and other factors when the Japanese market is not open. On things like the ETF—XLF—on the other hand, nobody has built the logic to trade it when the stocks in that basket are not open because, frankly, it virtually never happens. People don't invest time in building algorithms for situations that occur once in a blue moon. In fact, when those once in a blue moon situations happen, we have Reg SCI which we haven't talked about.[102]

Reg SCI is for participants when they are looking for market stability. Well guess what? One of the things that creates stability is when the electronic market makers say that, if my market data is bad, I don't want to trade. And that's generally a good thing. There's been at least one day when that would have been a really good thing.[103] But it's hard to distinguish between bad market data because your systems are bad, or bad market data because there's something really strange going on in the market.

MAHONEY: I have one last question. Do you think the markets are too complex? We talked on our conference call for this panel, about how it's about choice, competition, complexity and conflict, I guess. But are we too complex in our current structure?

WEISBERGER [Holding up his iPhone]: Does everyone see this? How many people in this room know how Google Maps or Uber work? I don't, but it works. I

---

[101] In a follow-up, describing this trading day, Stephen Cavoli recalled how on August 24, his desk engaged a lockdown out of pure caution, and as the market seemed to run awry. "We stopped trading because we figured we calculated the NAV incorrectly," he said. "We would actually have made more money by continuing to trade—so we figured we had to be wrong."

[102] Regulation Systems Compliance and Integrity (Regulation SCI) is a set of rules created by the US Securities and Exchange Commission to monitor the security and capabilities of US securities markets technological infrastructure. The Commission adopted *Regulation SCI* and Form SCI ("Form") in November 2014.

[103] August 24 as referred to previously.

don't think complexity is generically bad, if we understand it, it's architectured. The good idea of complexity is redundancy.

I thoroughly agree with the point made earlier that we shouldn't have single points of failure, and the complexity of the current system eliminates most. The one we were talking about earlier was the close on the NYSE—and presumably NASDAQ—which is not complex, but it is a single point of failure. As a result, the actual number of outages we've experienced that affect all investors is dramatically lower now. That's precisely because we have a lot of redundancy in the system.

So, it's really more about redundancy and resiliency, than necessarily arguing complexity. Clearly, complexity for the sake of complexity is a terrible idea just in general. But it's hard to say it's too complex when the up time is as good as it is.

MAHONEY: Joe, is there too much choice?

GAWRONSKI: Generally, things work. I'd dial it down a bit by doing some things like looking at venues; and saying if you don't have a certain percentage of market share—and we as an industry can decide what that is—you don't get all the same privileges. I generally agree with that. If you're going to get the benefit of the Order Protection Rule, if you're going to get market data revenues, then you have to be a contributor to the process.[104]

If it's the same old exchange, if it's the same old venue, then no. So, I would look at things like that, to take it down a notch. I don't think you put the genie back in the bottle, generally speaking, because we're kind of stuck with this complex market.

MAHONEY: Steve, too complex, too much choice?

CAVOLI: Yes. But to Joe's point, when you have this complex market, is this the moment you set up another committee to examine it? Who, for example, decides who has order protection and who doesn't? Inherently, it's just way too difficult having industry committees tackle this level of complexity.

I think that is a bridge too far. Let the industry compete without unnecessary interference by committees.

MAHONEY: Bryan, too complex?

CHRISTIAN: Yes, ultimately competition allows people to vote with their feet, and move their business around, and that was sort of my point before. You know, customers are ultimately looking for where they're going to trade; and why they trade where they trade. If they feel comfortable in a venue, they will trade there. That's because they like that venue's model.

From the market structure side of things, it's maybe more of a wish than anything else. But good market structure helps our markets. We talked about large-cap versus small-cap; and we've got a pretty complex tick pilot coming out.[105] Is that what we need? Is that going to answer the questions we have? I don't know. I mean good regulation will help our markets, and technology is there to support that as well.

[104] See, footnote 53.

[105] See, SEC Approves Pilot Program to Assess Tick Size Impact for Smaller Companies. Press Release. Securities and Exchange Commission. May 6, 2015. https://www.sec.gov/news/pressrelease/2015-82.html

MAHONEY: Sila, we've been given the big hooks. I know you'll be concise. You are conflicted here because complexity makes your job. You have a job now on complexity to write about. So, you can't say anything bad, right?

ALAN: Yes, complexity is bad from from a governance perspective. It makes it too hard to monitor the market, to surveil the market, and to bring good governance rules. As long as it's manageable. As Dave pointed out, we should have seen less of these extreme volatility situations. But it is not the case. And, even if was the case, if it is harder to regulate the markets, I think that complexity is bad in that sense.

That said, we came to a point where there is a little bit of leveling off. Here is one of the things I noticed coming to this conference for the past couple of years. Right after Reg NMS went into effect, we started saying we now have 13 exchanges and 40-plus alternative trading systems. The number of exchanges now is about 11. And so, it's still the same 10-plus exchanges, 40-plus ATSs.[106] So the level of fragmentation seems to have leveled off. In that sense, it seems like the markets have reached saturation. Maybe we've become as complex as could be. Then from this point on, it's about being able to manage it, govern it, and surveil it.

MAHONEY: Thank you.

[106] Referring to this same "levelling off" in the number of exchanges.

Chapter 5
Fair and Level Playing Fields: A Good Regulatory Goal?

Amber Anand, Alan Hill, Bill Harts, Nina Mehta, Gary Stone, and Adam Sussman

ROBERT SCHWARTZ: My professional colleague, academic collaborator and dear friend, Amber Anand, is our next moderator. It's always my great pleasure to introduce him.

AMBER ANAND: Thank you, Bob. Many different constituencies are represented on our superb panel. To begin, let's go back to the period leading up to the 1975 Amendments to the Exchange Act.[1] Nina, you will pick it up from there.

MEHTA: Let me take us back just before 1975, to recap some of the events that led up to the SEC's mandate from Congress to create a National Market System.[2]

---

[1] Federal legislation of June 4, 1975, to amend the Securities Exchange Act of 1934. The 1975 amendments instructed the Securities and Exchange Commission to cooperate with the industry in creating a National Market System, along with an ambitious system for the clearance and settlement of securities transactions nationwide. The amendments also provided for the prohibition of fixed-commission rates, promulgated earlier by the SEC in its Rule 19b-3.

[2] Ibid.

A. Anand (✉)
Syracuse University, Syracuse, NY, USA

A. Hill
Jones Trading, New York, NY, USA

B. Harts
Modern Markets Initiative, Washington, DC, USA

N. Mehta
New York, NY, USA

G. Stone
Bloomberg, New York, NY, USA

A. Sussman
Liquidnet, New York, NY, USA

R. A. Schwartz et al. (eds.), *40 Years of Experience with the National Market System (NMS)*, Zicklin School of Business Financial Markets Series,
https://doi.org/10.1007/978-3-030-91912-2_5

The late 1950s was a period for hot issues. In other words, many companies were going public, and stocks often surged on the first day, the first couple of days, or even the first few weeks of trading. At the same time, the SEC was concerned about financial disclosure and misrepresentation in registration statements, so it examined some of these companies. A lot of misconduct was taking place in stocks traded on the American Stock Exchange (AMEX). It turned out that some companies had the same Amex specialist firm, Re, Re and Sagarese.[3] The SEC officials investigated and discovered fraud, illegal distribution of securities, and a lot of price manipulation.

It was a bad scandal because the SEC was very focused on disclosure and transparency issues, and it wasn't paying as much attention to exchanges. Here was a case of a specialist firm accused of abusing its power and trust, and an exchange not living up to its basic self-regulatory function to oversee its members.

In 1961, the SEC began an investigation of the American Stock Exchange. Congress was so outraged about this that, in response, it gave the SEC $750,000 to conduct a thorough study of the securities markets. This was the first study of its kind since shortly after the Crash of 1929. To this end, the SEC had a team of 65 people working for 18 months to figure out how the securities markets really worked.

The Special Study of Securities Markets, published in 1963, was an enormous undertaking.[4] It gave the SEC deep knowledge about the rules and functioning of the markets. It changed in some ways the course of the SEC, as the agency pivoted away from some of the transparency issues, and more towards enforcement and market structure issues.

Then there was a bull market in the '60s, as well as a huge surge in institutional investor trading. The back offices at many brokerage firms had not been updated, nor automated to handle the physical clearance and settlement that resulted from all this new volume. As many of you know, there was a paperwork crisis in 1968.[5] At this time, so that the back offices could try to get caught up, the New York Stock Exchange and all of the markets in the United States closed every Wednesday and had shorter hours on other days.

Many of those events led to some of the stuff that everyone takes for granted nowadays. The Special Study—along with more attention being paid to the chaotic over-the-counter market in the mid-60s led to the development and launch of NASDAQ in 1971. The paperwork crisis then led directly to the formation of the

[3] Wall Street: Underground Combine. TIME. Friday, May 05, 1961.

[4] The Bright Image: The SEC, 1961–1973. Securities and Exchange Commission. Historical Society. http://www.sechistorical.org/museum/galleries/tbi/special_a.php

[5] How a blizzard of paperwork paralyzed Wall Street in the 1960s. https://www.businessinsider.com/wall-street-paperwork-crisis-in-1960s-2015-10

Paper Paralyzed Wall Street: Remembering the 1960s Paperwork Crisis. FINRA Staff. August 19, 2015. When paper paralyzed Wall Street. Remembering 1960spaperwork crisis.

Depository Trust Association in 1973.[6] The failure of brokerage firms in the aftermath of the paperwork crisis brought in SIPC regulation to protect investors.[7]

On the last panel, Joe Gawronski of Rosenblatt Securities mentioned that, when Dick Rosenblatt started his career at the exchange in 1969 people told him that more technology was coming, so it wasn't a good time for your career to stay on the floor.[8] He was referring to this: In 1969, Instinet and AUTEX were launched to address the needs of institutions that wanted to trade big blocks but couldn't do so on the New York Stock Exchange, and on the regional floors.[9]

Because of the rapid growth of institutional investors, and their difficulty in executing, and the volume and price swings in the stock market, Congress again became concerned and wanted another study, this time to figure out what impact institutions were having on the stability of the market. Unlike the Special Study, which was done mainly by lawyers, this latest was conducted by economists.

The Institutional Investor Study was subsequently released in 1971. One of the purposes of this study was figuring out whether institutional investors back then were essentially the high-frequency traders of their day.

Those were the go-go years, and the institutional investors were actually called in and out traders. They were fast traders; they were buying stuff; they were dumping it in a week or two, or in a couple of days. So, there was much concern about whether institutions were disrupting the markets.

In any event, the economists conducted the study, and the letter that accompanied the ensuing report to Congress raised, for the first time, the idea of a central market system. And then, within the next few years, there were Congressional studies, more reports, a lot of hearings and arguments back and forth. Eventually, the concept became that of a National Market System, which Congress mandated the SEC to establish in 1975 in the Securities Act Amendments.[10]

As you may recall, there were five components, or goals, of this National Market System: First, the economically efficient executions of securities. Second, the fostering of more competition among brokers, dealers and exchanges, and between exchanges and non-exchange markets. Third, the broad dissemination of information, which means price and quote data, so brokers and investors would have access to relevant prices across markets. Fourth, the practicability of executing an investor's order in the best market; and finally, the opportunity to execute without the intervention of a dealer. The SEC's overall goal was to maintain fair and orderly markets, and to protect investors.

ANAND: We've had some conversation about what fairness means.

---

[6] The Depository Tust & Clearing Corporation. http://www.dtcc.com/

[7] Securities Investor Protection Corporation (SIPC). https://www.google.com/search?q=sipc&oq=SIPC&aqs=chrome.0.0j69i59j0l4.4806j0j8&sourceid=chrome&ie=UTF-8

[8] Dick (Richard) Rosenblatt is the CEO and founder of Rosenblatt Securities.

[9] See, About Instinet. https://www.instinet.com/about-instinet/history.html

[10] See, footnote 1.

MEHTA: In a way, the entire concept of the National Market System emerged from the effort to deal with problems that institutions represented and were facing.

ANAND: How has the National Market System worked out for institutions? Have we solved their problems?

SUSSMAN: The market has improved since those days. But that would be a pretty low bar to set. I don't think the market will ever fully solve the challenges the institutional investors face, because, of course, they're trying to achieve a large percentage of ADV for most of their trades.[11]

Innovations have helped. Some of that was facilitated by regulations like Reg ATS.[12] But I would argue, similar to what folks argued on the previous panel, some of the regulations made it more difficult for institutions to execute. Maybe not in comparison to what they had to deal with in the 1970s, but probably relative to what they had to deal with prior to Reg NMS.

Under the current rules, it is very difficult for two naturals to execute outside the NBBO.[13] That's one thing that isn't quite in favor of the institutions these days.

HARTS: I'm a little surprised. It seems to me the goal of the National Market System that Nina talked about is allowing institutions to trade with each other without a dealer interpositioning (being a classic market maker and taking risk). This goal has been largely fulfilled.[14] There are plenty of places where institutions trade directly with each other including, for instance, on Liquidnet or BIDS.[15] And yet, even though you have all those places, it seems like institutions still, for the vast majority of their trading, go to the continuous markets where you do have dealers, especially high-frequency trading dealers.

SUSSMAN: I don't think we're contradicting each other.

STONE: The question actually is what happened between 1975 and today? The commission structure, for the most part, looks at the needs of the individual investor rather than the institution. That goes back to 1995–1996 when the Order Handling Rules were enacted.[16] The Order Handling Rules stemmed from dealers having a two-tiered market—a tighter market was displayed on the Instinet system. The pub-

[11] ADV is the acronym for Average Daily Volume.

[12] Regulation of Alternative Trading System (ATS) was enacted by the Securities and Exchange Commission in 1998. Regulation of Exchanges and Alternative Trading Systems. https://www.sec.gov/rules/final/34-40760.txt

[13] In simple terms, the National Best Bid and Offer, NBBO, requires brokers under US regulation, to guarantee customers receive the best prevailing ask price when they buy securities, and the best prevailing bid price when they sell.

[14] Referring to the historical role of market makers in fulfilling their role as dealers and capital risk takers. On exchanges, or an ATS in many instances, a transaction traditionally was handled by an institutional customer via a dealer buying or selling stock, and often holding and selling inventory based on market supply and demand, and on profit and loss opportunities. By contrast, on other ATS platforms, a transaction is handled directly between institutional customers, so in this sense there is no "interpositioning" by the dealer.

[15] Liquidnet. https://www.liquidnet.com/. BIDS. http://www.bidstrading.com/about/company/

[16] See, the SEC's Order Handling Rules of 1997 and Beyond: Perspective and Outcomes of the Landmark Regulation RICHARD LINDSEY, JOHN AIDAN BYRNE,AND ROBERT

lic, meanwhile, saw a wider market that was displayed on the NASDAQ system. Instinet was on the inside back then, and you had a two-tiered market.

The SEC's position was individual investor protection. Now we are considering the institution. Have we gone too far focusing regulation on solely one constituency, which is the retail investor?

From that perspective, we talked about this at the Equity Market Structure Advisory Committee meetings.[17] We were talking about block trade exemptions, which the last panel talked a little bit about. Also, we talked about not being able to move the entire market because you want to do a block. One of the issues we discussed at the first meeting this year on May 13th was that institutions, for the most part, are pooled retail money. You have a different constituency, and a different setup in the marketplace than you had back in 1975, 1995 and today.

Culturally, we have an SEC that is starting to change its focus it appears, and is looking at the fairness of the different groups in the marketplace, rather than focusing on just one.

HILL: I agree 100 percent. But it seems to me that regulation is a bit overly politicized. In politics, Wall Street is often seen as the big bad institution. The reality, in fact, is different. My brother, for instance, works for the government in California, so his pension money is at CalPERS.[18] But somehow CalPERS is a bad guy in today's political sound bite environment. How do we get to where politicians stay out of regulation, or can actually understand the concepts and help? US Presidential candidate, Hillary Clinton, has proposed tinkering with the trading markets, yet I don't think she necessarily understands market structure.

SUSSMAN: If we want politicians out of regulations, the first thing we need to do is legalize pot! [laughter]

ANAND: I thought institutions were no longer the big, bad guys. We have high-frequency trading now. Haven't we moved on from that?[19]

STONE: In Europe we haven't. Under MiFID II, both the buy- and sell-side are regarded as investment companies.[20] Therefore, the regulatory regime has changed from "side" to "activity." In other words, regulation is not based on the buy-side or sell-side any longer. Rather it's the activity you are performing that determines your

---

A. SCHWARTZ. The Journal of Portfolio Management. Spring 2016. http://www.iijournals.com/doi/pdfplus/10.3905/jpm.2016.42.3.056

[17] See, Securities and Exchange Commission Archives: https://www.sec.gov/spotlight/emsac/emsac-archives.htm

[18] The California Public Employees' Retirement System manages pension and health benefits for over 1.6 million California public employees, retirees, and their families.

[19] "That" is referring to the institutions.

"The point was that at some point, the conversation used to be about protecting retail customers from institutional traders," Anand explained in a follow-up. "By the time of this conference, the focus seemed to have shifted towards HFT, or High Frequency Trading."

[20] What is Mifid II and how will it affect EU's financial industry? Far-reaching rules will have a big impact on everything from banks to brokers. *Financial Times*. September 15, 2017. https://www.ft.com/content/ae935520-96ff-11e7-b83c-9588e51488a0

regulatory obligations. It's a very different way of looking at regulation than what we have here in the US.

MiFID II went through a political process. The politicians wrote the tone and broad strokes of the rules. The high-frequency traders, or HFTs, are viewed as the big bad guys in parts of the regulation.

HARTS: Can I jump in, being the big, bad guy [laughter]? Let me take this on just a slight detour of what Alan said. There have been some political statements. Of course. We're in the midst of a hair-raising presidential campaign right now. People say a lot of things to get elected.

But some of the proposals for financial transaction taxes that seem to seek change in market behavior through things like a tax on cancellations, really could have a tremendous negative impact on our market structure.[21] People haven't paid that enough attention.

One of the taxes would equate to about 42 cents a share on the average S&P stock.[22] That's not 42 mils—that's 42 cents. Secretary Clinton's tax would be smaller, and only on cancellations. But think about the effect that would have on the ability of dealers and market participants to compete with each other.

We want people to have more competition so that prices can better reflect the true value of stocks. The idea is also to narrow spreads.[23] Any impediment that you put in the way of that will be bad for investors.

SUSSMAN: It would level the playing field, in that one sense of the word level.[24]

HILL: Indeed, Adam, both your firm and mine have an institutional client base. The fact is the market is being regulated, to your point, for the retail person. Hence, everything is in hundred share lots now. Despite the fact that 80 percent of the equities are owned by institutions who care about real price discovery at size (500,000 shares) or a million, or a 5 million share order. I don't know if you can ever level the playing field between someone who wants to buy 5 million shares of something, and somebody who wants to buy 100 shares of something. Handcuffing the person who wants to buy 5 million shares of something because someone out there wants to buy 100 of something at a sub-penny, or a penny a share better. That seems kind of a silly market.

---

[21] Night of the living tax: It's time to bury Ellison's Inclusive Prosperity Act. Bill Hart. *The Hill*. February 23, 2017. https://thehill.com/blogs/pundits-blog/economy-budget/320891-night-of-the-living-tax-its-time-to-bury-ellisons-inclusive

[22] Calculated as 0.5 percent on the notional value. Thus with average price of an S&P stock was $80, which would equate then to around 42 cents.

[23] In a follow-up, Bill Hart elaborated: "There should be as little friction or impediment" as possible in the buying and selling interest of each stock, which the market should reflect. "Any time you start talking about taxes and fees, for example, that gets in the way of figuring out the appropriate price," he said. Factoring in fees and taxes, he added, market makers instead of bidding and offering one cent spreads are, in effect, faced with additional 42 cents spreads in the proposed tax outlined.

[24] The speakers comment here was delivered with sarcasm. He confirmed later that the aforementioned "impediment" would hurt market structure in his view.

Imagine if you tried to apply that to Walmart. Say Walmart wanted to buy 10 million pairs of jeans from China, but I wanted to buy 1 pair at a better price, and China had to fill me first! You have such massively different goals here between a retail individual investor versus an institution. It's hard to say we're going to level that, and that everyone will end up with the exact same good outcome. It just doesn't seem like it's possible.

SUSSMAN: It comes down to this: Are we treating the investors equally and fairly, or are we treating the orders fairly and equally? When we say retail customers, they might be placing block orders; they might be placing hundred share lots, same for the institutions. That's why it's nice to envision a world where customer orders would be treated ahead of professionals' orders. But that would add such a degree of complexity in the marketplace that I would rather see regulations, if any, go more towards treating orders with different characteristics. This would be better than trying to get back to who the end investor is.

HARTS: I agree. It would be an exercise in futility trying to distinguish who is a customer, and when a hedge fund becomes a professional and so on.

ANAND: Any thoughts beyond the block trading exemption from Reg NMS?[25]

SUSSMAN: That's all we want.[26] [laughter]

MEHTA: I have an observation about dark pools. I was writing about some of them back in 2005, 2006 and 2007, as they emerged. One of the arguments for dark pools by many of the brokers and banks creating them was that institutional investors complained about information leakage when sales traders were working their orders. The sell-side firms thought that if they had an automated trading facility that humans weren't touching, the naturals would be able to meet up, and clients wouldn't have the same concern about information leaking out all over the Street. Of course, these sell-side firms also wanted to compete with Liquidnet, which was charging 2 cents a share, a very high number for an execution-only electronic trade around 2005. These sell-side firms wanted that flow, and they didn't want it going to Pipeline, Harborside or POSIT.[27]

From the beginning, many of these bank-owned dark pools were not doing blocks. I remember asking several people in this room, 'Why isn't your average trade size larger? Why is it 600 or 700 sharers?' Now, of course, it's 400 or 300 shares. But the broker crossing systems all said that the goal was to match up

[25] Reg NMS (Regulation National Market System) was adopted by the Securities and Exchange Commission in 2005 and introduced two years later to further advance the ideals of a national market system. The regulation includes the order protection, or trade-through rule; access rule (fair access) to market data including quotations; rules on sub-penny trading and on market data.

[26] Laughter was triggered because the speaker represents the block trading platform, Liquidnet, so the exemption would presumably benefit Liquidnet.

[27] Pipeline Trading Systems, aprivate equities and options trading system from 2004 to 2012. In 2011, it agreed to settle an action brought by the Securities and Exchange Commission over charges in the disclosure of the activities of its liquidity providing affiliate between 2004 and 2010. Pipeline was shuttered following the SEC action.

Harborside, offering crossing services, was launched in 2002.

ITG's POSIT launched in 1987, provides anonymous matching of non-displayed equity orders.

naturals. Instead, what institutional investors got were reports that said we are showing you that you are getting a better execution in our dark pools through the use of our algos, even though you're not doing actual blocks. At the same time, institutions were increasingly focused on implementation shortfall and TCA, so they didn't necessarily have the same incentive to trade blocks in a fast, electronic market as they did earlier.[28]

Some dark pools had what were called, 'I-would-if-I-could buttons' that gave customers a chance to do a block if the opportunity arose, rather than dribbling out smaller pieces of the order. But they just weren't being used. I do think there was a lot of lip-service paid to the needs of institutions. But blocks never really panned out in most of the ATS venues.

ANAND: So their market solution is that there are specific venues focused on institutions, and that may not have worked out? Does that mean that institutions prefer going to the continuous markets and trading there?

HARTS: It certainly seems that way based on volume. Probably the ratio of institutional flow that is executed in the continuous markets, versus block crossing systems, is very lopsided.

MEHTA: They would rather trade amongst themselves if that were possible, and not go to dealers, and to the market. Instinet, when it was created, was supposed to be a platform just for buy-side firms. But then it included Weeden & Co., and a few market makers, because there wasn't enough liquidity.[29] Liquidnet started H2O because their clients weren't always willing or able to wait to trade large blocks.[30] Pipeline had done something similar.[31] Institutions certainly have hurdles trading with institutions. There's a cost. The contra side may not come, the market may move away from them; they may not be able to trade in the size they need.

SUSSMAN: Institutions need to have the ability to choose the venues and participants they trade with.

To Nina's point, in our second ATS—Liquidnet H20—we have broker flow coming in. But the information asymmetry is all in favor of the institution, which is a positive for them. They get to see the order; and they can then choose whether they want to engage with it or not. They're happy to engage with broker flow in our platform. But it's on their own terms.

---

[28] Implementation shortfall is the difference between the decision price and the final execution price, which includes commissions and taxes and any other charges, for a trade. Also known as the "slippage."

Transaction Cost Analysis (TCA) measures the effectiveness of a portfolio's transactions in trade executions.

[29] See, About Weeden. https://www.weedenco.com/about-weeden/

[30] In 2006, Liquidnet established H20, an "automated trading system [that] allowed brokers and exchange partners to send retail orders to Liquidnet, a first step in turning the firm into a well-rounded agency brokerage that offered more than matched orders in a dark pool."

See, Liquidnet's Merrin Wants Main Street to Dump Wall Street. Frances Denmark. *Institutional Investor.* March 21, 2012. https://www.institutionalinvestor.com/article/b14zplx0hj0rzb/liquidnets-merrin-wants-main-street-to-dump-wall-street

[31] See, footnote 27.

Depending on their strategy and urgency, if a PM instructs a traders to get a trade done within say the next five minutes, the odds of that occurring on a passive network like Liquidnet—where you have to wait 5, 10, 15 minutes for a natural match—is just not likely.[32] As mentioned, it comes down to the urgency levels (along with a bunch of other factors).

HARTS: Let's be clear. The problems of institutions trading amongst each other are related more to liquidity than to market structure.

If they're all going in the same direction then, of course, there will not be a lot of trades happening. As you pointed out, they might have to wait. That's when you go to a continuous market, and there are dealers.

HILL: That's absolutely right. Gary touched on European regulation. If MiFID, is passed, it will be interesting to watch for the separation of institutional order flow to pay for things like research and corporate access. I think one of the big reasons why there isn't more crossing is because, you might, for example, like Goldman Sachs research and pay them $150,000 (or whatever) and send Goldman a million share trade along with this. Goldman Sachs isn't going to call up JP Morgan and say, hey, let's cross these one million shares! Goldman is thinking of how it will make more money off this one million share order. How, for example, it can internalize it. That's a huge issue, and it explains why there isn't more crossing, if you want to call it that. Jones is an execution-only firm and we're trading with people. Our institutional clients come to us because they believe we can find the other side and cross a block of stock independently with a natural buyer. On the other hand, I think a lot of the brokers who receive order flow purely because of other things besides best execution are not the ones willing to share order flow.

The first time I went into IEX I was under the impression that it was going to be talking about crossing 10,000 lots; or 50,000 lots.[33] And yet IEX was saying, well, actually the brokers are just sending us over 100 share orders because they don't want us to look good, and they can actually have 25,000 share crosses on the table. Certainly, an interesting idea.

STONE: There is absolutely nothing in Reg NMS that prescribes price-time priority.[34] There's none. You can actually have batch auctions where liquidity or orders can build up over a period of time. But when the cross happens, the clearing price has to respect Rule 611, the order protection rule of the trade-through rule in Reg NMS. So this whole batch auction concept yes, you can do it now, there's nothing

[32] As Adam Sussman explained in a follow-up, because Liquidet has a limited amount of participants allowed into its system, liquidity is also effectively limited. If a portfolio manager instructs a trader to work an order in Liquidnet in say "5 minutes," a trader is hardly likely to wait that period of time to work his order. The trader will likely move to other platforms to handle the order.

[33] Also known as the Investors Exchange. The US-based stock exchange was founded in 2012 amidst much fanfare, and is the subject of Michael Lewis' bestseller, Flashboys: A Wall Street Revolt (W. W. Norton & Company 2014). https://iextrading.com/

[34] "The principle of price/time priority refers to how orders are prioritized for execution. Orders are first ranked according to their price; orders of the same price are then ranked depending on when they were entered." Source: Marketswiki.com

in the rules that says you can't. Look at NASDAQ in the Philadelphia experiment.[35] First, they should be commended for all it is doing. It is putting real money up. But Philadelphia went with price and size priority—and it failed. It didn't work.

Why is it that most matching engines are price time priority? The reason is because that's the way people want to trade. Traders put a value on immediacy. There's a lot more slippage when you're sitting and trying to get a block done, than when you are sitting there nibbling in the market to get it done.

Maybe the problem to solve is when an order is in the market. We haven't quite figured out how to get blocks, which are sitting upstairs in the algorithms, or on the portfolio manager's blotter, to come down and interact with each other. We have had conditional orders in the market for a long time.[36] Those were supposed to help solve that problem. But they haven't done it as much as many would have liked.

I'm very, very reticent about introducing regulation—especially if it is prescriptive. I don't think it works. If we look at many parts of Reg NMS, and read the Commissions' Atkins' and Glassman's dissent published with Reg NMS, that's what they talk about. They find that Rules 611 and 610 of Reg NMS, are very prescriptive, and were not going to work. In fact, if you read the dissent and look at the reasons why they said Reg NMS was not going to work, we're actually back now at the exact same conversations that we had then. I find it fascinating to look back at history, and see what people said.

ANAND: In terms of market innovation to solve these kinds of problems, it seems we are stuck with exchanges either tweaking their pricing, or introducing new order types. What other market innovations are there besides these?

STONE: There's more that can be done. One size doesn't fit all. We need to split the universe into liquid and illiquid stocks. The market structure debate then becomes a discussion between the top 120 most liquid stocks, and everything else. The reality is (and I get a lot of pushback on this comment) that no market, no asset class across the globe has solved the illiquid security trading problems. Fixed income has probably come the closest but we are still seeing the comments about liquidity problems in corporate bonds. Futures have not fixed it; we still have illiquid futures markets. In general, we haven't figured out that part yet.

---

[35] NASDAQ OMX LAUNCHES FIRST US EQUITY PRICE-SIZE EXCHANGE. NASDAQ Press Release. September 20, 2010. Philly—price-size priority. http://ir.nasdaq.com/news-releases/news-release-details/nasdaq-omx-announces-third-equity-trading-platform-us

> The NASDAQ OMX Group, Inc. (Nasdaq:NDAQ), the world's largest exchange company, today announced that it plans to launch a third equity trading platform during the second half of 2010, pending SEC approval. NASDAQ OMX will offer this equity trading platform with a new price/size priority model using the license acquired from its 2007 acquisition of the former Philadelphia Stock Exchange, known today as NASDAQ OMX PHLX.

[36] A conditional order is a type of order that will be submitted or canceled if set criteria are met, which are defined by the trader/investor entering the order. This allows for a greater customization of the order to meet the specific needs of the investor. Source: Investopedia.

As much as we want to say that we actually have solutions, they generally just don't work. That's where there is room for innovation. That's the interesting part. Europe may be on to something in that respect, insofar as best execution is not simply back stopped by best price, which is what we have in the US with Rule 611. Best execution is actually five different components. It's speed, cost, likelihood of execution, cost of execution, cost of settlement, and any other factors specific to the nature of the trade.[37]

I think that was the way we viewed best execution before Reg NMS. That's the way NASDAQ and OTC trading was set up. Under MiFID II, you have to create and disclose an order execution policy, and then demonstrate that you are following it. Europe will be a very interesting case under MiFID II. We will see whether or not best execution can be demonstrated with an order execution policy governed by those guidelines. Maybe an exchange brings back its floor to solve the illiquid securities problems, to have a place where liquidity can coalesce and actually get people talking with each other to arrange trades.

As someone has already said, maybe the illiquid security problem isn't spreads, isn't rebates. Maybe it's the research? Maybe the Global Analyst Research Settlement knocked out the leg that decreased the amount of interest in these stocks. Institutions, retail and others—just don't know the companies stories.[38] We've never, ever gone back and asked whether the agreement disrupted the liquidity ecosystem. You could do a great study of Germany and France which did not implement the Myner's recommendations, and the UK's FCA which did.[39] Was there a decline in the amount of small and mid-cap coverage in the UK, versus the rest of Europe? It's a great test case to see whether or not research declined and liquidity was adversely impact. The Myner's agreement led to the unbundling process.[40]

Personally, I find those types of things really interesting. But I simply don't have the data, the time, or the econometric stuff to figure it all out.

HARTS: There is certainly a lot more room for innovation. In the fixed-income markets and so on, even in the equity markets, I think that you'll continue to see participants drive down spreads; and drive down the cost of trading. These are real innovations that are a benefit for all investors. We'll continue to see that. It's not just about pricing.

ANAND: What is the innovation there?

---

[37] MEMORANDUM: SEC Market Structure Advisory Committee FROM: SEC Division of Trading and Markets1 DATE: April 30, 2015. RE: Rule 611 of Regulation NMS. https://www.sec.gov/spotlight/emsac/memo-rule-611-regulation-nms.pdf

[38] SEC Fact Sheet on Global Analyst Research Settlements. https://www.sec.gov/news/speech/factsheet.htm

[39] Report by Paul Myners, March 06, 2001. https://webarchive.nationalarchives.gov.uk/20070506151732/http://www.hm-treasury.gov.uk/media/2F9/02/31.pdf

[40] Further context, see, Unpicking the research unbundling conundrum. Hayley McDowell, *The Trade*, April 15, 2019. https://www.thetradenews.com/unpicking-research-unbundling-conundrum/

HARTS: Better and faster and cheaper technology, executing trades with less intervention or less overhead, for example.

STONE: IEX is an innovation.[41] There's innovation by the ATSs. Sometimes they grow up to be exchanges, or they don't. BATS, Direct Edge, were clearly a technology innovation; IEX is a methodology innovation.[42]

SUSSMAN: You've got the SNAP auctions. You've got LSE doing a midday auction.[43] It's hard for those platforms to gain traction under the kind of tyranny of price time.[44] I'm not sure how you break away from it. Maybe that's because it's market demand. Or maybe it's because the rules are so tilted in favor of price time. But I agree with you, I'd rather see the change come about by market-led solutions. That maybe pushes the envelope of the regulatory structure rather than an overhaul.

MEHTA: Price time also works because flow is portable. One upshot of Reg NMS was that the exchanges all discovered that no flow is static, that none of it is captive anymore. You change the fees, rebates and volume tiers, and the flow shifts somewhere else. The way the exchanges innovated was through their pricing schedules; and through order types whose characteristics allowed them to appeal to certain investors or traders so as to tailor who was on their platforms.

So this kind of competition was a vicious circle. There is much more competition than there was 10, 20, 30 years ago, and at the time of the Securities Act Amendments. But there's less variety. There were totally different markets in the past. You had the listed market, you had NASDAQ dealers, you had the third market, and electronic efforts to bring blocks together.[45] Now it's essentially one big liquidity pool the shape of which shifts depending on the pricing. And the same market-making firms are the ones providing the liquidity everywhere. You don't have different specialist firms or different market makers in different regions with their own book in that market. The market makers, high-frequency traders, prop firms, have a single P&L that they're managing across different venues and asset classes. So they're providing a certain amount of liquidity, and it's represented simultaneously in a lot of different places. But they definitely don't want to execute all of what they're showing.

There's been more standardization, not just in the markets, but in how stocks trade. When the NMS was being created, the idea in Congress and at the SEC was that certain securities that met various qualifications or characteristics would be

[41] See, footnote 33.

[42] BATS Global Market and Direct Edge are part of the CBOE Global Markets. http://markets.cboe.com/

[43] Chicago Stock Exchange set to decommission SNAP and outbound routing service. Maria Nikolova. FinanceFeeds. December 20, 2018. https://financefeeds.com/chicago-stock-exchange-set-decommission-snap-outbound-routing-service/

[44] Adam Sussman explained in a follow up that, as he noted earlier on the panel, that if two naturals want to interact, they have to use the pricing in the marketplace; two institutions have to pay attention and abide by the best bid or offer in the marketplace under this, "tyranny of price time."

[45] Referring to the trading of exchange-listed securities in the over-the-counter-market.

considered NMS securities; and that their trades and quotes would be disseminated over the SIPS.[46]

In the mid- to late- '80s, they decided that all NASDAQ and all listed securities would have their quotes and trades disseminated, and that made them NMS securities. There was a difference in which stocks were participating in this interlinked competitive marketplace. The tick size study is a way to get back to that earlier idea that not all stocks should be subject to these standardized rules.[47] Now everything is an NMS security, and there's been standardization not just on exchanges, but in these other rules.

HILL: You might have a great idea, but it might subsequently be hard to generate liquidity from that idea, or to generate a critical mass of liquidity if you put that idea into action. Several interesting companies have emerged with different ways of trading, but they have never gotten enough adoption. It seems like the innovation will come from people who already have existing pools of liquidity.

To your point, there's only just so much flow there. If I'm going to put trades into that new idea, then it can work, but it's hard. It's not like Silicon Valley, where some guy can come up with some idea and suddenly move forward.

If 80 percent of the stocks are owned by institutions, it's very hard for a guy who is under-capitalized and doesn't necessarily have a track record, to get into a large financial institution and say, 'Hey, you need to start using my cool new exchange. They're going to say that there is already 14 exchanges and some 40 dark pools.'

Who are some of the participants who've come up with successful ideas? Liquidnet obviously was very successful at building a pool. IEX was very successful after a book came out.[48]

ANAND: Switching gears, I want to talk about best execution. In terms of Reg NMS, one alternate scenario looks at imposing a best execution standard and letting participants figure out if they are getting a good execution or not. Alan, you have mentioned one impediment to that, which is that trades may be routed for other reasons, in which case execution becomes less important.

HILL: Yes, absolutely.

ANAND: Have we made progress in the last 10 years? Is best execution easier to get? Are institutions better able to measure it?

HILL: I would argue it has gotten way too hard to measure, and for anyone to even know if they're getting best execution anymore. I mean you can say what the concept of best execution is. But there are so many venues, there's so much complexity in the market, and it's so fast moving. There's a perception in my mind—and I'm sure Bill would argue this—that there's a lot of liquidity out there, and that spreads are tight. But if spreads are tight in hundred share lots, and 80 percent of

---

[46] Securities Industry Processor (SIP) See Consolidated Trade Association Fact Sheet: https://www.ctaplan.com/index

[47] See, Investor Alert. Tick Size Pilot Program. What Investors Need to Know. Securities and Exchange Commission. October 03, 2016. https://www.sec.gov/oiea/investor-alerts-bulletins/ia_ticksize.html

[48] See, Flash Boys: A Wall Street Revolt. Michael Lewis (2015, WW Norton & Company, LLC).

equities are owned by institutions who realistically don't care about the hundred share lots, there isn't as much liquidity. And if it can vanish on days when things go bad, then that hurts the selling point that there's a ton of liquidity out there. And it's difficult to measure best execution.

SUSSMAN: But it goes back to what Gary was talking about earlier. What they're doing in MiFID II is that best execution isn't one thing, it's five things as defined under MiFID. It's a framework. We have the technology and the systems to help traders document and track the choices they are making. We have the technology to provide the trader with an audit trail of their decisions. As long as you go through that process, and if you can document that you've done it, you will have met at least the regulatory definition of best execution.

I do think that we're closer now, at least in Europe, given that framework. I think it will wind up being adopted globally by those firms that operate on a global basis at least to have this audit trail of buy-side decision-making.

ANAND: There is a proposal in MiFID II to get rid of soft dollars. Is that likely to happen?[49]

STONE: We'll find out in December.[50]

SUSSMAN: It's probably not going to happen. I think that CSAs (commission sharing arrangements) will still be allowed under the final rules. It will just be a more transparent process that you'll have to go through to document the value that you assign to the research and the payment mechanism that you use to pay for it.

HARTS: I want to respond to what Alan has said. Not that I necessarily disagree as much as you might think. It's true that generally the size, the quantity at the bid and the offer may not be in say, the 10,000 share range. But, I will note going back to the days before high-frequency trading, you didn't really have those kinds of sizes either from the specialists on the exchange, or from the NASDAQ market makers. Also, it really is a myth that high-frequency traders somehow abandon the markets when things get tough, and that they are responsible for phantom liquidity.[51]

Numerous studies seem to confirm that that's just not true. Just yesterday, another study based on NASDAQ data found that it is not true, that HFTs did stay in the markets. The same thing appeared in a report about a year ago on the Treasury Flash Rally.[52] The CFTC, the Fed, and a few other agencies came together, and said that HFTs were the only ones left in that market when things went awry.

---

[49] See, Wall Street Caves on MiFID, Allows Separate Payment for Research. Benjamin Bain. Bloomberg. January 24, 2020. https://www.bloomberg.com/news/articles/2020-01-24/wall-street-caves-on-mifid-allows-separate-payment-for-research

Unpicking the research unbundling conundrum. Hayley McDowell, *The Trade*, April 15, 2019. https://www.thetradenews.com/unpicking-research-unbundling-conundrum/

[50] December 2015 was the official deadline for MiFid 11.

[51] Vanderbilt study debunks "phantom liquidity" problem caused by high-frequency traders. Vanderbilt University. July 27, 2017. https://news.vanderbilt.edu/2016/07/27/vanderbilt-study-debunks-phantom-liquidity-problem-caused-by-high-frequency-traders/

[52] See, Once-in-4,800-Year Shock Is Bond Market's Cold Case Two Years On. *Bloomberg*. Rebecca Spalding and Eliza Ronalds-Hannon. October 13, 2016. https://www.bloomberg.com/news/articles/2016-10-13/bond-market-s-biggest-cold-case-leaves-questions-two-years-on

ANAND: I will take a little bit of an issue with that (laughter). It's fair to say that there are market makers who are in the business of market making, and will profit from volatility. So it is not surprising that they step up when volatility goes up. But they do step away when market making is not as profitable. It could be on days when volatility is actually low which is kind of counterintuitive. They are not going to hold large overnight inventories. They're not going to trade when it's just not profitable to do so.

HARTS: I think most traders would say we're not going to trade when it's not profitable.

ANAND: That brings me to the next question: regarding traders, who has an obligation to trade?

HARTS: In the days when the New York Stock Exchange specialist had affirmative obligations, there were certain benefits, largely for retail order flow.[53] For instance, when a specialist prevented a stock from trading with large price gaps, the intermediate trades were usually of small size.[54] No specialist was going to stand in front of a moving freight train, buying when everyone else in the market was selling. There just aren't enough incentives for anyone to do that.

If we want to open up that discussion again about how to provide incentives for market making, fine, let's do that. But it seems like the markets have moved away from that for a reason.

STONE: The advantage that market makers always had was their proximity to the marketplace. That is why they had obligations. Therefore, the fact that market making algorithms are co-located near the matching engine does afford certain advantages in terms of speed, in terms of being able to receive data quicker and being able to respond.[55] Market makers that are co-located do not have such

[53] The obligation of NYSE specialists to enter the market on a particular security (either by posting or bidding and ask) when there is not sufficient market demand and supply to efficiently match orders. The affirmative obligation required specialists to create a market for a security when public demand or supply is ineffective and cannot create it for itself. Today, the NYSE special has been succeeded by the Designated Market Makers which has altered—and in some cases expanded—their affirmative obligations. Source: Investopedia.

[54] In a follow-up Bill Harts offered this example as an explanation. "Let's say that the order book is $20 bid for 1,000; $19.00 bid for 5,000. An order then comes in to sell a 6,000 shares market. So technically, the NYSE specialist could execute 1,000 at $20 and 5,000 at $19—a big jump of $1 for just 5,000 shares.

And that would make him look really bad if there was other buying interest 'in the crowd' that is not reflected on the book. Say a buyer of 500 at 19.75 and a buyer of 2,000 are 19.50.

To accommodate this extra interest the specialist, back in the day, would often 'walk the stock down,' by first executing 1,000 at $20; then asking around the crowd for other buyers, finding the $19.75 buyer; executing that trade, finding the $19.50 buyer, executing that trade, etc.

In conclusion, on the tape the prices posted in this case were $20, $19.75, $19.50, $19. In other words, this was a 'walk' rather than a price 'jump.'"

[55] This refers to the ability of market participants to gain advantages in the speed of their trade executions and the price-quote data through advanced technology, specifically "co-location" of their computer servers near stock exchanges' computers. That lowers so-called latency, a critical factor in high-speed trade executions. The practice is regarded as legal though it has many critics.

obligations. What if you had to step in as a co-located participant in the marketplace when things start getting very volatile and crazy. Your proximity gives you advantages that provide a subsidy that has to be deployed during volatile times. It gives you an ability to provide a cushion when, for example, the markets sell-off.

Most of the studies I've seen say that Bill is right. HFTs do stand their ground in volatile markets. Indeed, the Eurex Exchange has market maker obligations as tactic confirmation that with co-location comes certain advantages such as proximity, market data, and clearing.[56] In order to have those advantages, or preference over a period of time, HFTs do stand when the market starts going crazy. It is actually during volatile times that the industry gets a black eye. Because everyone sits there and says, Oh, the market structure is all messed up because it got really volatile. Which isn't disingenuous.

SUSSMAN: Are you saying you think that co-location is such an advantage? That it should only be conferred upon those that have some kind of market making obligation? I kind of feel like you almost said that, but you didn't quite say it.

STONE: Yes. Co-location provides advantages, and there should be an obligation for that advantage.

SUSSMAN: But, getting back to something we talked about earlier, the challenge of that, is that we would then be treating one class of participants differently than another, a separate class.

STONE: We do now.

SUSSMAN: All orders should be treated equally, regardless of the firm that is generating the orders, or indeed their affirmative obligations.[57]

STONE: Yes, but unfortunately, the structure that we have right now creates those advantages, and that's really the point. It's Rule 611, the trade-through rule that creates some of those advantages. For example, speed and proximity are important. Proximity matters and introduces another set of conflicts. For example, there are different data feeds, so what should the cost be for those data feeds? What is the cost of the ports? The '75 Act said that the cost had to be fair, reasonable and not unreasonably discriminatory. I'll put words in the Commission's mouth even though I don't represent them. I would say that it should be more widely affordable, that is to say, a cost-utility model. Now we have a separation between the two. Today, only certain participants can afford certain amounts of the market data. The last panel talked about a big, huge conflict of interest between the public's SIP feeds and direct feeds. And that's not sustainable.

HARTS: If you're saying that we should put caps on market data revenue, we will absolutely back you 100 percent. I mean it's way overpriced.[58] I'm sure NASDAQ will disagree. But that's our marketplace. To Adam's point, I don't think

---

[56] Eurex Exchange. https://www.eurexchange.com/exchange-en/

[57] "Affirmative obligations" refers to the obligations established by an exchange to be a market maker.

[58] "Disclosures from ICE, Nasdaq and Cboe show that their combined stock-market data revenues were around $560 million in 2017, although those don't include connection fees that traders and brokers pay to access the data."

we should exclude anyone. NASDAQ makes those feeds, and co-location space, and everything else available to everyone on an equal basis. Anyone who wants to buy it can buy it.

STONE: You know, it's interesting, the SEC chair, Mary Jo White, talked in recent times about how we need to look at co-location, whether or not everybody actually does have fair access into it, and whether or not only certain participants can actually leverage the co-location facility.

ANAND: Questions?

SCHWARTZ: I would like to circle back to block trading. In going after a fair and level playing field, has that resulted in the breaking up of blocks? Do you think it's good to have blocks? What would it take to get blocks back? Do we have to be a bit more relaxed about enforcing a fair and level playing field?

I see a market doing two things: Price discovery and quantity discovery. Price discovery is well done, or as well as possible in the lit market.[59] That's what you look to. I'd see blocks as an approach to quantity discovery. It seems to me in that, in our current environment, price discovery, and quantity discovery have disconnected. It seems to me that if you could bring back the blocks, and have it work more efficiently, you'd have better integration, and better discovery on both fronts.

SUSSMAN: On an exchange, from a holistic perspective, I think we've already covered the ground. There are some tweaks—of the existing regulation that would allow for some block activity to occur with less friction. Aside from that, I would go back to what we said earlier. Regulations treat all participants the same—and they shouldn't.

I don't think that all orders, or all securities should be treated the same. It should be based on the characteristics of the orders. I don't want to get back to a place where we're treating different participants separately. But it would be useful to say that different orders in different types of securities can be handled outside of the existing Reg NMS framework. That would be useful, not just for blocks but for all sorts of other activities in the marketplace.

STONE: There is quantity, or size discovery right now. The problem is that there is not enough of a buffer for a capital commitment discovery. You don't have the ability as a market maker take down a block, and still have either a time or a price cushion to be able to either hedge or work out of the position without moving the market. That is something, I think, that we need to look at more.

"'Costs for exchanges' data have grown over the past eight years at a compound average growth rate 11.7%, according to industry consultant Larry Tabb." Source: *Wall Street Journal*. Dave Michaels. Wall Street Fractures Over Stock Exchanges' Data Sales. Some traders say exchanges have a monopoly over certain data, allowing them to charge too much. October 25, 2018. https://www.wsj.com/articles/traders-exchanges-to-square-off-in-market-data-fee-fight-1540465201

[59]A lit market refers to venues that display the various bids and offers in stocks. By contrast, dark markets, or dark pools, do not display prices.

When you look at the fixed-income market with TRACE, big sizes are printed.[60] But they're printed obscurely in some ways, so that the true size isn't there. Right now, if I take down a block of stock, I have a winner's curse immediately. All of a sudden the market could start going against me because everyone knows that the block trade just occurred. That's what we're trying to bring back—a profitable market for the market maker who is willing to put up the capital to move those big blocks.

Some market makers exist to provide immediacy in the trading of blocks. That can be a fleeting phenomenon because the likelihood of a block seller and a block buyer arriving at the decision to trade at the same time can indeed, be, fleeting. Sometimes a market maker needs to stand in the middle to bridge a time gap, to assemble different parties together, to either create or to distribute a block.

HILL: TCA is an interesting dynamic in the block discussion in terms of how TCA has changed the behavior of traders on the buy-side. The best execution committee at a buy-side firm, or managers at the firm, will often say, 'Well, we will bring in outside consultants to measure performance on our trading desk each quarter.' That decision to bring in outside consultants will ultimately drive your best execution rating much as it drives how traders are rated for their year-end performance. In this instance, if VWAP is selected as the measurement of quality by some firms, suddenly the entire trading of these firms will be influenced by VWAP.[61] In this scenario, Jones, for example, may call a firm working a large order and say, 'Hey, we'll sell you five days of volume, or we may have a natural on the other side for this order.' Because this firm is tied to VWAP, it may be constrained because the stock offered is, for example, at 2 cents away from the VWAP. The firm is therefore handcuffed, afraid to act.

Maybe the stock price rises a bit. We may then turnaround and sell it to a firm who previously didn't want the stock because it was constrained by VWAP. Behavior is being driven a lot because of this dynamic. Every day I spend visiting clients, I think behavior has been driven a lot by that dynamic. That has made some people fearful in their trading approach.

Larry Tabb and the TABB Group have done a lot of industry studies. Every single time it emerges from these studies that a huge percentage of institutional traders want to trade more blocks. But they have a fear in the back of their minds that there will be some bias against that block in a very short period of time.

Then some guy at an outside consulting firm says, 'Oh, that was a very bad trade you just did.' But the reality is, you have a PM at a fund that thinks, 'Hey, that stock was a buy, and it's for a long holding period.' He thinks the stock is going to go up 20 percent in the next year, so who cares if you step a penny away from the NBBO? If you have someone on the outside essentially contradicting that, saying that's bad and, hence, the trader on that trade is not a good trader, that's a negative dynamic the industry needs to think more about.

[60] TRACE is FINRA's system for collecting transactions in corporate bonds and other fixed income instruments from FINRA members and disseminating them to the public.

[61] Volume Weighted Average Price, or VWAP.

SUSSMAN: That's why I think that the best execution framework that's evolving based on the MiFID II regs, will change that. On top of that, you have the MiFid dark pool cap.[62] So those two things combined will change the attitudes towards TCA, and block trading in Europe.

HILL: But, again, everything has been measured off of a quote that's 100 shares wide on either side. To me, this isn't real discovery of any kind. Certainly not if you are trying to trade 5 million shares.

STONE: I want to clear something up. The actual best execution rules in the U S set forth by the FINRA Rule 5310 best execution rules, as well as the lawsuit, *Newton v. Merrill Lynch* in '98, have the five same components that we have in Europe.[63] The difference is that, in the US, SEC Rule 611 back-stops best execution to best price which is the National Best Bid and Offer (NBBO). It is Rule 611 that puts such a focus on price versus other best execution components.

An institution can define what it sees as best-execution, given the investment goals of the fund (it's alpha strategy). Best-ex can be defined in the context of the investment goal. For example, if I'm a portfolio manager who wants to buy five days of volume because I expect the price to rise and—I will exaggerate—to return 200 percent, my execution strategy may favor volume capture, that is to say, size over average price. If I am dealing in an illiquid stock, I may wish to pay up for a block. In this case, buying a large block of stock at the height of the market on a particular day because it became available. This may be the better investment implementation strategy, rather than trying to hit the VWAP for that day.

HARTS: To your point about 611. We've talked here today about complexity in the markets, and some of the reasons. If we all agreed to eliminate the prohibition on locked markets—that doing so would simplify a lot of the problems we're talking about here—it would probably lead to fewer markets as well.[64] If markets weren't able to force or to attract order flow just by virtue of blocking a market, I think there would probably be fewer markets.

STONE: I'm not sure I agree. One of the things we should probably do is a pilot, or study of whether or not eliminating the prohibition on locked markets would be good for market structure.

One of the problems we have in the marketplace is that we sit there, talking about how great displayed markets are; and how important it is to incentivize the display. But blocks are different from average trade size interactions. Average size trade

---

[62] Refers to the dark pool volume cap proposals under MiFID in Europe, proposals such as permitting just 4 percent of the total trading in an individual stock in a dark pool. At the time of writing, in late 2019, cap rules had come into effect.

[63] See, NEWTON v MERRILL LYNCH. https://www.leagle.com/decision/2001413259f3d1541400

[64] Market makers may not enter quotes that would lock or cross the market. A locked market is one where the bid and offer are equal in price. A crossed market is one where a bid is entered that is higher than the offer or, one where an offer is entered that is lower than the bid. Source: Investopedia.

Regarding the "ban" on locked and crossed markets, see, To Lock or Not to Lock. Terry Flanagan. MarketsMedia. July 07, 2014. http://marketsmedia.com/to-lock-or-not-to-lock

UPDATE ON OUR EFFORTS TO REVITALIZE U.S. EQUITY MARKETS, APRIL 10, 2019. NASDAQ PRESS RELEASE. https://business.nasdaq.com/totalmarkets

orders are a few hundred shares. In addition, there are obstacles to block executions—from the Intermarket Sweep Orders (ISOs), to hidden orders having preferences, and mid-points having preferences over the guy who is actually displaying—which is setting the price—to the fact that reserve doesn't have preference in the repainting of several of the exchanges.[65]

We have to have a discussion at the commission level on what is the display, and are we really incentivizing the display order? Should we be collapsing the threshold of an ATS, in order to bring more, not necessarily out of the dark pools or the ATSs, but to make the ATSs more lit?[66]

It's funny. I go back to when Bloomberg Tradebook first started. Every single one of the ECNs' quotes always had a displayed component to it. Dark pools didn't come in until around when Island was introduced. Island had a big spat in the ETFs, and so Island went dark on them.[67] Then all of a sudden, we had a wave of consolidation. At the end, when NASDAQ applied to become an exchange rather than a stock market, NASDAQ formalized the hidden order types in their rule book. Every venue then began to introduce hidden order types. Market microstructure order preference in matching engines subsequently became much more complicated.

MEHTA: Institutions always want to hide their interest. That was why 2 dollar brokers existed on the NYSE floor. They didn't want their information revealed. And what Alan was saying is right, that with the implementation of Reg NMS, there were shifts in how people look at blocks. Institutions were used to trading within the spread when the tick was larger, and they didn't want to trade two ticks or three ticks away because that just felt lousy. Even on Liquidnet, buy-side firms preferred that mid-point, and were reluctant to negotiate price.

But Reg NMS also changed intermediation. At the same time that banks and brokers were telling their customers that they would address their concerns about information leakage on the sales desk, they were basically saying we will intermediate in another way through this dark pool. We will give you algos, which is another form of intermediation, and then we'll give you TCA reports that say, hey, you're doing great.

ANAND: Question?

ENRICO CACCIATORE [Voya Financial]: Two questions: Gary, if we gave direct feeds to everyone, for free, how will that really give you an advantage? I think you are just trying to nitpick on something miniscule.

---

[65] Re-painting the screen is a term adapted by traders for replenishing the display, or redisplaying. For example, let's say there are 100 shares on display; 500 on reserve. Then, a 100-share order comes in, so the electronic book matches 100 vs display, and then "redisplays 100" leaving 400 shares in reserve.

[66] Referring to the threshold, or volume limits permitted for individual stocks traded on Alternative Trading Systems (ATSs).

[67] See, Island Goes Dark: Transparency, Fragmentation, and Regulation. Terence Hendeshott, Univertsity of Calrifornia at Berkeley. Charles M Jones. Columbia University. January 05. 2005. http://faculty.haas.berkeley.edu/hender/Island_Dark.pdf

Second question: Everybody should define what is a block? For example, if multiple 1,000 shares, or 1,000 share prints, go up in 500 milliseconds, is that considered a virtual block?[68]

STONE: I'll take the SIP related question. I think Larry's Clarity project is showing a couple of things.[69] One, we have several exchanges that still use the SIP in order to be able to match, as do a lot of the ATSs. That appears to cause significant slippage in terms of where the mid-point is at any point in time. Because of that, there is an advantage. There is something that does occur, that is disadvantaging participants who deal in those pools.

If everybody got direct feeds, would it change? If you go back and read Reg NMS, one of the things it said was that Instinet asked the question, are we supposed to synchronize to a point and place where all our quotes are supposed to land? The SEC said no, you wouldn't be able to technologically do it reliably. I tend to agree. So information has to leave the venue at the same time, and then you can put yourself where you want it to be. But the slippage between the SIP and the direct feeds is occurring because of the processing slowness of the SIP. Also because quotes need to travel from data processing centers in north Jersey to data processing centers in south Jersey for aggregation before they are sent back out to the marketplace. Direct feeds go directly to a source for aggregation.

Why is it that everybody hasn't gone to direct feeds when this slippage occurs? I will argue that there is a bit of a regulatory bias towards the SIP. For some, it's easier to comply with Rule 611 using the SIP. Reg NMS says that you can have policies and procedures to create your own electronic order book, or view (that is a snapshot) of the market at a particular point in time when you made your routing/matching decisions. But what ends up happening is that a regulator will walk into a trading firm, looking at the SIP as a benchmark, and say that it's trading outside the inside. That it's in violation of 611.

In these hundreds of instances when the SIP is slow, the direct feeds aren't. So, consequently, a firm in this situation described will have to sit there, and actually go back and reconstruct the view that the electronic order book had of the market at the time that it was said to be in violation of 611. But the standard in Reg NMS is very different. You simply need reasonable policies and procedures to show you are receiving market quotes in a manner that provides a reasonable view of the best bid and offer off of the market to match orders, or a reasonable view of the market when you send orders to other market venues. And so we've gotten to this way of looking at the SIP—that it's the regulatory benchmark; and that's why a lot of institutions still use the SIP, and some of the exchanges do, too.

SUSSMAN: On your block question, were all of the executions done at the same price?

---

[68] Virtual blocks are, in effect, block trades, and a phenomena of advanced electronic trading markets.

[69] https://www.globenewswire.com/news-release/2017/01/10/904859/0/en/TABB-Group-Announces-Spinoff-of-Clarity-Service.html

CACCIATORE: The same price.

SUSSMAN: And were they all agreed to ahead of time? For each print was there an agreement to trade?[70]

CACCIATORE: In my example, we're talking about five different trades.

SUSSMAN: I don't think that time is really a function of the block. If I said yes to that, and then you were like, well what about over one second, what about two seconds, ten seconds? I would say no. The agreement has to be at a single point in time otherwise we'd get into a kind of Pandora's Box.[71]

ANAND: Bob Schwartz has stood up, so we must go! Thank you all very much.

[70] The speaker is referring to how he is defining a "block" trade. In his view, a block trade needs to occur at a single point in time, that you can't take multiple executions for one larger order—even if they occurred within a brief period, e.g., a second.

[71] Ibid.

Chapter 6
What Have We Learned?

Bob Pisani, William Brodsky, Arthur Cashin, and Richard Lindsey

ROBERT SCHWARTZ: Bob Pisani has honored us many times as a moderator at past conferences. So I can confidently predict he will be a splendid moderator, once again, for this next panel.

I invited him back today because, like many of you, I follow Bob closely on CNBC broadcasts, from my home and office, and yet he never sees me watching him. So by having him here today, we are both finally face to face [laughter]! And the same thing has happened with Art Cashin, I see him on the floor of the New York Stock Exchange on CNBC broadcasts. As for Bill Brodsky and Rich Lindsey, we go back a long way, as friends and as professional colleagues.

PISANI: Nina Mehta on an earlier panel today, gave a typically thorough history of NMS.[1] Between these three guys on the panel, we have about 130 years of collective industry experience. All of them go back to the 1970s. Art Cashin was on the floor of the New York Stock Exchange in 1965. Bill Brodsky, a long-time friend, is executive chair of the Chicago Board Options Exchange. Richard Lindsey at the

[1] Federal legislation launched on June 4, 1975, to amend the Securities Exchange Act of 1934. The 1975 Amendments instructed the Securities and Exchange Commission to cooperate with the industry in creating a National Market System, alongside an ambitious system for the clearance and settlement of securities transactions nationwide. The Amendments also provided for the prohibition of fixed-commission rates, promulgated earlier by the SEC in its Rule 19b-3.

B. Pisani (✉)
CNBC, New York, NY, USA

W. Brodsky
CBOE Holdings, Inc., Chicago, IL, USA

A. Cashin
UBS, New York, NY, USA

R. Lindsey
Callcott Group, New York, NY, USA

R. A. Schwartz et al. (eds.), *40 Years of Experience with the National Market System (NMS)*, Zicklin School of Business Financial Markets Series,
https://doi.org/10.1007/978-3-030-91912-2_6

Callcott Group, is chief investment strategist for liquid alternatives at Janus. More importantly, he was director of market regulation at the SEC until 1999, witnessing a lot of the changes that ultimately led to Reg NMS.[2]

The topic today is what have we learned? That's why I mentioned the 130 years of collective panel experience of the national market system, which is our system in the US for trading equities. What is the difference between, say, 40 years ago and today? What was good and bad, what drove the change?

Bill Brodsky said he'll start by sending me two lists. One has terms very prevalent on trading floors in 1975, the second is a list of terms prevalent today.

According to the first list: In 1975, there were odd lots, 5-day settlement, tape watchers, floor traders, the ITS system, and a bunch of other terms and names.[3] You get the idea. Terms today include index funds, exchange-traded funds, high-frequency trading, payment for order flow, co-location, and dark pools.[4] The point is the terminology is completely different today. Bill, things have changed a lot. What have we learned in the past 40 years?

WILLIAM BRODSKY: So much has changed. I could argue that even without Reg NMS, the march of technology has been so breathtaking that change would have occurred anyway. My perspective is that Reg NMS came about because the SEC conducted a special study of the securities markets back in '63.[5] Quite frankly, my view is that the SEC had wanted to break the monopoly of the New York Stock Exchange, and particularly the power of the New York Stock Exchange specialist. A lot of those things did occur (actually I think during Richard Lindsey's watch) with the introduction of Reg ATS, and other things.[6]

So, you had the combination of the government push, plus the march of technology in which certain things were going to happen anyway. But Reg NMS tried to

[2] Reg NMS (Regulation National Market System) was adopted by the Securities and Exchange Commission in 2005, and introduced two years later, to further advance the ideals of a national market system. The regulation includes the order protection, or trade-through rule; access rule (fair access to market data including quotations); rules on sub-penny trading, and on market data.

[3] For odd lots see, FLASHBACK FRIDAY: Odd Lots in Focus. John A'Antona. *Markets Media*. November 17, 2017. https://www.marketsmedia.com/flashback-friday-odd-lots-focus/

Some years ago, the settlement date for stocks was T+5, or five business days after the transaction date. Watching the (Ticker) Tape explained. https://www.investopedia.com/articles/01/070401.asp

[4] This refers to the ability of market participants to gain advantages in the speed of their trade executions, and price-quote data through advanced technology, specifically the "co-location" of their computer servers near stock exchanges' computers. That lowers so-called latency, a critical factor in high-speed trade executions.

The practice is regarded as legal though it has many critics.

Payment for Order Flow is the compensation and benefit a brokerage receives by directing orders to different parties to be executed, typically for a penny per share, or a fraction of a penny.

[5] Congress authorized the Securities and Exchange Commission to conduct this *Special Study of the Securities Markets*.

[6] Regulation Alternative Trading Systems, or Reg ATS. See, https://www.sec.gov/rules/final/34-40760.txt

homogenize it by creating common standards for quotes, intermarket trading, more efficient clearing and so on.

Looking back, I could say it was really a much simpler world, much more collegial- in the same way that in the old days you knew your travel agent. You'd call up and you would order tickets. Maybe a week later, you'd get the tickets in the mail. My feeling is that everything now is instant.

As with other things in life, we've learned that the financial markets have, in fact, moved very quickly to a digitized standard. A lot of people will say that this is bad. They'll talk about high-frequency trading as a bogeyman, or as other things. In reality, my belief is that investors are really much better off overall than they ever were. The market has been democratized in my view. I would say, overall, we're better off today. But we still have to grapple with a lot of the changes, and with how people perceive what's happened. Indeed, the negative perception is a big issue.

PISANI: Art, when I came on the floor in the mid-'90s, trading was still done in eighths, as I recall.[7] It was very obvious to me at the time that the SEC was somewhat hostile to the New York Stock Exchange. Also, I think that was the SEC attitude to the NASDAQ. Here's my impression: The SEC thought the NYSE was too slow to adopt changes that the SEC saw as good. The SEC was more interested in electronic trading than in other things, and it smelled a lot of resistance to electronic trading at the NYSE, I think rightfully so. Tell us a little bit about the origin of that hostility. How did that hostility, if I'm characterizing it correctly, shape our market structure?

ART CASHIN: A couple of minor points. I'm not here to represent UBS, I'm not here to represent the New York Stock Exchange. And at the request of my sons, I'm not here to represent the family (laughter)! But my friend Bob Pisani said that since I became a member of the NYSE over 50 years ago, I might have some historic perspective. I'm honored to be with these gentlemen who have almost had an equal amount of industry experience.

---

[7] Prior to 2001, markets in the US traded in fractional increments, such as eighths, in their stock price quotes. Since the introduction of decimalization, all quotes appear in decimal trading format.

Arthur Cashin pointed out in a follow-up, that for well over 200 years after its founding, the NYSE traded in fractions, that is eighths of a dollar. "Folklore says that was because the early American currency was so suspect that people used other currencies," he said. "One that was popular was said to be the Viennese Johanthaler. Like the Spanish pieces of eight [term for the old Spanish dollar], you could break off one of the pieces to make change. Think of a pizza with eight slices. One bit was 12.5 cents, and two bits was a quarter—a reference still heard around the country today."

Cashin went on to explain that as the twenty-first century approached, there was pressure to decrease the increments, in the hope that the quote spread could then narrow. "The first attempt was to cut the eighth in half—and we so began to trade in sixteenths, or 6.25 cents (called teenies)," he said. "Next they went from fractions to decimals, and that allowed shrinking the increment to a penny."

Cashin concluded by recalling how the week before decimal pricing was introduced, traders were happy to pay up 6.25 cents since that was a single increment. "Once we went to pennies," he added, "they were aghast to pay up three increments, even though that represented only 3 cents less than half the increment they were happy with the week before. Illogical, but true."

The hostility goes back to several things. It even went back further, to some degree, to the '40s and the '30s, when the SEC was founded. You have to recall that the New York Stock Exchange, in the SEC's view was, in some ways, too big to regulate. There was a somewhat apocryphal story, well believed, that in the late '40s the SEC called the NYSE on a Friday afternoon, and asked to speak to the chairman and several board members. The SEC said, effective Monday, we are introducing a rule that will separate the role of principal and agent. In effect, that rule would have separated the two functions of an NYSE specialist. The specialist could then trade for his own account as principal, or execute for others and charge a commission, as agent. And purportedly the SEC was told by the chairman, that in that case the exchange wouldn't open on Monday![8] Lo and behold, that was enough to send the SEC back to the negotiating table.

So, if you are dealing with an 800-pound gorilla, you certainly want to make sure you have some way to handle that gorilla. To your point, Bob, I don't know if it was outright hostility. The SEC always wanted to get the NYSE to be somewhat less dominant. In the watering holes of Wall Street, particularly those down around 11 Wall Street, the SEC always felt that it bent over backward to champion any David who would take on the Goliath. And sometimes that David was Mr. Madoff.[9]

The NYSE has had a history of looking at competition. Obviously, the competitors have had a history of looking at a dominant market. The NYSE in its heyday, had about 85 percent of the order flow. In the 1960s that meant an NYSE trade had the *Parents Magazine's* seal of approval. If you couldn't get it up in New York, and you had to take it to the Midwest Stock Exchange, or somewhere else, that raised questions about pricing because the New York Stock Exchange was the most centralized market.[10] The NYSE was, theoretically, where the best bids and offers were. If the person who was trading your block couldn't get you up in New York, maybe you weren't getting the best price.

When you get that kind of dominant position, when your order flow is over 85 percent of total volume of stocks listed on the NYSE, and people give you that kind of credibility, both your competitors and your regulator think they want to see things change.

---

[8] The Chairman and Board's threat not to open on that following Monday would have been very disruptive to markets, with the NYSE having an 80 percent market share in trading, as Arthur Cashing explained in a follow up. Consequently, he added, the SEC, "had to back down and re-negotiate with the NYSE, producing a much milder version of the rule."

[9] 11 Wall Street refers to the address for the New York Stock Exchange. Mr. Madoff, of course is Bernard Madoff, who was a rival of the NYSE at the time, and in this context, is considered a David taking on the epic might of the Goliath, NYSE.

[10] As Arthur Cashin explained in a follow-up: "If you [trader] had to go to a different market [exchange] to execute [print] your order, odds are it was mispriced since someone on the NYSE would likely pay higher, or sell lower." The Midwest Stock Exchange changed its name back to the Chicago Stock Exchange in 1993.

Now I will pass it off. I will tell you the first step that I recall in NMS was, as my friend, Mr. Brodsky, pointed out, not the most efficient. But it was somewhat effective. It was the ITS, or Intermarket Trading System.[11]

We had emerged from a period of small regional exchanges, such as the Chicago and Philadelphia Exchanges, trying to get everything back together through the ITS. The one good thing about ITS, I recall, was one of its very first rules, which meant you couldn't block a market.[12] And as we went further into NMS, as I recall the early stages, people were allowed to lock markets, causing trading to freeze.

PISANI: Richard, you were director of market regulation for the SEC until 1999. You had a whole front row seat to the changes that were occurring in the late 1990s. Is it fair to say that the SEC was hostile to the New York Stock Exchange, and the NASDAQ? Why was that?

RICHARD LINDSEY: I don't think it's actually fair to say that there was hostility. Before I joined the SEC, I was on sabbatical at the New York Stock Exchange and a professor at Yale.[13] And I can tell you how the NYSE operated. Indeed, there were the regionals at that time. The New York Stock Exchange philosophy was that they wanted the regionals to be there for competition, but they also wanted the regional exchanges on life support. Because if the NYSE could keep the regionals on life support, then these regionals really weren't competition. But the NYSE could always point to this and say, look, we've got all this competition!

The reality was there was no competition for the New York Stock Exchange, or really for NASDAQ at that point in time. So a lot of the change back then was really all about a fairly simple idea.

Because what happens over time in a regulated environment is that for the institutions that are the dominant players in the regulated environment, regulations become barriers to new entrants in the market. They become barriers to innovation. Regulations allow incumbent institutions to keep out new entrants, and prevent innovation and competition. Those barriers to competition were really what we were looking to remove.

[11] Electronic network linking the trading floors of US registered exchanges, to permit trading among them in stocks listed on either the NYSE, or the former standalone American Stock Exchange, and one or more regional exchanges. The ITS was created so that a broker or market maker on the floor of any participating exchange could reach other participants for an execution, whenever the nationwide quote showed a better price available. A floor broker on the exchange could enter an ITS order to assure execution of all of an offering or bid, instead of splitting it with competing brokers. Sources: NASDAQ definition. Industry Research

[12] As Arthur Cashin noted in a follow-up, the correct term referring to "block" the market is "lock the market," meaning that "you could not offer at a price bid on another exchange nor could you bid at another exchange's offer." Cashed added: "The rule forced you [the trader] to ship the order to the exchange that was bidding or offering. That caused that order to be executed on that exchange. And that increased their market share so other exchanges tried to avoid."

[13] Richard Lindsey was director of market regulation at the Securities and Exchange Commission from November 1995 to February 1999. He was a visiting economist at the NYSE from August 1994 to July 1995.

We created the order handling rules, and ECNs, and then Reg ATS that followed. We were all about trying to increase competition in the marketplace.[14] At least from my perspective as an economist, competition regulates much better than lawyers or regulation does. If you try to write rules, you are going to get it wrong.

For the most part, if you instead can engender competition in the marketplace, then it will naturally start to find a reasonable place to be. Competition, of course, has an ill effect for many incumbents in the marketplace. What happens to them changes, sometimes for the good, sometimes for the bad. The old saying is that you can tell competition works by counting the dead bodies. It is generally true.

PISANI: If it's not hostility, there at least was a sense that they were actively trying to block change, or block competition. Your purpose was to increase the competition, which is why we got ECNs and ATSs, and the whole panoply of systems we see now.[15]

LINDSEY: Right, combined with the fact that the system wasn't working really.

PISANI: How was it not working?

LINDSEY: This was talked about a little bit on the last panel. In particular, think about what was happening in the NASDAQ market back then, where odd eighths were essentially not being displayed to the public, and instead you had Instinet.[16] And no fault of Instinet's, but I've always said it: Instinet gave a way to kind of break that coalition, of not displaying those prices. So, if you put Instinet and the market together, you actually had what looked like a normal market. But only the market makers were dealing really in Instinet. There weren't actually that many institutional players in Instinet at the time. The market makers were using it as a way to enforce the avoidance of odd eighths.

So part of what we needed to do was this: Find a way to bring the quotes from a place like Instinet, into the marketplace. And that was done through the order handling rules.[17] Now the order handling rules also had an impact that people seemed to neglect, on the New York Stock Exchange. In fact, orders there also had to be displayed if they, indeed, improved the quote. Because previously orders didn't necessarily have to be displayed.

PISANI: Bill, do you want to pick up on that?

BRODSKY: Well, there were other changes at the time. You had the advent of discount brokers.[18] I recall vividly that a firm like Charles Schwab not only repre-

---

[14] SEC's Order Handling Rules and Beyond. Richard Lindsey, John Aidan Byrne, Robert Schwartz. Rapidly Changing Securities Markets, Springer, August 2017. https://link.springer.com/chapter/10.1007/978-3-319-54588-2_1

[15] Ibid.

[16] Institutional Networks, founding name of today's Instinet, was launched in 1969 as the first automated system that, in practice, allowed institutions to trade directly with each other. See history of Instinet, and as of writing, now part of Nomura. https://www.instinet.com/about-instinet/history.html

[17] See footnote 9.

[18] On May 1, 1975, the brokerage industry deregulated commissions, as part of the National Market System, a change that ushered in the era of discount brokers like Charles Schwab.

sented smaller customers, but didn't particularly like doing business on the New York Stock Exchange. And so firms like Charles Schwab would try to give business out elsewhere, so market fragmentation started in ways that hadn't existed before.

PISANI: Fixed commissions were abolished in '75, right?[19]

BRODSKY: Yes, and the elimination of fixed commissions is really what gave rise to the discount brokers. There were many more between '75 and '80, than there are today. But, of course, many of those firms now have gotten very, very large. But there was a desire to find places to do business, other than the New York Stock Exchange. For many years, if you were a member of the NYSE, you had to do all your business on the NYSE, unless later on you were a member of other exchanges.[20]

Firms like Schwab would find ways to do business off the New York Stock Exchange. And that created other, what I would call, very intense issues that, again, helped force these changes. There weren't dark pools at the time, but there were competing markets on the regional exchanges, and ultimately on some of the ECNs.

CASHIN: But you can't overlook the fact that many of those discount brokers were involved in a practice that some people thought was payment for order flow. They were shipping orders to particular brokers, the aforementioned Mr. Madoff being a classic example. And that was one of the reasons these firms also wanted to step away from the stock exchange. They were getting a rebate and, therefore, it was better for them to trade away from the New York Stock Exchange.[21]

LINDSEY: Well, even that was bifurcated to some extent. Not to pick on Schwab, but as a prime example, Schwab bought specialist units on the floor of the Pacific, and on the floor of the Boston exchanges.[22] If Schwab was the specialist in a particular security, then Schwab routed the order to their specialist unit, and its specialist unit could then capture the spread associated with it. And if they couldn't,

---

[19] See, Federal legislation launched on June 4, 1975, to amend the Securities Exchange Act of 1934. The 1975 amendments instructed the Securities and Exchange Commission to cooperate with the industry in creating a National Market System along with an ambitious system for the clearance and settlement of securities transactions nationwide. The amendments also provided for the prohibition of fixed-commission rates, promulgated earlier by the SEC in its Rule 19b-3.

[20] Competing With the New York Stock Exchange. William O. Brown Jr., J Harold Mulhern, Marc D Weidenmeir. *The Quarterly Journal of Economics*, Volume 123, Issue 4, 1 November 2008, Pages Pages 1679–1719, https://doi.org/10.1162/qjec.2008.123.4.1679. November 1, 2008.

[21] Firms like Bernard L. Madoff Securities paid firms to send their order flow directly to them. The key targets, as Arthur Cashin explained in a follow-up, were often discount brokers because the payments added to their income. When complaints arose that Madoff and others were executing these orders to their advantage, and not for the advantage of their clients, these payments began to fade away.

"As payment for order flow began to fade under criticism," added Cashin,"a new factor has emerged. It is a system of rebates in which market centers pay people for certain types of orders, and charge others who took the liquidity provided."

[22] The Pacific Exchange was a regional stock exchange in California acquired by Archipelago Holdings in 2005, which merged in 2006 with the New York Stock Exchange.

The Boston Stock Exchange, a regional stock exchange based in Boston, Masachusetts, was acquired by NASDAQ in a deal announced in 2007.

then they would route to Bernie Madoff, or to other third market makers, and accept a rebate payment for order flow.[23]

PISANI: This was not uncommon. Quick & Reilly was on the floor, as well.[24]

BRODSKY: Then you had the advent of 'unfixed', or negotiated commissions. Later, the spreads went from eighths to sixteenths, and ultimately to pennies. It was like a mosaic, although not necessarily called for by the national market system.

PISANI: You had, number one, changes in market structure, going from eighths to sixteenths and pennies. Then you had the desire of the SEC to foster competition, and next you had the advanced technology changes, which meant the sheer ability to conduct computerized trading.

I remember in 1999 when I got a call from Matt Andresen.[25] Matt said, "Mr. Pisani, I want you to come and take a look at our operation, it's called Island. We're at 30 Broad, we're right next door to you.'[26]

When I had heard about these guys, I sort of had Dick Grasso's attitude-why should I come and see you?.[27] And Matt said, because we're going to take down the New York Stock Exchange—and we don't like NASDAQ either! I'm thinking, I've got a real nut case here on my hands, this is going to be great. In any event, I decided I would come over and take a look at Island in lower Manhattan, near the NYSE building.

So I go over, and I walk upstairs. There's this kid working at Island, standing there, his name is Chris Concannon, and he introduced himself.[28] I asked, "Could I see your operations?" There is a pause. "Operations?" Chris asked. "Can I see the guts of this thing," I explained? Chris replied, "All right, but you're not going to be impressed." I nodded and said, "I still want to see it."

Chris then takes me into a room on the second floor. It was this tiny little room filled with off-the-shelf Dell computers, strung together with wires. I gave it one look, and muttered: "You're going to take down the New York Stock Exchange with this?" And I'll never forget this next moment, when Chris crisply responded, "Bob, it's not the hardware, it's the software. There are people trading algorithms using software through our systems".

So I asked Chris to name one of Island's clients, in fact, to name its biggest client. He replied, "You don't know any of our clients because they're new." I asked,

---

[23] Referring to Bernard Madoff of Bernard L Madoff Investment Securities. See historical background, and the role played by Bernie Madoff in the so-called "third market", see footnote 9.

[24] Referring to Quick & Reilly's JJC Specialist Corp. on the floor of the New York Stock Exchange.

[25] Matt (Matthew) Andresen, founder and CEO of Headlands Technologies. Richard Lindsey is recalling when Andresen was President and CEO of Island ECN. See Andresen's Bio, http://www.headlandstech.com/about/matthew-andresen/

[26] Paper on how NYSE floor operated for more historical context: http://people.stern.nyu.edu/jhasbrou/Research/Working%20Papers/NYSE.PDF

[27] Dick (Richard) Grasso, Chairman and CEO, New York Stock Exchange, 1995 to 2003.

[28] At time of writing, Chris (Christopher) Concannon is President and Chief Operating Officer of Cboe Global Markets, Inc.

"What's the name of your biggest client?" He shot back the name of a fellow named Steve Swanson at Automated Trading Desk.[29]

I soon went down to visit Island's client, Automated Trading Desk in Charleston, South Carolina, where they had their operations. I walked into the building where it was housed. The place looked like something out of 2001: A Space Odyssey. I met this guy Steve Swanson. "Can I see your operations?" I asked. And the guy looked at me and said, "Operations?" I replied, "Yeah, I want to see your trading desk." He said, "Okay, I'll show you my trading desk, but you're not going to be impressed." Now this is the second guy who says you're not going to be impressed!

He walks into a room with two guys sitting in front of a computer terminal on either side of each other. One of them is reading *USA Today*, and there is nothing else on the desk. The other guy is staring at a computer screen, looking very bored. I said, "This is it?" He said, "Bob, you don't get it, it's an algorithm that people are using with our system. These guys are here to make sure the system is operating properly, because we need human eyes on it. But everything in the software is behind the walls."

That was my ah-ha moment, when I finally understood what they were doing. I went back and wrote a report, and kind of regret it. Because it was a little bit snarky. I was so in deep in the weeds at the New York Stock Exchange that it was hard for me to see, even back in 1999, the sort of revolutionary implication of what firms like Island were doing. And, of course, they were paying for order flow by then. Island was very instrumental in helping push that.

My point is the role technology played in helping revolutionize everything. It's what you were saying, Bill. It's like a skyscraper comes together when several things happened in the 1880s. Suddenly, you have the telephone; you have the elevator; you have plate glass; and you have a skyscraper. Without those things, you don't have a skyscraper. You needed them to come together to have the modern system, the skyscraper.

CASHIN: I would like to get back to a point you made. Here is what is enormously important: The reality is one thing, the perception is something completely different. And as we morphed into NMS, one of the aspects, not necessarily mandated, but evolving, was a switch to pennies. And it was an absolutely stunning event.

The week before we went to pennies, we were trading in teenies, that's increments of 6-1/4 cents. The day we started trading in pennies, I was executing an order. And I finished the order by moving up 3 cents. The guy on the desk upstairs screamed, "You idiot, you paid up 3 increments, how could you do that?" And I responded, "Wait a minute, Friday you were trading very happy to pay up 6-1/4 cents. But now because the increments are different you're incensed?" The point on perception is that everybody began to look at this switch to pennies, as if liquidity had absolutely disappeared.

[29]ATD, based in Mt. Pleasant, SC., was founded in 1988 as a trading-technology company for automated limit-order trading, and it was sold to Citi in 2007. ATD is the abbreviation for ATD's Automated Trading Desk Brokerage Services. Steve Swanson was the co-founder of ATD.

The example I use is simple. Say you live in a town of some size, and on the west side of town the bus stops only every 8 blocks. If you want to sell hotdogs, or get a political petition signed, you've got a good idea where you'll find some people. They'll be at one of the bus stops. On the east side of town, the bus stops whenever you wave your hand. There could be the same number of riders, but people have no perception where they can find that pocket of liquidity they're looking for. And that misperception exists to this day. People talk about liquidity having completely disappeared from the marketplace.

PISANI: Richard, did switching to pennies reduce liquidity?

LINDSEY: No. I think all studies actually show that they don't reduce liquidity. But I'll come back to your technology question. And it wasn't just the idea of the application of technology; it was also people who could apply it. I go back even earlier in time than Bob with Island. And I can tell you about my first time walking into Island's office when, there were three people in bare feet working there. In the middle of the floor was a pile of pizza boxes and empty Yoo-hoo bottles. It looked more like a college dorm room than what later became an exchange.

I was there because Merrill Lynch had approached me, and said there is something going on over at Island—and that there was something wrong there. And I responded, "What makes you think that?" And Merrill came back, "We have three communication lines to service all of our order flow into the NASDAQ market. Island has eight, and they're much smaller than we are. We have this huge retail kind of net that brings in lots of order flow, and we have only three lines, and Island has eight."[30] Merrill added: "There's something wrong here. Island is doing something in the marketplace."[31]

So I went and asked Island. I said to Island, "You've got eight lines, Merrill's got three, why?" They responded, "Well, we ran throughput capacity on the communication lines, and found that the throughput is much faster if you could run the lines at 12 percent capacity." Island added: "We can put much more through 8 lines at 12 percent each, than the 3 lines that they, Merrill, are trying to cram everything threw."

Part of it is a change in thinking in terms of the way to apply technology to the marketplace; the way to think about what to do, and how to do things. At the same time, there was a disagreement between Island and NASDAQ. Island claimed that NASDAQ could create a centralized order book, but NASDAQ said it wasn't possible.

I had the boys from Island sit down with the chief technology officer of NASDAQ, and he said you can't create a consolidated limit order book.[32] Island said, "Sure, you can. You pull this from this feed, this from that feed, and this from that feed, and you combine them together and you have your order book." And the chief technol-

[30] This refers to three direct communications links.

[31] In a follow up note, Richard Lindsey explained that this refers to something supposedly "nefarious" though what Island was actually doing that might have had hints of this, hadn't seemingly been specified by Merrill.

[32] Otherwise known as a Central Limit Order Book, or CLOB, this system once proposed by regulators met with industry opposition in the late 1990s, and early part of the twenty-first century.

ogy officer at NASDAQ was stunned. Of course, you could do it. The data is there; you just had to be able to access and use it.

PISANI: Let's move forward a little from 1999 into the early 2000s, when we had the debate about fast versus slow markets.[33] In a way, it hasn't gone away, we're still having this debate. But there was a very awkward, very difficult period for the NYSE right around the time Dick Grasso, former Chairman and CEO of the exchange, had left, and was succeeded by John Thain.[34] At the time, Thain immediately set it up for the purchase of Archipelago.[35] Thain had come from Goldman Sachs where thinking was very close to Archipelago, generally very pro-fast markets. And there was that awkward period there which Art Cashin remembers well. I remember it as particularly painful for the NYSE, because we had a dual fast versus slow market, essentially, or they tried to create one that wasn't very successful.[36] So there was this transitional stage. In a sense we're still dealing with that.

Art, was there anything in your recollection that could have been done to improve the whole process?

CASHIN: John Thain came to the NYSE with a pre-conceived notion. He had made speeches about a hybrid market before he was even mentioned as the person to succeed Dick Grasso. That was a Goldman Sachs concept. John Thain came in and tried to implement it, but without really being able to pull the technology fully together.

There are to this day some people who worked at the NYSE who thought that Mr. Thain may have gone to the SEC, behind closed doors, and said, "If you want to pull these guys at the NYSE into the 21st century, you're going to have to mandate electronic trading".[37] That idea may have come out of that because like Venus, electronic trading sprang out fully formed, and the market was in no way ready for it. That itself created greater difficulty. As the NYSE began to advance it further, they missed out on a variety of things. Today, the markets are so dissipated in terms of order flow. I think the Commission at one point allowed—and may have said it out

---

[33] See, Trading Fast and Slow: Colocation and Market Quality* Jonathan Brogaard Björn Hagströmer Lars Nordén Ryan Riordan First Draft: August 2013 Current Draft: November 2013. https://research.mbs.ac.uk/accounting-finance/Portals/0/docs/Trading%20Fast%20and%20Slow%20Colocation%20and%20Market%20Quality%202.pdf

[34] For background on this major leadership change, see, The Brain in Thain. New York magazine. Noam Scheiber 24, 2007. http://nymag.com/news/businessfinance/25991/

[35] NYSE completes acquisition of Archipelago Holdings. Carolyn Pritchard. *MarketWatch*. March 7, 2006 5:26 p.m. https://www.marketwatch.com/story/nyse-completes-acquisition-of-archipelago-holdings

[36] Referring to the so-called Hybrid Market at the NYSE. See, SEC Approves NYSE Hybride Market Proposal. SEC Press Release. March 22, 2006. https://www.sec.gov/news/press/2006-41.htm

[37] As of writing, John Thain could not be reached to respond to this comment, or to offer perspective on the matter.

loudly (and certainly it was roundly believed by some people) that nobody should have more than 40 percent of the order flow.[38]

In any event, the SEC has roundly succeeded.[39] But it has done a variety of other things. Aspects of the marketplace have grown up, such as rebates for shipping order flow, which I believe was a primary cause of the Flash Crash.[40] Computers, for instance, had been set to send orders to a certain place in suburban New Jersey, to get a rebate. When everything hit the fan during the Flash Crash, the people in that place in New Jersey, weren't staying around to trade. They left marker bids of a penny in place just to prove they were still making a market.[41]

Now I'm an old fogie. I like humans because I happen to be one, despite what my kids say, and before the changeover, nothing had previously traded for a penny increment on the New York Stock Exchange. Now the algorithms don't have anybody to talk to. We saw that again, very unfortunately, with the blowup of Knight Trading.[42] That's when even the orders were coming down, and the people on the floor of the New York Stock Exchange tried to reach the people at Knight to tell Tommy that the situation had run amuck.[43] But nobody wanted to talk to other people. They just wanted the machines to talk to each other.

PISANI: As you know, stub quotes have been eliminated. We're definitely all moving towards kill switches.[44]

---

[38] In its heyday, the New York Stock Exchange executed between 75 percent and 85 percent of all orders in stocks listed on the NYSE.

[39] Referring to statistical reality that the NYSE's share of trading in its own listed stocks was hovering in the mid-20 percent range by the time of the conference. NYSE's market share continued to dip further into the low-20 percent range in the following years.

[40] Flash Crash of May 6, 2010 lasted about 36 minutes, erasing 998.5 points in the Dow Jones Industrial Average and then quickly recouped much of the losses as the various indexes rapidly rebounded in this high-speed, electronic trading phenomena.

[41] Here Arthur Cashin is referring to aspects of the Flash Crash studied by market practitioners and academicians, including the role of "rebates" and "access fees," and how these may have contributed a noticeable downside. At the time of writing, many US equity transactions, in effect, still occur, in data centers operated by trading firms and brokerages in suburban New Jersey where complicated rebate and access fees are computed by algorithms. For more, See, A Look Back at the Flash Crash and Regulatory Initiatives. Roberta S. Karmel. *New York Law Journal*. June 18, 2015. https://www.brooklaw.edu/newsandevents/news/2015/~/media/8CC4393DD2A7470F976 5E66558D606EB.ashx

[42] Aug. 1 stock trading fiasco costs Knight $604M, *USA Today*, October 17, 2012. According to the opening paragraph in this AP story: "The Knight Capital Group trading firm said it lost $764.3 million in the third quarter because of a software glitch that flooded the stock market with trades one day in August, causing dozens of stocks to fluctuate wildly." http://www.usatoday.com/story/money/markets/2012/10/17/knight-capital-earnings/1638817/

[43] "Tommy" here is Tom Joyce, then Chairman and CEO of Knight Capital Group.

[44] See, SEC Approves New Rules Prohibiting Market Stub Quotes. SEC Release Nov 08, 2010. https://www.sec.gov/news/press/2010/2010-216.htm

See, Trading 'Kill Switch' Coming Soon: NYSE Exec. Dec. 18, 2012. CNBC. https://www.cnbc.com/id/100324817

BRODSKY: Let me offer a little bit of a different perspective on the hybrid.[45] While the New York Stock Exchange was dealing with the advent of technology, we at the CBOE were in the same situation, being a traditional exchange with a large trading floor. There were many traders who didn't want to see automation come to the floor.

We were pushed harder because of the advent of ISE, which itself was an automated way of trading options.[46] We developed a hybrid system at the CBOE, and I recall showing John Thain what we were doing.[47] He immediately reacted by saying, "We have to do that!" The reality is that the New York Stock Exchange didn't have the time to develop the necessary system, and so they really had their backs against the wall. And that's when Thain went out and bought PSA/Arca because he really didn't have a choice.[48]

My point is that the march of technology, regardless of regulation, and regardless of the SEC, is going to mandate what people really want. What we found—and we had a term for it at the time—was WYSIWYG, our way of saying, 'what you see is what you get.' And that's the world we live in today.

Someone said to me today that they only buy their shoes on Amazon. People have made decisions on how they'll live. If they find electronic alternatives more efficient than dealing with market participants they are accustomed to dealing with, then these people will use electronic alternatives. Reg NMS notwithstanding, because this actually occurred before Reg NMS was introduced. We had been living through a period where the world had understood that computers worked, that you could use a computer to get instantaneous fills. For the smaller orders that computerization was absolutely necessary. For the larger orders, it became more of a challenge due to a lack of liquidity.

It was said here earlier today about pennies and liquidity, it's harder for large institutions to get the kind of fills they got when the spreads were wider. That's because when you have penny markets you're not able to fill a large order within the spread.

PISANI: That's a common complaint today, Richard, that there is no liquidity at all. Is that a legitimate complaint? As a market watcher, I'm moving forward a little bit, but I want to address the way the market is right now.

LINDSEY: I mean it can go back to the overarching topic, and that is, what have we learned? We've learned, first of all, that market structure can't stay stationary. The technology is evolving, the participants in the market are evolving, changing

---

[45] See footnote 36.

[46] International Securities Exchange (ISE). https://business.nasdaq.com/trade/US-Options/index.html

[47] See footnote 35. Clearly, the "hybrid" at the NYSE operated in a different marketplace than the "hybrid" referenced by Bill Brodsky. Both, however, would have combined elements of electronic and human-base trading functionalities.

[48] NYSE completes acquisition of Archipelago Holdings. Carolyn Pritchard. *MarketWatch*. March 7, 2006 5:26 p.m. https://www.marketwatch.com/story/nyse-completes-acquisition-of-archipelago-holdings

through time, so market structure actually needs to evolve. We went through a fairly rapid pace of change in the late 1990s/early 2000s. We haven't had much of change since, other than certain innovations in recent years. But it may be time, indeed, to change again.

Looking back at over the forty years or so of NMS, you can say this: A bunch of things never change. And one of the things that never changes is the institutional view. The institutional view almost always is that the institution always wants to trade in size at the price, and does not want to reveal any of its order flow. But I do want everybody else to reveal theirs! You know, the institutions say it today; they said it a decade ago; they said it three decades ago, so it is something that you are never going to be able to achieve.

There is liquidity in the market. You have to access it differently. You have to work at it a bit differently than you used to. It's not just the narrowing of spreads that means that people can't do block orders and go to the institutions; the sell-side, and do it. It's also that the sell-side isn't going to put up the money anymore. The sell-side has other capital constraints and other concerns; and that's not necessarily the best and first use of their capital.

The sell-side isn't committing capital; the sell-side wasn't committing capital really in the late '90s. It just kind of looked like it did.

PISANI: I'm glad you brought that up. Things have not changed that much. What's interesting to me, is how much the buy-side hated the sell-side then, and still does. I just came on the floor in the mid-90s. I recall how they would call me up, these mutual fund guys, big buy-side guys. They hated the specialists, and they hated the NASDAQ market makers. They would say, "Pisani, you know, you're so interested in this. Did you see what the Pepsi specialist did to me today? Why don't you investigate that for a change?" These are names of people you would know. They'd call me up, and they would scream like crazy. Now they call me up and say, "You know, Pisani, you know these high-frequency traders, the machines, blah, blah, blah, why don't you investigate that?"

I just keep thinking, was there ever a golden moment when everybody was sort of happy? I actually wrote an article for the Museum of American Financial History called, "An Early History of High Speed Trading," noting how back then you could very easily see the hostility of any new technology that came around.[49] We're referring to the likes of the telegraph systems in the 1830s, the ticker tape. With each of these technologies, I showed how there was hostility on the part of the trading community. Somebody out there had gotten a step ahead, and was taking advantage! Somebody knew something he or she didn't know somewhere; and something awful was going on somewhere! I'm glad you brought that out. I don't think things have changed that much.

Are we expecting too much from technology? When the NYSE recently had an outage, I spent the whole day on the floor. It was practically the entire CNBC

[49] Plundered by Harpies. An Early History of High-Speed Trading. Bob Pisani. *Museum of American Financial History*. Fall 2014. https://www.moaf.org/publications-collections/financial-history-magazine/111/_res/id=Attachments/index=0/Plundered_by_Harpies.pdf

broadcast for an afternoon. We were shocked, Shocked that there could be a technological problem. Of course, Knight's snafu practically brought down Knight.[50] The question is, are we sort of expecting a little too much from technology?

I remember parts of the DOT system, and the SuperDOT system, that routinely went down when I was on the floor in the '90s.[51] I never recorded it because it was so routine, and we didn't even notice it. But today we have an eye on everybody and everything, so there's a sort of expectation that everything is going to work perfectly. When it doesn't, we're shocked and dismayed about what's happening around it. Any thoughts?

BRODSKY: Think about what happened on that day recently [relative to November 11, 2015] when the systems failure occurred on the NYSE. With the exception of the close, when people were concerned about certain pricing issues, the markets worked just fine.

Who remembers days when there was a blizzard or a hurricane in New York, and the New York Stock Exchange closed and the whole country couldn't trade? Was that better than what we now have? Or when the New York Stock Exchange was down, investors were still able to trade stocks with liquidity? In my view, it made the news because it was the New York Stock Exchange.

PISANI: I'm lonely, because I spent too much time on market structure, that's why.

LINDSEY: Bill said it perfectly.

CASHIN: Well, I also would like to see how that works on expiration days. It tends not to happen.[52] When there is real demand for liquidity, that's when the market share of the New York Stock Exchange goes up. But to your point, we will soon have cars that drive themselves. By the same token, you won't ever have a market that makes itself. Because somebody's got to put up money, and somebody's got to make the decision as to how much risk they will take.

One of the earlier panels today talked about market makers having affirmative responsibility, and how that is not around anymore. To that point, I remember in the '87 Crash when one specialist put itself out of business making too good a market as a specialist.[53] I know this because I was with PaineWebber at the time. After the close, we found out that this specialist had gone broke. Sometimes people do follow

---

[50] See footnote 41.

[51] The electronic system of the New York Stock Exchange once used to route market and limit orders from customers, or their agents, to a specialist on the floor of the exchange. SuperDOT succeeded the Designated Order Turnaround (DOT) system. By 2009, SuperDOT was replaced by the NYSE's Super Display Book system.

[52] Referring to options expiration. The expiration date for listed stock options in the US is typically the third Friday of the contract month.

[53] "The first contemporary global financial crisis unfolded in the autumn of 1987 on a day known infamously as "Black Monday." A chain reaction of market distress sent global stock exchanges plummeting in a matter of hours. In the United States, the Dow Jones Industrial Average (DJIA) dropped 22.6 percent in a single trading session, a loss that remains the largest one-day stock market decline in history. At the time, it also marked the sharpest market downturn in the United States since the Great Depression." Source: Stock Market Crash of 1987. Federal Reserve History.

up, and make good markets. But the market will never be fully automatic because there's money involved.

PISANI: Unless we get an artificial intelligence system that can trade by itself.

CASHIN: It's got to have its own bank account!

LINDSEY: I remember the first time ICE came to me at the SEC, saying it was thinking about creating this electronic options exchange, and how it wasn't going to have market makers.[54] Indeed, it was going to all be priced off of a formula, presumably the Black Scholes formula, at least at that time. I looked at them and said, "Well, you could do that, but I think you are just going to lose lots of money if you try to do something like that." Because, you know, really what a market maker does is try to balance supply and demand to a large extent. It's not priced off a formula, and it's not, geez, a fixed price that everybody can trade at. I agree 100 percent with Art that unless there is some massive leap in technology, we really do have to have people at some point saying this is about where the market is.

STEVEN SACHS: [FBN Securities]: Where does the Dow Jones, the S&P, and the Russell, get their prices from? I came across this after the Flash Crash.[55] As Art mentioned, many of the stocks at the New York Stock Exchange then stopped trading, including Procter & Gamble, which basically stopped at $56 a share. But it traded on other exchanges at $39. But the indexes still get their prices from the primary market. Except on this one aforementioned day when the exchange went down, and they went to the consolidated tape. In my opinion, that made sense.

Why do we still get the prices strictly from the primary market?

CASHIN: The idea of a primary market, and the fragmentation, is part of this discussion. It's very concerning. Because if you went down and convinced the SEC after the meltdown we'd seen, that we should revert back to the plus tick rule for shorting, I doubt that you could implement it.[56] Because no one would know what the real last sale was. There are too many markets around, so there is no solid primary market that everybody follows.

The idea of using the NYSE is more tradition. I think they are ahead on order flow of the next closest competitor, but not by a heck of a lot.

BRODSKY: If the SEC makes a list of things to deal with, this and what happens at the close on expiration are some of the things I would hope the SEC looks at. There are things that, because of fragmented markets, changes the dynamic of how

---

Donald Bernhardt and Marshall Eckblad, Federal Reserve Bank of Chicago. https://www.federalreservehistory.org/essays/stock_market_crash_of_1987

[54] Intercontinental Exchange (ICE). https://www.theice.com/index

[55] Flash Crash of May 6, 2010 lasted about 36 minutes, erasing 998.5 points in the Dow Jones Industrial Average and then quickly recouped much of the losses as the various indexes rapidly rebounded in this high-speed, electronic trading phenomena.

[56] The Uptick Rule (also known as the "plus tick rule") is a former law established by the Securities Exchange Commission (SEC) that requires every short sale transaction to be entered at a higher price than the previous trade. This rule was introduced in the *Securities Exchange Act* of 1934 as Rule 10a-1 and implemented in 1938. It prevents short sellers from adding to the downward momentum of an asset already experiencing sharp declines. Source: Investopedia.

certain things are done. These are very, very important issues to address. I don't think they are insurmountable. But I think we tend to fall back to what used to be; and the markets of today are not as they used to be. The SEC, to its credit, has created the market structure working group, or task force.[57]

PISANI: In conclusion, I ask each of you to offer a short impression of what we've learned after 40 years of changing market structure. Richard, one of the theories (sort of), or concepts, floated is that competition is good; and that seems to be one of the things people keep saying we've learned. Is it axiomatic that all competition is necessarily good? Are there things you see in terms of what competition exists today that you don't like, for example?

LINDSEY: There are forms of competition I don't like. We haven't really talked about high-frequency trading. People paint high-frequency trading, or HFT, with too broad a brush. Because when people say HFT, there are lots of different styles, and lots of different approaches.

Some of them are probably not so good for the marketplace, and have to do with a lot of rapid order placement and cancellation.[58] I tend to think that dark pools aren't particularly good for the marketplace. Dark pools detract from the quality of a visual and open market, where people can see the prices, and see price discovery.

Personally, I think that a quote is a quote, is a quote. So, if it's something that you can execute against, it should be displayed in the marketplace, not hidden in a dark pool. If I had to worry about something, there is the proliferation of dark pools. Somebody mentioned we have some forty of them now. From a purely theoretical standpoint, with the proliferation of dark pools, you could probably reach a tipping point where the price that you observe in the marketplace doesn't really represent much of a price. And, as a result, there is not really much price discovery. Because it's all being discovered someplace else, or at least executed someplace else. Those are things that we have to think about. We have to think about what the structure should look like going forward; and about how to incorporate and make room for additional technology. So no, not all competition is necessarily good for, or in the public's benefit. But much of it is.

CASHIN: Be careful what you wish for. That's what we've learned from NMS. The road to hell is truly paved with good intentions. While we've seen some real improvements, we've seen some things that can cause problems. Richard just began listing a few of them. But as Bill points out, it's an evolving system.

I am concerned that even though, in theory, the retail investor can get a fast, relatively efficient and relatively cheap execution, as Bill said before we got up here, the retail investor really feels the market is not friendly to him, and that's critical. Now that everybody is living off 401(k)s and self-directed plans, we need to assure them we have an efficient market structure they feel is not working terribly against them. As you pointed out, Bob, there's never been a golden age where somebody thinks

---

[57] The SEC's Equity Market Structure Advisory Committee held its first meeting earlier in 2015.

[58] This refers to "spoofing," defined under the 2010 Dodd-Frank Act as, "the illegal practice of bidding or offering with intent to cancel before execution." Some regulators use the terms "spoofing" and "layering" interchangeably in describing this illegal high frequency trading practice.

this is perfection, that this is all working, because there is money involved. When money is transferred, somebody always thinks: What did he know that I didn't know?

PISANI: Bill, this is what I always get back to. When was this golden period that everyone is sort of nostalgically referring to? Thirty years ago, if you wanted to buy 1,000 shares of IBM, it would have cost you hundreds, maybe even thousands of dollars, depending on how it was done; and you would have got a confirmation later, anywhere from 20 minutes to the next day? And today a trade costs $7.99 on E*Trade, with a sub-second confirmation. This is one of the reasons the SEC is not acting like there's a crisis. The SEC sees that at least the consumer is getting a better deal. The SEC is concerned, however, about the rickety nature of the market.

But let me ask you a broad question, Bill, because you're a bit of a philosopher. Art opened the door on this. Have we scared the average investor a little bit? I hate it when people come on air at CNBC, and say the machines are taking over, without sort of qualifying exactly what they're saying. Do you think there is any reason why we should be concerned about market structure, scaring away the average investor, or thinking that it's not a market that they can participate in?

BRODSKY: I don't think it's the market structure that's the problem. It's the rhetoric, and the hysteria that occurs when certain things happen. I put some thoughts together in preparation for this. Art and I were involved a long time ago observing the markets. If we look at where we are, versus where we were, then sure, you can wax poetic about how it was nice. Back in the day, they had a wonderful luncheon club at the New York Stock Exchange, and they played backgammon after the close. It was kind of nice, but that's not the world we live in today.

The world we live in now is a very high-speed, highly technological, precise world. Although institutions might complain, these investors certainly have the ability to fend for themselves. But the average investor who has a 401(k), who has an IRA, who doesn't have the GM pension plan of 30 years ago, has a more competitive market, a more transparent market, a less expensive market, a more innovative market with the best products in the world.

The failure isn't the HFT, and all these other things. It's the failure of the community in the broadest sense of the term, whether it's the graduate schools, the colleges, the high schools, to teach people financial literacy. Because, ultimately, they have to deal with their financial futures. And I believe we have the best system in the world in the US, with the best products in the world; and we don't train our people how to use them. And we all have that responsibility, and it starts at a very basic educational level.

Once again, there is so much rhetoric. But there's no real fundamental education on financial literacy. And if we did that better, investors would appreciate the products more.

PISANI: I completely agree. You've touched a raw nerve. One of the reasons CNBC was founded 25 years ago, was that management at NBC felt that there was a market niche for teaching financial literacy better. And I have to say, I've been there the whole time, 25 years. If you ask me is the United States a more financially literate society than 25 years ago, "no" is my opinion. I have nothing, other than my own opinion to back that up. I have no research, but I don't think many people would disagree with me. And it's somewhat disappointing.

The truth is people spend more time thinking about the Giants game on the weekend, than what their retirement might look like. We've all become behavioral economists. We know how resistant people are to understanding things that they think are opaque and difficult. This goes back to your idea, maybe making markets less opaque, and less difficult to understand. But let's face it, they are difficult to understand. And when we look for retirement issues, that's why I always tell people if you are baffled, pay somebody 1 percent to manage your money. It is worth it to have a professional do that for you, even if you're paying 1 percent. I wish it was different, but I share your concerns.

On that note, thank you all very much for a very interesting panel.

Chapter 7
The Buy-Side Responds

Pete Jenkins, Andy Brooks, Enrico Cacciatore, Curt Engler, and Frank Loughlin

ROBERT SCHWARTZ: Pete Jenkins and I go back a long way. As many of you know, Pete is a regular participant at this annual conference. His contributions here as an experienced practitioner, and as a distinguished industry leader, is always welcome. It is my great pleasure to introduce our moderator, Pete Jenkins.

PETE JENKINS: Thank you, Bob, for having CODA Markets on this institutional panel.[1] As many of you also know, I am an ex-buy-sider. And now as a sell-sider, Bob Pisani's statement that all buy-siders hate sell-siders, actually frightens me! We'll soon hear what the panel has to say today!

Before we turn to that, let me first share one very interesting statistic, about how the institutions have a tougher job today than they've ever had. The amount of assets they hold is substantial: 80 percent of large-cap equities alone are now held by institutions. That's up 50 percent from 15 years ago. And the assets held by institutions keep growing.

[1] CODA Markets, formerly PDQ, is a subsidiary of PDQ Enterprises.

P. Jenkins (✉)
CODA Markets, Westport, CT, USA

A. Brooks
T. Rowe Price, Baltimore, MD, USA

E. Cacciatore
Voya Investment Management, New York, NY, USA

C. Engler
JP Morgan Asset Management, New York, NY, USA

F. Loughlin
Alliance Bernstein, New York, NY, USA

R. A. Schwartz et al. (eds.), *40 Years of Experience with the National Market System (NMS)*, Zicklin School of Business Financial Markets Series,
https://doi.org/10.1007/978-3-030-91912-2_7

We have witnessed a huge change in market structure over time. In that regard, the job for institutions is more challenging than ever before. So we'll look today at their concerns and at how they view Reg NMS, and the national market system.[2] There are certainly some positives from the institutions.

This conference is timely since the SEC right now, through its SEC Equity Market Structure Advisory Committee, has cast a spotlight on these things.[3] The debate has begun and the institutions are part of it, thank goodness. I'll start with some very broad questions. Let me first paraphrase the Vanguard Group. The Vanguard Group has said the US equity markets are now the most efficient in the world; that regulatory changes and technological advances over the past 20 years have benefitted all investors as transaction costs have come down and as access is better than ever before.[4]

I've heard mixed views on this. And I'm very interested, very broadly, in the panels' comments on where we are today; and on how well Reg NMS is working.

ANDY BROOKS: We have a lot of respect for Vanguard. But it has a different business model than many of us. If you're an active manager, I don't know if today's market structure is such a good deal. I mean, it's a good deal if you're trading mega caps; and you're trading on the close when there's a lot more liquidity than in other periods of the trading day. But if you're in the small and mid-cap space, things are pretty challenging. In fact, I think transaction costs have gone higher there.

It was very interesting to hear how the aforementioned SEC Advisory Committee discusses the compression in transaction costs, acknowledging that a lot of the compression is really the compression of commission rates. You take that out of the equation, and it's a different story. Depending on what you're trading, and how it's going, some of this change is great; some of it is not so good. If your order size is bigger than the typical retail share sizes coming into Charles Schwab or E*Trade, it's a challenging environment.

It's always been challenging, Pete, even back when you were trading it was challenging. We at the institutions want immediacy. We don't want to disclose our trading intentions; we don't want to move stocks; we want a fill; we want, we want, we want! That's a classic buy-side sort of mantra. But there's a lot happening behind

[2] Reg NMS (Regulation National Market System) was adopted by the Securities and Exchange Commission in 2005 and introduced two years later to further advance the ideals of a national market system. The regulation includes the order protection, or trade-through rule; access rule (fair access) to market data including quotations; rules on sub-penny trading and on market data.

National Market System: Federal legislation launched on June 4, 1975, to amend the Securities Exchange Act of 1934. The 1975 amendments instructed the Securities and Exchange Commission to cooperate with the industry in creating a National Market System along with an ambitious system for the clearance and settlement of securities transactions nationwide. The amendments also provided for the prohibition of fixed-commission rates, promulgated earlier by the SEC in its Rule 19b-3.

[3] Equity Market Structure Advisory Committee. https://www.sec.gov/spotlight/equity-market-structure-advisory-committee.shtml

[4] Proposed rules and amendments to joint industry plans. https://www.sec.gov/rules/proposed/34-50870.pdf

the curtain that doesn't seem so good when we think about market structure. It's that excess, it seems to me, we ought to discuss, or at least acknowledge it could do with some improvement.[5]

CURT ENGLER: This conference is the first time we're really getting to hear what people think about the buy-side—that we're unrealistic, grumpy people! But I do think Bob Pisani owes you a big apology for his horrible impersonation of you earlier.

JENKINS: Curt, I thought he was impersonating you [laughter]!

ENGLER: He could have been impersonating any of us. In any event, Reg NMS, for sure, has complicated our lives. But that's a good thing because in that complication there is also an opportunity of sorts. The amount of control the buy-side has today is unparalleled. There is certainly a lot of work for us, and a responsibility to look at all the routing, at all the different configurations, to try to tailor the trading strategies for our portfolio managers. That is one of the winners, and hence the title of this conference. On balance, I think that the buy-side are the winners, even as our job has gotten more complicated. We have the resources and the skills to manage the consequences, even though we're grumpy about it at the same time!

FRANK LOUGHLIN: It wouldn't be a panel if we didn't have an opportunity to disagree. You can put us squarely in the camp of agreeing with Vanguard.

Bill Brodsky said it earlier, the US is probably the most evolved, the most sophisticated, the most robust, and the most liquid market in the world.[6] It sort of reminds me of the quote from Churchill about democracy, how it's the worst form of government except for all the rest. We could probably say something similar about the US market.

Whether it's from technological advances, competition spurred by technology, NMS specifically, other regulation more generally, or whether each individual change benefits the institutional trader and the clients we represent, the fact is the sum total has been a huge benefit in the form of innovation and lower cost.[7]

And that's whether those costs are the result of commission compression, or lower impact costs. We think it's a combination of both. It would be hard to dispute that even for large institutions, because it's never been cheaper to trade.

When we debate market structure internally, we always think about market structure as a continuum, from the highly functional to the highly dysfunctional.

With that in mind, when the industry considers recommendations and changes in market structure, we subscribe the 'do no harm' rule. In other words, you have to

[5]"Excess" here refers to challenges the buy-side has historically raised about the marketplace, challenges such as excess volatility, and the difficulty in buying and selling large institutional orders.

[6]At the time of the conference, Bill Brodsky was executive chair of the Chicago Board Options Exchange. He was on the 2015 Conference panel, "What Have We Learned?".

[7]Federal legislation launched on June 4, 1975, to amend the Securities Exchange Act of 1934. The 1975 amendments instructed the Securities and Exchange Commission to cooperate with the industry in creating a National Market System along with an ambitious system for the clearance and settlement of securities transactions nationwide. The amendments also provided for the prohibition of fixed-commission rates, promulgated earlier by the SEC in its Rule 19b-3.

allow for the possibility that any changes you make that you think are in the industry's best interests actually may move market structure further to the dysfunctional spectrum, away from all the good things and benefits we've had over the years.

We do not subscribe to the idea that the market structure is unfair (even if we had asked investors we represent for their outlook on a market structure that others have deemed imperfect). Although it is true, some of our own investors may agree with the assessment of a market structure that is certainly kind of imperfect.

Assume you told an institutional investor we have an imperfect market structure, but that it's never been cheaper for a pension plan to invest its assets, and have them professionally managed. I doubt if this investor would sign up for a market structure that seems more fair and more transparent—but where costs are going to go up!

ENRICO CACCIATORE: The markets are amazing right now. Looking where we came from. It's a fantastic place. And we're only in the first of nine innings. What the future holds for this market is beyond belief. We talk about artificial intelligence, or AI, in automated trading. We're just at the beginning in virtual reality. And look at many of the firms that have a lot of capital to throw around. They are hiring AI people that work for IBM. That's an indication of where things are going.

And from this distinguished group here on the panel, we throw around a lot of AUM, (assets under management). We manage a lot of money for retail and institutional investors. When we say we're institutional investors, that means we're really the mutual funds, for example—and we represent retirees, the entire spectrum of the populous. It's not just large institutions. With our fiduciary responsibility to uphold, we're looking at every individual, including the retail investor. The buy-side on this panel manages 401(k) plans and mutual funds. We're looking out for the best interest of not just firms and institutions, but also of the retail investor as well.

JENKINS: One thing today that wasn't happening when I was on the buy-side, is very interesting. That is that buy-side firms are actually investing, putting their money into, Alternative Trading Systems (ATSs) such as Luminex and IEX.[8] That would indicate to me that a lot of those firms are investing in ATSs, and many are also unhappy with the market structure at the same time. Three out of four on this panel have said the market structure is much better. Andy, you are a little bit more negative. Three here on this panel have said the markets are much, much better. Why are institutions investing this money in these alternative systems?

BROOKS: We have some investors up here on the panel on some of those systems. Full disclosure: T. Rowe Price made an investment in Luminex, now owning under five percent of that entity. If Luminex is able to consolidate, perhaps, and provide a better experience for those trades that really are appropriate, and best suited for block trades, that would be terrific.

That is a modest percentage of our order flow. I don't think we wanted to disintermediate anyone, or any entity. The current construct on Wall Street works pretty well for us. Yes, we're upset with some parts of market structure. But, for example,

[8] Luminex: https://luminextrading.com/
IEX Group: https://iextrading.com/about/

we think we get great value from the regional firm Robert Baird, which is one of our broker dealers. We also think we get great value from Morgan Stanley, and we have a process to identify that and reward them appropriately.

I don't think we want Luminex to run the world. But if it did nothing other than cause better behavior from the sell-side, if it did nothing better than make the process of presenting order flow more legitimate, more genuine, that would be a win. By the way, I usually like the sell-side, they're okay. And they like me a lot, so they tell me! Part of Luminex is designed to eliminate the fall down. And the fall down is this: When two market participants both acknowledge they want to trade with each other but then suddenly one of them doesn't want to trade, and runs away, that's a bad experience.[9] In this scenario, one person has expressed his or her interest in trading with the other side, which then cancels. It is disingenuous if I see your trading interest, and then cancel my own trading interest or vice versa, after we have both acknowledged we want to trade with each other. It is not playing by the rules if you have flushed me out for information, and then you cancel your order. Most of this behavior happens in dark pools and electronic venues.

Other things we are unhappy about are incentives for order flow routing. There will undoubtedly be more analysis and research on that process. There will be studies on participants' behavior. The complexity of where people send orders; and where they keep sending them and don't get executions, really begs the question, who are you operating for, whose interest is it?

Believe me, we make plenty of mistakes. But to identify the conflict of interest is important. The current market structure is doing a lousy job of that. If it's doing anything, it's enabling even more conflict, so nobody really knows what's going on.

I agree with my panelists. Frank and I take turns on which side we're going to be on. We have a big coin, and we flip it! But a lot of good things happen. There's innovation, and a lot of competition. I worry about what's going on behind the curtain. A lot of stuff doesn't sound so good to me. We ought to deal with and truly understand that, because that might make the experiences better.

The buy-side senses that there's a better way to do some things, and perhaps to identify and eliminate some of these conflicts.

JENKINS: Any other view on IEX, or on the buy-side investing in market structure? Is that money well spent from your perspective? We've talked about how institutions may be slower to respond with their technology. They may not have the same budgets as some other, more nimble players. But you catch up, eventually through your intermediaries who have the tools to trade the way you need to trade.

LOUGHLIN: You can probably interpret it two ways. One potential interpretation is unhappiness with the current state of affairs. Another is recognition that if you think things are generally highly functional and work well and part of the

[9] "Fall down" is an industry term used when either the buyer or seller in a trade on a matching platform does not engage, or "firm up" the other side, after initially demonstrating its interest to either buy or sell. In this scenario, the party that has pulled its interest, is often considered to be "trolling" for information.

reason is increased competition over time. Then is this just the next iteration of increased competition?

To Andy's point, one of the big features of Luminex is aimed at mitigating the fall down behavior he described.[10] Systems like Luminex may not be a reflection of how we're unhappy with market stricture. Instead, it might be that there's certain tweaks that could make it better.

CACCIATORE: We have to look at all the ATSs, and the exchanges. They're all storefronts for some general purpose. Look at the exchanges, and the market makers. We really need to kill the term HFT, or high frequency trading, because it's out of date; it's not applicable in today's market structure. It shouldn't be around anymore. We really need to better define market maker, stat arb, or latency arbitrage for today's markets. They all serve a different purpose today than they did in the past. If you break it down, HFT, which includes market makers, and firms like Virtu and Two Sigma, all serve a very strong purpose in the marketplace. They're the heartbeat of the marketplace.[11] All right, they're the heartbeat of the retail investor who provides tight spreads to the marketplace when wanting to buy 100, 200 shares and so on. And while they're doing that 100, 200 shares, they're creating and redeeming ETFs. They're arbitraging other asset classes at the same time. The markets today are set up for speed, unlike in the past when there was much more human intervention.

When it looks like a flickering quote before you on the computer screen, that flickering quote might involve, for example, two ETFs, such as IWO and IWP, based on the Russell 2000. That flickering quote in turn would require you to look at 2000 other instruments at the same time since there are, of course, 2000 stocks in the Russell 2000. In other words, market participants are constantly doing a risk assessment, which is feeding back into the individual underlying stocks. So you have that piece of market structure to consider today.

I trade for both quant and fundamental active funds. And there are two separate scenarios for each. The quant funds are looking at a very different systematic risk function than our fundamental active funds. Liquidity constraints apply in both cases. That's where ATSs/dark pools come into play. Because we are talking about liquidity constraints, it means a participant like me will check ATSs, alternative trading systems such as dark pools, for liquidity. For example, say I go on a lit market—that is a protected market, and I am showing 100 shares with a million shares hidden. In this example, I'm going to hold up that 100-share publicly displayed quote.[12] It's not going to move the market. But if I go into an ATS and show a minimum trade size of 300 shares, at the mid-point with those same 300 shares, I may

---

[10] See footnote 9.

[11] Virtu Financial: https://www.virtu.com/

Two Sigma: https://www.twosigma.com/

[12] A lit market refers to venues that display the various bids and offers in stocks. By contrast, dark markets, or dark pools, do not display prices.

Lit pools are effectively the opposite of 'dark' pools or dark liquidity. Whereas 'dark' venues do not display prices at which participants are willing to trade, lit pools do show these various bids and offers in different stocks. Primary exchanges operate in such a way that available liquidity is

not move those 300 shares immediately. I am going to slide down various price levels on the lit market with those 300 shares. Therefore, I'm passively participating in price discovery. Essentially, the ATS is sort of a byproduct of the protected lit market—-because it allows me to trade in a manner where I'm not going to stop the directional flow of a market. For example, if there is a seller in the lit protected market, and the seller starts driving the quote down, and starts hitting bids, and the price goes down 10 cents, I am not going to impact that price discovery movement. I am not going to impact price directly.

Then we have the growth of conditional order flow, which permits me to potentially trade, for example, one million shares with a conditional order of say, 10,000 shares, via various ATSs.[13] If a trader on the other side shows interest in those 10,000 shares, I can move my order from a conditional to a firm order of 1 million shares. In effect, I am not locked into a specific quantity of shares, as I can trade any quantity, conditional on certain parameters. And I have a higher probability of getting a larger print than in the past.

You are going to start seeing more systems like PDQ—which is on our panel here today. For example, say I want to let the market know about my need for liquidity in a certain stock. If I go to the lit markets to work my order in this stock, PDQ has a way to know electronically—via its algorithms—that it's a participant like me at Virtu working the order. PDQ is going to understand my profile. It'll be willing to provide much larger liquidity to me. PDQ is not going to know me directly. But indirectly it will know. Hey, I'm an institution and it knows my general intentions and profile, so it's going to provide me with liquidity.

You're going to see a lot more different trading venues emerge to serve different purposes. We have to accept them all.

JENKINS: By the way, I did not ask Enrico to say that [laughter]. Let's switch gears on the overall market. Andy, you touched on it, small-cap, mid-cap stocks. I mean we've lived with a one-size-fits-all market. I've always been astounded that has not changed. In the ATS world, individual firms have made efforts to create a different structure to trade those stocks. But give me some commentary on small caps, what needs to be done here? The exchanges don't seem to be listening. I know we're going through a pilot program, that could last another five years or so.[14] What are some of the other changes that could be made?[15]

---

displayed at all times, and form the bulk of the lit pools available to traders. However, an Alternative Trading Systems, ATS can operate on a displayed basis if it and its members choose to do so.

[13] A conditional order is a type of order that will be submitted or canceled if set criteria are met, which are defined by the trader/investor entering the order. This allows for a greater customization of the order to meet the specific needs of the investor. Source: Investopedia

[14] See, Investor Alert. Tick Size Pilot Program. What Investors Need to Know. Securities and Exchange Commission. October 03, 2016. https://www.sec.gov/oiea/investor-alerts-bulletins/ia_ticksize.html

[15] Ibid.

BROOKS: We're pretty active in that space. Pete, you're right, you can't make these stocks trade, and invariably they don't trade well. That's the nature of small company investing, so you've got to deal with that.

There are probably some things we could do. On your reference to one-size-fits-all, it seems like we might want to try and take some of these smaller stocks, and widen the spreads there, or do something to increase displayed liquidity.

I'm surprised that Richard Lindsey agreed with me on this.[16] I'm delighted, he's a smart guy. A minimum trade size in a dark pool is something we ought to do.[17] If you are really interested in price formation and price discovery, 40 percent of the volume being reported off board in a TRF through dark pools and other entities, doesn't sound so good to me, especially in regards to small-cap stocks.[18] Some way to aggregate things back, or encourage a little more transparency would be helpful.

I'm speaking my own book here in the sense that I might be countermanding what I just said.[19] In any event, some of these block trading facilities are probably ideal for small company investing. We always say that, and invariably the biggest volume in these block trading facilities are large-cap stocks, so that's perverse in itself.

That is an area that could deal with some experimentation, and something a little different, because it's hard to trade those small-cap stocks.

ENGLER: Some of the regional differences came up in an earlier panel. For instance, our EMEA desk uses significantly more capital than we do.[20] One of the primary drivers is that they don't have to print to the tape right away. So, maybe there are exemptions, or changes that could help resolve these differences.

BROOKS: Via capital, meaning putting people—the broker dealer and position trader—at risk so the buy-side wouldn't have to expose themselves?

ENGLER: Correct.

LOUGHLIN: We're sizable in the small and mid-cap stocks, the so-called SMID space. It is tough. Although, I think we would say that it wasn't any easier going back to the mid-'90s when the majority of these stocks were NASDAQ driven, and it was a quote-driven market, and not an order driven market—and spreads were typically at a quarter, or at a half point (25 or 50 cents). There's this perception that it's harder now, but it was never that easy. We think the idea that liquidity provision could be offered away from the visibility of the broader market is good. Because it provides an incentive on both sides of the equation. It provides incentive for

---

[16] See, Chap. 6. WHAT HAVE WE LEARNED?

[17] Andy Brooks elaborated in a follow-up that with some 40 percent of trading conducted off board at the time of the conference, a certain minimum trade size would be sensible since participants were already able to trade "100 to 200 share lots" in dark pools, away from the primary market, and without widespread transparency to other participants.

[18] As of writing, there were three active Trade Reporting Facilities, or TRFs: FINRA/Nasdaq TRF Carteret, FINRA/Nasdaq TRF Chicago, and FINRA/NYSE TRF.

[19] That is to say, Andy Brooks is speaking from his own professional work experience and what he had so far witnessed.

[20] EMEA desk is for markets that cover Europe, the Middle East and Africa.

institutions like ourselves to seek out size, and to want to trade in blocks. And it incents liquidity providers to be willing to take the risk, without having holes blown in them. So that's a potential option.

We think that the tick pilot is probably worth doing, though we are not very hopeful that it changes things a lot.[21] All that is probably a short way of saying, yeah, it's tough. We don't really think we have a good answer, but certainly something similar to a European model is worth noting. In Europe, there are markets where you don't have to print to a tape right away, so that approach here might work and incent participants.[22]

CACCIATORE: The nature of small-cap stocks is difficult, and it's priced into the return model for small- cap funds. I trade specifically for our small-cap active funds that are benchmarked to the Russell 2000. We're one of the top holders of the stocks in the market. But we're only holding 200 of those names at a time.

There are a limited number of participants willing to trade in size. The only way you can really trade in those names is to trade slowly. You can be 30 percent of the volume in these small-cap names. If you're looking at the market impact, it's not really costing you that much. Or, alternatively, you can trade dynamically and with flexibility. When there's news out, you might see four, five, or ten times the average daily volume occur because, hey, news has come out. Suddenly there's repricing, and the volume is there by then. You want to keep the market structure as free as possible. When you start capping spreads at 5 cents, you do harm because you disincentivize an institution like myself from wanting to close the spread to one penny. You want to avoid that.

JENKINS: Switching gears, SEC Commissioner Luis Aguilar, at the SEC Equity Market Committee Meeting on October 20· referred to the Flash Crash. He said, "The August 24 event showed how acute volatility can wreak havoc on the market."[23] He said, "There are issues with how trading is resumed after it is halted, limit up, limit down."[24] He also suggested relooking at the opening auction process. With the growth in ETFs, are there any views on how to avoid some of the things the trading community ran into that day? Andy, I liked your recent comment at the National Organization of Investment Professionals (NOIP). You emphasized the importance

---

[21] See, SEC Approves Pilot Program to Assess Tick Size Impact for Smaller Companies. Press Release. Securities and Exchange Commission.

[22] Frank Loughlin explained in a follow-up that in this European arrangement, trades did not have to print to a tape immediately like the arrangement in the US. Therefore, if a broker in Europe was willing to commit capital, the fact that a trade could occur without other participants seeing it hit the tape, would be much more of an incentive-inducing arrangement than in other places to take that risk.

[23] Flash Crash on August 24, 2015. See, What happened during the Aug 24 'flash crash'. Bob Pisani. *CNBC*. https://www.cnbc.com/2015/09/25/what-happened-during-the-aug-24-flash-crash.html

[24] See. FAQ on Limit Up/Limit Down. https://www.nasdaqtrader.com/content/MarketRegulation/LULD_FAQ.pdf

of opening at the right price, rather than opening quicker.[25] There is this viewpoint, about getting these things open and trading quicker. Should the industry takes its time with an auction process, and find the right price?

BROOKS: It's a complicated issue. When you have a lot of instruments that are derivatives of single stocks, it's really a challenge in terms of what people think might happen in a period where there is extreme dislocation.

Some of us have wondered, for instance, whether ETFs ought to open at 10:00 in the morning. Just get all the individual stocks open beforehand. The New York Stock Exchange does not have the manpower to open individual stocks manually, so they're trying to figure out how to do it. They open a lot of stocks automatically today. NASDAQ has issues with its opening. And what was the most troubling thing for me as an observer that day, and as a participant? It was the derivative print.

Now here's my pal, Curt. Let's just take JP Morgan, which closed at 62-3/4 or thereabouts on August 23. Then on the 24th, the day of the Flash Crash, it opened at 57-3/4 or 57-1/2, within 2 minutes after the open, between 9:32 and 9:34. Some 180,000 shares traded down to $50. Now that's a 7-1/2 or 7-3/4 point swing (call it 15 percent), and it's dysfunctional. Where did that volume come from? What was going on there? Were those limit orders, or stop orders, or were those other orders coming in? And now that JP Morgan was open, I could extrapolate that this would happen to other stocks. There is no way that a stock should have traded down 15 additional percent. Something is pretty dysfunctional.

Ironically, the NYSE specialist—now known as the Designated Market Maker—doesn't get to see any of that with our present market structure. This is because we don't trust them! We're so interested in speed. We're so committed to speed, and yet that's the wrong price as outlined. So, what do you do there? In Europe you can't open, you can't trade a stock until the primary market is open. That's a thoughtful approach because you don't have all this pre-market trading like in the US. Another stock is at, say, $37, and then it's suddenly trading at $5 by 9:40 AM, for no explicable reason. Why? I'm telling you, if you called me and said I sold it at $5, I'd say you're fired, or that I'm suing you or something.

We've some issues here. Invariably, you don't really know how things are going to work until you stress it. That's what happened with the plus-tick rule.[26] We experimented for a year and a half in a period of an absolute glassy ocean. No ripples, no waves, no nothing. Then we get into it, and a lot of things went on.

JENKINS: Any other thoughts on the opening process?

---

[25] Pete Jenkins, noted in a follow-up, that liqudity in ETFs dried up in the Flash Crash because market makers were unable to hedge. As noted in an analysis there were a total of 1,278 trading halts on the day of the Flash Crash, August 24, in 471 separate ETFS and stocks. "Because of this, it was not possible to calculate the value of many ETFs, or hedge or trade ETFs and stocks at a 'correct' price." See, footnote 15.

[26] The Uptick Rule (also known as the "plus tick rule") is a law created by the Securities Exchange Commission that requires each short sale transaction to be entered at a higher price than the previous trade. This rule was introduced in the *Securities Exchange Act* of 1934 as Rule 10a-1, and enacted in 1938. The rule, in effect, prevents short sellers from adding to the downward momentum of an asset already experiencing sharp declines.

ENGLER: The lack of harmony across openings was raised on another panel today. As Andy pointed out, how New York opens is different from how NASDAQ opens, and there is a period where a perfect storm can be created based on disinformation and other factors.

JENKINS: I am not sure I wanted to get into a big discussion about the maker-taker model.[27] Kevin Cronin, who is a well-known trading industry executive, was quoted saying "investors need to put in limit orders." He suggested it would be sensible to consider incentives for posting more liquidity. We've tried that. I've heard this discussion on exchange committees for years. How do we incent institutions? Everybody wants the institution to put in that transparent limit order. I mean, in the end, are the liquidity providers in the marketplace? How do we incent the institutions to put out their limit orders?

LOUGHLIN: It's always a curious conversation to us because the words need and should are always attached to displaying liquidity. Pete just said everybody besides the institutions wants the institutions themselves to display their order flow. It seems like, if everybody else wants you to do something, maybe it's not in your best interest to do it. Or it's not in your client's best interest. It's kind of a pretty simple formula, to the extent that you can measure it. You can measure your efficacy in trading orders when you display. You can measure your efficacy in trading orders when you don't display. If you come to the conclusion that your results are better when you do display, that's probably an incentive to keep doing so. If your results, regardless of how you measure them, are not better when you display, then somebody else saying you need to, or you should, ought to make you run for the door.

BROOKS: Frank, staying with that, if we display, are we advantaged? Not really, because there's not a trade-at rule.[28] You say you're going to buy shares at a price and everybody says, "Oh, he's in at that price, I'm not going to sell it there." I, the executing broker, will do it over here, I'm not going to respect that, I'll just internalize it.[29] That sounds bad to me. But you're right. We've been talking about this for a long, long time.

LOUGHLIN: I'll be the first to say I don't know what the commonly accepted metric for displayed order size is in the US. They say the average displayed order size in the US is X number of shares. On the average, you hear talk of an equal weighted number of shares put at 740 shares; time weighted maybe of 300 shares. We could increase that 10-fold and it's still an insignificant number. Look at the

---

[27] In a competitive program to encourage trading on exchanges, maker-taker fees offer a transaction rebate to trading participants who provide liquidity, charging customers who take liquidity. Read more: What Maker-Taker Fees Mean To You | Investopedia. http://www.investopedia.com/articles/active-trading/042414/what-makertaker-fees-mean-you.asp#ixzz4IvzckkIR. Follow us: Investopedia on Facebook.

[28] "Exchanges have been lobbying US regulator the Securities and Exchange Commission (SEC) to introduce a rule that would force equities transactions onto lit exchanges unless dark pools or internalizing matching engines operated by brokers could prove meaningful price improvement had been achieved." From *The Trade News*.

[29] See, Your Broker's Choice. Trade Execution: Jan. 16, 2013 Securities and Exchange Commission. https://www.sec.gov/reportspubs/investor-publications/investorpubstradexechtm.html

collective assets that this panel represents. Are we saying our problems would be solved if the display size went from 300 to 3,000? When was the last time, Andy, your trading blotter had an order for 3,000 shares?[30] What's the argument here really? It feels artificial.

ENGLER: This is related to the price discovery that every panel before us touched on. I may have it wrong but it's less of a concern for me. I don't see putting caps on dark orders. You could be aggressive in the dark, and you could move the quote. Firms such as Virtu are everywhere on the lit and dark markets, and weaving the whole picture of liquidity together. Maybe that's why I was destined for management—I could actually move a quote trading in the dark.

I don't think that price discovery improves by putting caps on dark, or on lit markets, or by incenting more limit orders, or bigger limit orders on exchanges. So I'm missing the point there. The ecosystem of liquidity is pretty efficient at finding the right price, and matching that supply and demand. Is it perfect? No. It is imperfect. I like that term, but it works.

LOUGHLIN: If you assume people act in the best interest of their investors, then trading in the dark speaks for itself. We get better results, that's why we do it. If you accept it at face value, it should sort of end the conversation about whether we should, or need to display.

CACCIATORE: We're thinking in a singular fashion. Most strategies we deploy are multi-functional in nature. We are typically participating in the market with some specific strategies to guide us. For instance, we'll layer the lit book with our orders; at the same time, we might post larger orders on inverted venues because on an inverted venue, orders are probably going to get hit first since participants are incentivized to take liquidity.[31]

Also, at the same time, our volume will be layered in the dark pools, looking for liquidity as well. All in all, there are multiple underlying strategies in our approach. It is not just always a simple matter of showing, for instance, 100,000 shares on the bid or offer.

We talked about the PSX—a price-size model exchange on NASDAQ. It hasn't been successful, because institutions don't really want to use it that way. There are other forums to trade. In any event, things are moving in the right direction. From a liquidity perspective, the sell-side is becoming much more of a partner because it is becoming smarter in how to use its own capital. Where the sell-side is providing two-sided markets say, for example, either a stop order or 5 cents up on a stock

[30] Pad is the trading term for "trading blotter." Put another way, Frank Loughlin was asking Andy Brooks when was the last time his desk had an order for 3,000 shares on his trading desk.

[31] As noted by one trading executive, traders use "inverted venues to 'cut the queue' because cost-sensitive smart order routers target inverted venues first." As he further elaborated, to trade passively in stocks with large queues at the primary exchange, "the only way to do so is by posting on a different exchange."

An inverted venue refers to an exchange that offers two models to lure more equity trading volume, the conventional maker taker model and a taker-maker model, or inverted rebate system where the liquidity taker is paid for handling a trade. Examples of exchanges offering inverted rebates have included Nasdaq BX, Bats BYX and Bats EDGA.

quoted at 50, the sell-side will get you a print on that order. In fact, the sell-side central risk books at the trading units at Goldman Sachs, JP Morgan and other firms are customer facilitation services. Their central risk books will each sweep their own books, in minimum penny increments, say 50.01, 50.02, and so on, to work the same aforementioned hypothetical orders.

BROOKS: Two things, Enrico. I'm glad you're in the game; you're a lot younger than I am. I'd be blowing a gasket if I had to do this stuff every day, and our guys do, on our team. But think about how complex that sounded, the scenario that you just described. I've got to be here, I've got to do this, I've got to do that. I'm like, what are we gaining from this? It sounds convoluted as hell.

CACCIATORE: By the way, I'm not doing it. That's a strategy, it's automated.

BROOKS: I'm sorry?

CACCIATORE: It's automated.

BROOKS: Right. A lot of those same things are automated, depending on what tools you use. Let me add, I'm always struck by how the buy-side is great about saying we want to trade in size until it gets close. And we're all guilty of this. It's going to be really interesting to watch this, as things evolve, and as there's more innovation. Are we still going to talk a good game, or are we actually going to do it? And I will be be fascinated by the outcome.

JENKINS: Enrico mentioned conditional orders and referenced IOIs.[32] It almost seems like the use of conditional orders is increasing, as well as IOIs, as people become more comfortable with the market. They almost seem like this is your way of indicating to the world that you want liquidity.

Why do you feel comfortable with these indications, these conditional orders, and IOIs? Is it because you're not firm, that you feel more comfortable with those? Do you even think that conditional orders will continue to be utilized?

LOUGHLIN: There may bepeople in the audience who could speak better to this. But it seems like the sell-side experience on conditional orders is that the firm up rate is pretty good, and the fall down rate is lower than what we experience in some other, venues? And so it seems like a win.[33]

There's sort of an element of control and anonymity, you're not posting necessarily. The whole concept of being conditional, I only have to act when there's a potential contra, right? So, you know, you're not fumbling around in the dark, metaphorically speaking, wondering whether there is another side.

LOUGHLIN: The evidence we see suggests that people are behaving much better around the firm up rate.

JENKINS: Right.

---

[32] In equities trading, an IOI stands for an Indication of Interest, usually by an electronic signal broadcast by a sell-side broker to various other market players (usually the clients of the broker dealer) *indicating* to them the positions he is currently dealing in and looking for latent interest in those positions from his clients. It is an indication and not a commitment. For conditional orders, see footnote 13.

[33] See, footnote 9.

LOUGHLIN: Look at an actionable IOI.[34] That actionable IOI is visible. If you see it, you certainly know before you engage it, who it is. You know going in what the result will be. Somebody rolls an actionable IOI and sells you 50,000 at 10 cents.[35] In a matching network, you do not know who the contra-side is. You can see all the IOIs. You can pick and choose which one you want to interact with. On the concept of being actionable. There's no haggling. You know, it's not a question of seeing a displayed quote somewhere else, and of trying to hit or take it, and not getting it all. It would seem those two innovations, if you want to call them that, are around here to stay.

CACCIATORE: It's automation, automation, automation. I can tell you once we get the human further out of the equation, you're going to see more of a ramp up in how trading is done systematically via automation. I don't mean human traders will be completely eliminated. But human traders will control the outliers, that is trades that have an exceptional situation that the machine can't handle. For example, historical data in the trading system may not be applicable to the parameters of a trade, so the human trader may have to step in.

Also, when there is extreme volatility, the human trader may get involved. But in a more highly automated trading environment, we don't need to worry as much about market participants' intentions. That's because information leakage by human traders becomes less of a factor, since the machines are doing more. There is much less of an issue about a human trader firming up a trade with a counterparty, since the market environment is more automated. It is a matter of the automated trades within an automated marketplace.

BROOKS: It is interesting. We're all part of this. We are fumbling around in the dark—metaphorically and indeed, in dark pools—a little bit on the conditional side. Let's say we have 100,000 shares to buy, and we send 10,000 to 10 different places conditionally.

CACCIATORE: Well, conditionally you could send 100,000 shares to 10 different venues.

BROOKS: Send 100,000 shares, but you're showing the order, and you wait to see where somebody might be. I don't know if that's good. I know it's automated. I don't know if it would be better to show it in three, mostly dark pools. I know that in the old days, if I've made myself look like five buyers, that was generally bad for me. Now this is anonymous, and maybe it's not shown unless there is somebody on the other side, so that is a little bit better. But it doesn't seem logical to show your hand in so many places.

[34] Actionable IOIs (Indications of Interest) are bids or offers for a stock that are in effect, available for execution.

[35] In the example, for the purposes of clarification, this 10 cents represents the price, not the spread, which will be obvious to traders reading this. The full dollar amount is not included in the quoted price, so the "dollar" price amount could be, for example, 25.10, 50.10, meaning $25.10 and $50.10. That is unimportant, since traders will often drop the full amount and only use the price after the decimal when negotiating.

CACCIATORE: And it's not reportable in OATS.[36]

BROOKS: Right. But it just doesn't seem like we're casting a big net here.

JENKINS: It is counter to the old manual world. But, as Enrico says, these are automated processes, so things are a little bit different.

Switching gears again, I don't want to get into a deep discussion about transaction cost analysis. But I was intrigued by the Capital Group's comment that, in terms of their costs, they have described a great lowering of their costs of executions as a result of changes, ranging from decimalization to Reg NMS. But post-Reg NMS, they said basically that their costs have not come down. That was interesting because most people I speak to say their costs of execution have slowly been coming down. The Capital Group almost made it sound like Reg NMS really did nothing for transaction costs.

LOUGHLIN: To the extent that it's a function of spreads and of full disclosure, we haven't measured it with that break point. Let me say this: If you think about it in terms of narrowing the spread, it seems like an unfair comparison? Because when the industry switched to decimals, we went from minimum increments of a teeny to a penny. If they were already at a penny, by and large, spreads had narrowed so much by the time of Reg NMS. It is like an unfair comparison because there was no additional narrowing to be had. And so, it's not surprising this was the conclusion.[37] Is it an indictment of Reg NMS? Hard to say, right?

JENKINS: I mean you would think that there were a lot of other things that came out of Reg NMS in terms of costs coming down.[38]

LOUGHLIN: The first time spreads could be as narrow as a penny was with decimalization. If it went there already, that was it, there was no more narrowing to be had.

ENGLER: It's extremely difficult to disentangle Reg NMS from a single desk's transaction cost analysis. The PM's alpha would probably dwarf any sort of micro effect. That said (and I wasn't at JP Morgan before pre-NMS) it still seems like it's extremely efficient. The word evolution was used three times in previous panels. But it's the buy-side's overall effort to understand all those complexities. We haven't seen an increase, but rather a leveling out of costs.

BROOKS: I would say, on the small and mid-cap side, our sense is that our costs have gone up. Certainly, they have not gotten less. And I don't know whether that's post Reg NMS. I can't disentangle that either. But it seems to us it's gotten more

[36] The Order Audit Trail System (OATS), an automated computer system owned by the National Association of Security Dealers to record information relating to orders, quotes, and other related trade data from all equities traded on the NASDAQ, including over-the-counter (OTC) stocks. In early 2017, FINRA proposed the phase out of OATS as a new system called the Consolidate Audit Trail (CAT) comes on line. Source: Investopedia.

[37] Referring to the Capital Group's assessment on its transaction costs.

[38] Pete Jenkins explained in a follow up that Reg NMS introduced further changes in market structure so as a practical matter, it begged the question, why had costs not come down further. "My question was referring to more than just spreads," he explained, "because Reg NMS introduced more efficiencies in market structure, it created more competition, and it actually tightened spreads overall even though you can't tighten a penny spread today."

expensive to trade smaller cap stocks. On the other side, large-cap stocks have probably stayed the same, or maybe even gotten a little cheaper, mostly spreads and commissions.

CACCIATORE: We have to define what TCA, transaction cost analysis is. We are looking at TCA in the wrong way. Because, for example, in some myopic way, we try to look at the VWAP, (or PWP) as our benchmark.[39] I think you want to look at your trading performance in a more multi-dimensional way. In this approach, we're looking for the intent of this trade. What was the portfolio manager's intention for the trade over the trading day? What did the PM want to do? Why did we buy, or sell this trade for the PM? Is it that the PM wants to buy a million shares? We are better off, for example, looking at the pre-trade estimate based on historic spread costs, volatility, and whether or not it will cost 300 basis points.

Based on the intention of the PM, I will then decide whether to trade at a particular time, and how I will trade a stock.

Things I should look out for as I trade: Is the market moving? Is there some sort of adverse reaction to my trades? And once I'm done with a trade, it might, for example, cost me 100 basis points in performance. So, it looks great. But what I want to do now is this: I want to analyze that post-trade data. I want to compare my performance by looking at post-trade data. Maybe there was adverse momentum in the name. Perhaps I should have actually had a positive return of 100 basis points because the stock was down, say over 3-1/2 days, by 500 basis points. And I bought it in the first 10 minutes of my trading in a block, because Andy had 5 million shares for sale when I really wanted to only buy 1 million?

That's how I think you have to look at it. We sometimes try to look at the simplistic method of doing TCA, and yet it's much more complex. We really have to decompose a trade, and look at it from that perspective.

JENKINS: This is the part that really confuses me. What you are talking about is complex enough. If you're going to do some of the stuff real time, you're spending a lot of money on analyzing it.

But studying a broker's order routing is supported by everybody. What is the panel's view on the cost to doing this? Are you really getting the bang for the buck? Dave Weisberger said it would, "be far better for buy-side traders to quantitatively measure the performance of their broker's routing methodologies instead of constraining them." That gets to this: What will you do with that information when you find out what happened on a single trade to a single route? What are you going to do with this data?

ENGLER: I'll break it up into two parts. There's one that's the generic broker's algos we use. We'll look at various destinations and the fees to see if there is any sort of bias. I like the SEC's overall approach of more transparency. Once you actually

[39] VWAP, or Volume Weighted Average Price, is calculated by adding up the dollars traded for every transaction (price multiplied by number of shares traded) and then dividing by the total shares traded for the day. Source: Investopedia.

The Participation-Weighted Price (PWP) determines the volume-weighted average price of a stock from the start of an order.

see the data and fees and rebates associated with that, you can start answering the question with data, rather than just speculating that they're only prefacing their dark pool. Where we are controlling the schedule on some other strategies, and are going directly to various ATSs. We look deeper at the before, during and after, to see what happens in stable markets when the quote changes. There is some value in doing that. Granted, it's fractions of basis points that we are fighting over. But that fraction is for our clients. It's important to get that micro, as well. But, if you have your overall schedule, no amount of micro will help if you don't have your overall trading strategy correct. There is some value there but it's a lot of work.

JENKINS: It seems like it will take quantitative teams to run through this stuff. Is that realistic and cost effective, at most firms, or even at a large firm such as JP Morgan asset management? Obviously, you have quantitative teams onboard.

ENGLER: It's a combination. In other words, you can do a certain amount in-house. There are vendors you can leverage to run the analysis, as well.

LOUGHLIN: In terms of Dave's quote, he's right, you absolutely should measure it. Not constraining it sounds a bit curious. If you measure it, and then you don't affect change as a result of the measurement you do, it becomes a really expensive exercise in data collection. If you measure and ignore the results what is the point?

Maybe I'm misunderstanding what he means, but the not constraining it part seems curious. Perhaps we have a pretty sizable private client business which generates a lot of smaller order flow, like the classic 80/20 (80 percent of the actual orders, 20 percent of the share volume). It's small order flow where the impact is expected to be generally low. Perhaps that's order flow that you should allow the brokers to compete unconstrained. Just tell them what you're trying to accomplish, let them build it, route it to them, and they compete. On order flow, where the potential to have bigger impact is more meaningful, not constraining an order routing strategy you know about and disagree with in advance, doesn't seem like the right answer. And whether that's not disagreeing in terms of how they lay out their routing methodology, or it's measuring the results and saying that, by comparison to peers, they're subpar, it would seem incumbent to make a change. The not constraining reference seems a little curious in this context.

But absolutely, we should measure the performance of the broker's routing methodologies. And it certainly does take a big investment in time and resources, on the quant side, because there is a huge amount of data involved.

CACCIATORE: Since the buy-side responds, we should applaud guys like Frank, Andy and Curt and other large institutions who've established a relationship with the sell-side. Because of guys like this, and places like the Tabb Group that aggregate industry data, we're able to have a dialog like this today. These guys were an impetus for bringing this relationship together.

About three years ago, we wouldn't be able to leverage some stuff we're talking about right now. These guys sort of made it happen. Thanks.

JENKINS: Questions?

Nazli Sila Alan, [Professor, Fairfield University]

I want to circle back to the small-cap issue. What is the panel's opinion on an idea of Bob Schwartz and I who, along with a co-author from Deutsche Borse, worked on together, based on an earlier paper by Bob? We looked into the idea of having the listed companies, themselves, involved in their secondary market trading. We tested the Dow stocks and the DAX 30 stocks.[40] Basically, the idea was to institute a program, which we called the Supplemental Liquidity Program, to get a listed company itself for its own stocks, to post large orders, not throughout the day, but just during the call auctions. The company's orders are there to "catch the market", if the market is going too low or too high. That is, post a buy order at a low price, and then the sell shares at a high price. The idea is basically to minimize price fluctuations. That would add this additional big liquidity into the market. It would be completely transparent, and based on a predetermined set of rules to minimize gaming opportunities obviously.

We looked at it as a way to improve liquidity, especially in small caps that you guys all have been alluding to. That is, very necessary. But it has been hard since the beginning, and it definitely hasn't gotten any easier after all this market fragmentation. What is your opinion on such a program of getting listed companies, themselves, involved in their own secondary market trading?

BROOKS: The company can't be on both sides, right, they could be a buyer.

ALAN: But they are buying at a low price, and selling at a high price.

BROOKS: I'm not sure they're allowed to do that.

ALAN: They are not regularly, but we are talking about it.

BROOKS: How much stock are they willing to sell, how much are they willing to buy? It could be interesting. Goldman Sachs used to do that, too, but they don't do it anymore. Now we've heard talk about market makers. I'm of that opinion that real market makers don't exist anymore, they're gone.

ALAN: But the idea is to make the companies, themselves, behave as if they are their own market makers. Because they're the ones that will ultimately have the most stake in the game. They're not there to profit. They are there to provide stability for their own secondary market.

LOUGHLIN: What was their appetite for doing so? I guess if you're the CFO, or the treasurer of one of these companies, there's sort of the catch the falling knife argument? I may think I'm putting a floor in the stock, but what if I'm not? And again, I'm not sure what the answer to this is. But obviously buybacks have been a significant part of the landscape in US equities for a number of years now, given the low interest rate environment. But does that hold across cap ranges? What if you're running a smaller business that you're trying to grow? Is part of your capital allocation plan buying back your own stock on a regular basis to sort of act as a *de facto* liquidity provider? I'm curious what the appetite is for doing so? Notwithstanding the results of your tests, if you take this plan to publicly traded companies, how onboard are they?

---

[40] A Liquidity Program to Stabilize Equity Markets, *Journal of Portfolio Management*, August, 2014. Nazli Sila Alan, Fairfield University, Deutsche Börse AG, Baruch College—CUNY. https://papers.ssrn.com/sol3/papers.cfm?abstract_id=2495819 and see Chap. 7.

ALAN: We tested the profitability of this. As long as there's trending in prices, meaning if the price is completely falling down, or completely going up, of course they'll be losing money. They won't be willing to do that. We conducted a five-year study, from 2008 to 2012, for Dow stocks and DAX stocks. For the most part, companies profited from instituting such a program. We couldn't test the pricing, then it's also going to have stability effects as well.

CACCIATORE: Sounds like a regulatory nightmare to me.

ALAN: Well, it is. It's not something that could be achieved overnight.

CACCIATORE: Could they buy and sell in the same day? Can they buy and sell the same week, the same month?

ALAN: Sure they can. But they're just attending the call auction, so if there's one call per day, they can only execute once, yes.

CACCIATORE: That's what the secondary market is for. We are involved in the small-cap market where the syndicate goes out and raises capital. We'll buy a lot of our liquid stocks through the secondary market. When you start trying to control the edge cases through using company stock, you're playing a game you shouldn't be doing.

BROOKS: It would be interesting to see what Valeant would have done in your framework.[41]

ALAN: Right, we'll keep that in mind.

JENKINS: Questions?

ATTENDEE: Trying to incentivize the market makers, to bring back some of that capital, was brought up earlier. Part of the problem is that you guys have all gotten bigger. We've seen a consolidation on the buy-side, and now there are these huge institutions on the buy-side. They outsize a lot of the market makers, the guys that used to provide the capital. But are there any other ways to incentivize them to bring back capital? It is really a risk transfer. You needed to get that 200,000 shares done because your portfolio manager really, really needed to get it done today, for some reason. You were transferring risk; you were paying a price for that transfer of risk. But do you guys have any other, incentive ideas?

LOUGHLIN: Are we talking about incentivizing Designated Market Makers?

ATTENDEE: I'm not talking about 5,000 shares.

LOUGHLIN: We're talking about getting the banks to provide balance sheets?[42]

ATTENDEE: Yes.

LOUGHLIN: I've been called crazy for saying this but I will say it again. We think they still do, to the extent that they're allowed to within the current regulatory framework. And maybe they do for people at this table, and maybe they don't for everybody. But we think they still do. It's not an everyday, all the time thing, because

---

[41] The 'Short' Who Sank Valeant Stock.

Andrew Left has long targeted firms that he thinks are overvalued or engaged in fraud. Matt Wirz, *The Wall Street Journal*, October 22, 2015. https://www.wsj.com/articles/the-short-who-sank-valeant-stock-1445557157.

[42] Referring to the banks and large brokerage houses taking more risk, acting as principal, in trading.

it's not every day all the time. Because we don't need it every day, all the time.[43] But when you need it, it's there. It is kind of full stop, period, end of story.

ENGLER: You may not like the price but liquidity is there.

BROOKS: I would agree. It's an expensive way to trade, so you've got to have some real conviction. You've got to be willing to pay for immediacy.

CACCIATORE: I would say that it's there. Regulation has taken capital away from firms and their balance sheets. Look at the Russell rebalance. The Russell rebalance has become much less of an opportunity for the sell-side to participate in the marketplace, since we now participate more on an agency and not on a principal basis.

But we're seeing increased capital exposure to larger asset managers, such as firms like us because the sell-side is able to better facilitate market risk exposure today. With their central risk books today, the buy-side is now able to facilitate trading, and deploy their capital on a larger scale than in the past. This essentially facilitates the transfer of risk, from the buy-side to the sell-side.

LOUGHLIN: Something important has changed in the risk game when we need liquidity in a specific name. Because providing liquidity in a different name doesn't really help me on the buy-side, in this instance. The sell-side thinks their risk and willingness to hold certain stocks, and aggregate order flow for much longer periods of time, allows them to be creative over time with risk. For example, they might sell Enrico 5 million shares of Microsoft, and then put a hedge on against it. And if they hold a certain stock long enough, they might catch the contra side; and then they unwind it at a much slower pace than they used to in the past. The fact that they do so means that at any point in time they're holding a fair amount of notional risk, and sometimes they get creative about the way they put that back out to the marketplace.

In some instances we have to be reactive. We don't get to choose the name necessarily, yet if it's a name you care about, and are offered that ability to engage with that kind of flow, it's really appealing.[44] It's an outsized actionable IOI, in effect, right? And for all intents and purposes, it's a natural.

BROOKS: They've gotten much more sophisticated on the sell-side in dealing with this, I would agree.

ATTENDEE: Is there anything the exchanges can do to keep some of the liquidity on the exchanges? Can we have that order flow interacting with naturals, or retail order flow?

ENGLER: Is there anything exchanges can do? I don't think so. I'll just be generic. We're investors. If any system out there can provide a safe place to rest liquidity and interact with other sides that come in, that's not an exchange right now. There are workflow considerations. There's immediacy considerations, and things like that. I think even if some of these block crossing networks just add to a little bit

[43] Ibid.

[44] For example, the portfolio manager wants to buy this certain stock that's suddenly offered by a seller.

of an increase of incremental crossing, then that's a home run, and we're willing to invest money to try to save our client's money. But absent that, we have access to the exchanges, and we'll just trade normally if that liquidity isn't there.

BROOKS: You know, in the old days some of the exchange specialists, or Designated Market Makers as they are known as today, were great market makers. And they really controlled the stocks. I don't think they're doing that anymore. What would make you want to go to their market? Why would they protect you better; or why would they attract your order flow better than a natural, or some other place where you could be anonymous? That's the challenge.

JENKINS: Bob has a couple of announcements.

SCHWARTZ: It's been a long and fruitful day. I don't want to keep you guys away any longer from the wine, our true liquidity!

Please thank our excellent panel.

Chapter 8
A Liquidity Program to Stabilize Equity Markets

Nazli Sila Alan, John S. Mask, and Robert A. Schwartz

Financial markets are an integral part of the operations of firms and markets, and equity markets are foundation players. Illiquidity and price instability, however, are Achilles heels of financial markets in general, and of equity markets in particular. A program that would bring needed liquidity to the equity markets would convey major benefits for market participants, listed companies, an exchange, and the broader economy. In this paper, we consider such a program, one that was originally set forth by Schwartz (1988). In so doing, we present empirical results obtained by simulation analysis on the daily cash flows generated by running such a program for a sample of 30 DOW stocks (27 NYSE and 3 NASDAQ) and 30 Deutsche Börse DAX stocks for the period, January 2, 2008 through December 31, 2012.

In an ideal world, share prices would respond quickly and efficiently to new information, but real world markets are characterized by noise that translates into prices that are excessively volatile over brief intervals of time (e.g., intra-day and from day-to-day). By "excess volatility," we are referring to price changes that can be attributed to price formation dynamics that include the bid-ask spread, market

---

Reprinted, with permission from "A Liquidity Program to Stabilize Equity Markets," Alan, N., Mask J.S., and Schwartz, R., the *Journal of Portfolio Management*, Winter 2015.41 (2) 113–125.
The views expressed in the paper are those of the authors and do not necessarily reflect the views of the Deutsche Börse Group. Any errors or omissions are the responsibility of the authors.

N. S. Alan (✉)
Dolan School of Business, Fairfield University, Fairfield, CT, USA

J. S. Mask
Deutsche Börse AG, Frankfurt am Main, Germany

R. A. Schwartz
Zicklin School of Business, Baruch College, CUNY, New York, NY, USA
e-mail: robert.schwartz@baruch.cuny.edu

R. A. Schwartz et al. (eds.), *40 Years of Experience with the National Market System (NMS)*, Zicklin School of Business Financial Markets Series,
https://doi.org/10.1007/978-3-030-91912-2_8

impact, and price discovery noise. The first two, spreads and market impact, do not appear substantial enough to account for the magnitude of excess volatility that has been documented in the literature.[1] We attribute much of the excess volatility to price formation being a dynamic, noisy process, replete with investor herding, overreacting, and mean reversion. An inherent dynamic of the marketplace is that buying begets buying, and selling begets selling. The opposite also applies: sellers can step aside when buying momentum heats up, and potential buyers can step aside when selling momentum heats up (who wants to step forward and catch a falling knife?).

Various proposals have been set forth in response to the high bouts of volatility that have been experienced in recent years. Imposition of a special transaction fee imposed on trading (the so called "Tobin Tax") is one such proposal. Alternatively, the MiFID II Regulation proposed that orders have minimum resting times. The idea has also been advanced that additional capital be injected by/for market makers so that they might provide greater liquidity and hence enhanced price stability when a market is under stress. Each of these proposals has been greeted with criticism. With regard to market makers supplying supplemental liquidity, additional compensation in the form of privileges would have to be offered to these firms, and it is not at all clear how this might be appropriately arranged.

In this paper, we consider an alternative approach that calls for the inclusion of listed companies as suppliers of liquidity. We note that price formation has public goods attributes that, as is true of public goods, are undersupplied by a free market, and we suggest that the listed companies are in the best position to be the suppliers of this public good. We empirically assess Schwartz's (1988) proposed program that is designed to supply liquidity and enhanced price stability to the markets without preventing share values from adjusting appropriately to new information. The program calls for listed companies to establish supplemental liquidity (SL) funds that will buy back their shares in a falling market, and sell their shares in a rising market.

Using simulation analysis, we have back tested the SL procedure using closing price data for 30 DOW stocks and 30 DAX stocks for the period January 2, 2008–December 31, 2012; we also repeated the tests using the open, midday, and closing auctions for the 30 DAX stocks. Comprehensively assessed across stocks and years, the program has generated cash flows that are predominantly positive. These findings suggest that short-run prices are indeed excessively volatile, and that the SL program, rather than operating at a cost, could generate profits for a firm that institutes it.

The paper is organized as follows. In the first section, we present a broad brush description of the SL program. In the second and third sections, respectively, we first address the SL program's public goods attributes and then describe our analytic context. Our empirical assessments of the cash flows associated with the procedure are presented in Section "Empirical Analysis". The SL program is contrasted with

[1] See Schwartz and Whitcomb (1977), Hasbrouck and Schwartz (1988), Lo and Craig MacKinlay (1988), Fleming and Remolina (1999), Stoll (2000), and Bessembinder and Rath (2008).

traditional market maker operations in Section "The SL Program Vis-À-Vis Traditional Market Maker Operations", and our concluding remarks are in Section "Conclusion". In an appendix, we present further rules, consider five issues relating to compliance with local regulations, discuss the relationship between call auction prices and equilibrium values, and assess the possibility of an SL program being subject to gaming.

The Supplemental Liquidity (SL) Proposal

Formally structured and maximally transparent, an SL program should be established by an issuer, managed by a third party broker-dealer intermediary, and both hosted and monitored by an exchange. An issuer would allocate both funds and shares for the purchase and sale of its stock at pre-announced price points. In so doing, the fund would commit capital to buying shares in a falling market, and it would receive proceeds from selling shares in a rising market. The parameters for the determination of its orders would be set well in advance and would be publicly known.[2] As we will explain, the SL purchases and sales are to be made in an exchange's call auctions only.

A properly structured SL program could convey major benefits for a listed company and its shareholders. Bringing more efficient price discovery to the market will translate into higher share values and, correspondently, into a lower cost of equity capital for issuers. A listed company is in a far better position than a traditional market maker firm to provide the optimal quantity of the public good that a broader population seeks: liquidity that results in price discovery that is reasonably accurate. As we discuss further below, a traditional market maker firm is not able to provide an equivalent amount of liquidity in an equivalently effectual way. Traditional market maker operations are geared for the continuous market while a periodic, price discovery call auction is the appropriate venue for the provision of supplemental liquidity (SL). The capital requirement for running an SL fund would be small relative to the value of a company's shares outstanding; this is largely because the very market dynamic that calls for the institution of an SL fund (i.e., excessive share price volatility and its associated mean reversion) can yield returns for the fund. Thus the program, when running, can be largely self-financing.

[2] This design feature would put our proposal above and beyond the level of transparency already established as "Accepted Market Practice" in France, Portugal, Netherlands, and Italy. (Source: http://www.esma.europa.eu/page/accepted-markets-practices)

Price Discovery is a Public Good

Our SL proposal is founded on the public goods properties of price formation in the equity markets. Market produced prices convey benefits to a far broader public than the participants in a trade, as the uses of an exchange produced price include marking-to-market, derivative pricing, valuations of mutual fund cash flows, estate valuations, and dark pool pricing. As noted by Alan and Schwartz (2013), "Because the beneficiaries include a wide range of people who are not participating in the transactions that establish a price, an economist would refer to an exchange produced price as a *public good*."

Regarding the various proposals that have been made in response to the high bouts of volatility that have been experienced in recent years, we suggest that their viability be assessed in light of the public goods attributes of greater price stability and the sharper price discovery that enhanced liquidity can provide.[3] The intention of the recent proposals is to ensure that sufficient liquidity be available during times of stress.[4] For instance, addressing those market makers who allegedly withdrew their liquidity when the market needed it most, the MiFID II Regulation has proposed that orders have minimum resting times. The idea has also been entertained that additional capital be injected by/for market makers so that they might provide greater liquidity and hence enhanced price stability when a market is under stress. Both of these proposals apply to continuous market operations, and they both require that market makers improve the quality of their markets for a considerably broader population.

Neither proposal is an efficient way to achieve a better output of the public good. No profit seeking, market maker firm operating in a continuous trading regime can be expected to act voluntarily as these proposals intend them to. When it is not in their own, profit maximizing self-interest to provide additional capital, market makers require additional perks, and it is not at all clear how best to do this.

Listed companies, on the other hand, are far better positioned to supply the public good. The value that greater price stability and sharper price discovery provides to a listed company is not trading profits per se, but the higher share values and correspondingly lower cost of capital that will be attributed to enhanced liquidity. From a public policy perspective, the listed companies best represent the interests of the broader public, and hence they are in the best position to supply the public good.

---

[3] See Schwartz (2009) for an earlier mention of the public good attribute of price formation that likens the public good provided by an exchange produced price (it sheds light on share value) and the public good provided by a lighthouse (it signals the location of a harbor or the presence of a rock).

[4] One proposal is a "Tobin" tax on trading, the primary objective being to discourage participants from flipping quickly in and out of positions. We see irony in this. First, HFT players have been thought of as the new market makers; if indeed they are, why make it more difficult for them to enter their orders in the first place? Further, in light of the considerable regulatory attention which has been given over the years to lowering transaction costs by reducing commissions and bid-ask spreads, why should government then impose a tax on trading that raises transaction costs?

Analytic Context

Because our empirical analysis is based on historic data, in our simulations the SL trades cannot impact the companies' share prices (i.e., the share prices are exogenous). In contrast, in a live market, the intension of the corporate buybacks in a falling market is to curb price declines and, in so doing, defend against market collapses. Equivalently, in a live market, the corporate sales are intended to contain price increases and, in so doing, defend against speculative bubbles. Accordingly, the liquidity brought by the corporate purchases and sales should combine to disinflate excessive price volatility without impeding the efficiency with which new information is translated into share values (we discuss this further in Section C of the Appendix). The magnitude of these desirable price effects can be assessed, however, only after a program has been instituted.

Price paths in historic data typically exhibit both mean reverting and trending behaviour. Mean reversion is cash flow generating for any market maker as purchases are made at lower bids, sales are made at higher offers, and net revenues are realized as price mean reverts between these lower bids and higher offers. Trending, on the other hand, is costly for a market maker who seeks to keep his inventory within predetermined bounds; shares sold in, e.g., a rising market, have to be bought back (or marked-to-market) at a yet higher price when the inventory is rebalanced. Hence, as is the case for any market maker, the trading cost of running an SL program depends on the relative strengths of these two pricing dynamics (mean reversion and trending). We capture the cost of trending by marking any long or short inventory position to market at the end of a simulation run.

As a more robust test of the profitability/cost of running an SL program in the presence of trending, in our empirical tests we reverse the trending patterns by running the simulations both forward and backward for each company in our sample; any positive (negative) trend for the forward analysis becomes a negative (positive) trend for the backward analysis. For the forward analysis, we start with the earliest day in our sample period (January 2, 2008) and advance one day at a time; for the backward analysis, we start with the last day in our sample period (December 31, 2012) and proceed backward one day at a time. Profitable trading for both the forward and the backward tests would strongly indicate that mean reversion dominates trending as a pricing dynamic.

Empirical Analysis

In this section, we present to our empirical analysis of the corporate supplemental liquidity proposal. In so doing, we provide further details on how such a program might be structured.

Test Design

Our tests are conducted with three data sets: DOW 30 stocks using closing prices only, DAX 30 stocks taking account of the closing call only (DAX 1-auction), and DAX 30 stocks taking account of the opening, mid-day, and closing calls (DAX 3-auction).[5] Each of our three data sets spans the five-year period, January 2, 2008 to December 31, 2012. The DOW sample includes the 30 stocks that were included in the index as of the end of 2013.[6] The DAX samples are formed by taking the 30 most consistently represented DAX constituents over our sample period.[7] We run all simulations both forward and backward, as described above.

We start a simulation for a stock with a pre-specified array of price points for SL buy orders and SL sell orders. For our forward simulations (the procedure for the backward simulations is comparable), these price points are located in relation to a *reference price* which is the first price in each of our three samples. When only closing auction prices are used, the reference price is the closing price on the first day of the sample period (this applies to both the DOW and DAX 1-Auction samples); when all three daily auction prices are included in the sample, the reference price is the opening auction price on the first day (this applies to the DAX 3-Auction sample).

With the initial reference price determined, SL orders to buy are entered at prices below it, and SL orders to sell are entered at prices above it. The array of established price points can be thought of as a ladder, with each rung of the ladder being a price point.

The price ladder remains intact until an SL order executes totally in a call auction. At that time, the execution price (not the price at which the order is submitted) becomes the new reference price, and the entire ladder of SL bid and offer prices shifts accordingly. The ladder shifts up following an SL sale, and it shifts down following an SL purchase. The distance between the array of price points (the rungs of the ladder) is set by a parameter that we refer to as the *SL spread*. Because there is no order entered at the rung corresponding to a reference price, the price difference between the lowest SL sell order and the highest SL buy order is twice the SL spread.

To illustrate, if a company has set an SL spread of 5% and its reference price is $50, the lowest priced (most aggressive) SL sell order will be at $52.50, and the highest priced (most aggressive) SL buy order will be at $47.50. If the SL buy order is hit and executes totally at a clearing price of $47.50, the new, most aggressive SL sell order is priced at (rounding off) $50, and the new, most aggressive SL buy order is priced at (rounding off) $45.

---

[5] We would like to thank the Deutsche Börse Group for having provided the data.

[6] The composition of the DOW index was changed four times throughout our sample period; for the latest constituent list, 26 stocks were included in the index for more than 90% of our sample period.

[7] Including the most prevalent DAX stocks resulted in 29 of the sample stocks being included in the index more than 80% of the time.

We run the SL program using SL spreads ranging in one percentage point increments from 1% to 10% of the reference price. Lower SL spread measures are expected to lead to more frequent order executions, but to lower profits per trade. We find that the SL program remains largely profitable across the SL spread range that we have used but, not surprisingly, that profitability decreases as the SL spread increases.

Further details of the procedure include the following. If the clearing price at the call is less than $47.50, the reference price and the price ladder shift further down to align with the new clearing price. If the order placed at a reference price does not execute fully, the unexecuted portion remains on the book for the next call auction, and neither the reference price nor the price ladder shift. (Partial execution does not occur in our simulation runs because we simply assume all or nothing executions.) If the clearing price at an auction has dropped to a yet lower value on the price ladder (e.g., $45), then the order at $47.50 will execute fully at the lower price, and the order at $45 will also execute, at least partially, at this price.

Each SL order is for a pre-specified number of shares (in our simulations, we have taken the number to be 100,000 shares). Order sizes can be modified as the SL program progresses. If, for instance, an SL fund has sold considerably more shares than it has purchased during a period when price has predominantly trended up, the size of its sell orders could be reduced until a desired inventory level has been regained. We call this procedure *tapering*. Specifically, the SL buy (sell) order size could be tapered when the SL inventory becomes unduly long (short). We have analysed tapering using 500,000 shares (short or long) as the taper trigger, and dropping the SL's buy (sell) order from 100,000 shares to 50,000 shares when a 500,000 share long (short) trigger has been reached.

Test Results

Our simulations were run separately for each of our sample years (2008–2012), and for the five years combined. We seek two insights from the runs. First, we wish to assess the general level of profitability/loss associated with an SL program. Second we are interested in the sensitivity of the profitability/loss results to (i) different approaches to measuring P&L (straight forward total dollar assessment versus marked-to-market total dollar assessment), and (ii) parameter settings (the size of the SL spread and the inclusion or not of tapering).

Table 8.1 presents, based on a 5% SL spread, (i) the average cross-stock simulation results for realized profit and for profit with inventory positions marked-to-market, and (ii) the number of buy and sell transactions and ending inventory. Panels A, B, and C of Table 8.1 present, respectively, the simulation results for the DOW, DAX 1-Auction, and DAX 3-Auction samples. Results for the forward and backward analyses are shown in separate columns for each year, and for the five years combined, while results without and with tapering are shown in separate rows. Throughout, positive profit results are shown in bold italics.

Regarding the overall level of realized P&L profitability presented in Table 8.1, the values are of mixed sign but are predominantly positive: In Panel A, of the ten DOW forward and backward simulations without tapering, six are positive, and the combined 2008–2012 P&L is positive for both forward ($61.95M) and backward runs ($23.08M). The results with tapered SL orders are stronger, with seven of the ten simulation runs being positive, and the combined, overall sample results staying positive at $35.63M for forward runs, and at $20.38M for backward runs. The marked-to-market P&L values are also mostly positive, with seven out of ten simulation runs being positive without tapering, and four out of ten being positive with tapering. Regarding the five-years combined, the forward simulation runs yield a $9.81M and $1.41M marked-to-market P&L for, respectively, the no tapering and with tapering scenarios. The only negative profit observed for the overall sample is much smaller than the positive P&L values, at −$0.08M for backward runs without tapering (this P&L is a positive $0.06M with tapering).

The DAX 1-Auction results in Panel B of Table 8.1 and the DAX 3-Auction results in Panel C are similar, yet stronger compared to those for the DOW. Of the ten forward and backward simulations for the DAX 1-Auction and the DAX 3-Auction, five have positive realized P&L without tapering. With tapering, the number of positive P&L simulations increases to six for the DAX 3-Auction and to seven for the DAX 1-Auction. Both with and without tapering, the DAX marked-to-market P&L values are positive for seven out of ten simulation runs. With one exception, the overall five year results are all positive (as we observed for the DOW stocks, both DAX samples have negative marked-to-market P&L for the backward run without tapering, but the amount was less than one million euros). Across all of the runs for five years combined, realized P&Ls for the DAX 1-Auction (DAX 3-Auction) range from a minimum of €32.71M (€32.64M) for the forward run without tapering to €74.19M (€74.68M) for the backward run without tapering. For all three samples, tapering tightens the range over which P&L varies. Lastly, for all three of our samples, the positive profitability results shown in Table 8.1 are considerably greater in magnitude than their negative counterparts.

Table 8.2 presents the results for the five sample years combined for different values of the SL spread that ranges from 1% to 10%. The table shows the average cross-stock simulation results for realized profit, and for profit with inventory positions marked-to-market, as well as the number of buy and sell transactions and ending inventory positions. Panels A, B, and C of Table 8.2 present, respectively, the results for the DOW, DAX 1-Auction, and DAX 3-Auction samples. Results for the forward and backward analyses are shown in separate columns.

In all three panels of Table 8.2, the forward simulation run results for all three samples indicate that the five-year combined profitability values, regardless of the chosen SL Spread, are positive. As expected, the realized P&L values decrease monotonically as the SL spread is widened. For example, for the DOW sample with no tapering, realized P&L decreases from $285M at a 1% spread to $27.66M at a 10% spread. This can largely be explained by a lower number of trades occurring at higher SL spread levels. The backward runs also indicate positive results for all no-tapering scenarios. And, even though a number of negative P&Ls are observed

Table 8.1 Simulation results by year

	Forward						Backward					
	2008	2009	2010	2011	2012	08–12	2008	2009	2010	2011	2012	08–12
Panel A: DOW Sample												
No Tapering												
P&L, realized (mil$)	−9.40	***27.54***	***14.57***	***13.08***	***16.16***	***61.95***	***43.94***	−9.83	−5.79	***1.89***	−6.35	***23.08***
P&L, M2Mkt (mil$)	***5.68***	***5.86***	−0.95	***0.73***	−1.51	***9.81***	***1.48***	−3.03	***1.28***	***0.72***	***0.68***	−0.08
No of Buys	22	12	6	9	4	52	17	16	8	10	5	55
No of Sells	17	16	8	10	6	58	22	13	6	9	4	55
End Inventory (‘000)	450	(37)	(253)	(420)	(660)	(660)	(83)	573	313	163	127	(83)
With Tapering												
P&L, realized (mil$)	***0.14***	***24.50***	***6.77***	−1.30	***5.50***	***35.63***	***25.32***	***2.89***	−4.80	***3.40***	−5.96	***20.38***
P&L, M2Mkt (mil$)	***5.95***	−1.08	−0.86	−0.45	−2.15	***1.41***	−0.32	−2.19	***0.76***	***0.91***	***0.67***	***0.06***
No of Buys	22	12	6	9	4	52	17	16	8	10	5	55
No of Sells	17	16	8	10	6	58	22	13	6	9	4	55
End Inventory (‘000)	200	(320)	(418)	(403)	(485)	(485)	(273)	82	222	113	122	(273)
Panel B: DAX 1-AUCTION Sample												
No Tapering												
P&L, realized (mil€)	−26.38	***20.67***	***14.10***	−1.81	***26.14***	***32.71***	***80.10***	−3.38	−3.62	***15.70***	−14.62	***74.19***
P&L, M2Mkt (mil€)	−2.42	***11.10***	***3.13***	***15.65***	***5.15***	***32.62***	−14.01	−18.68	***3.28***	***7.90***	***7.50***	−0.60
No of Buys	24	14	8	16	7	69	16	17	9	13	10	65
No of Sells	17	18	10	14	11	70	25	15	8	17	7	72
End Inventory (‘000)	1,008	660	560	872	584	584	(600)	656	400	216	400	(600)
With Tapering												
P&L, realized (mil€)	−11.31	***20.69***	***7.07***	−1.11	***21.22***	***36.56***	***45.64***	***4.85***	***0.26***	***19.65***	−13.36	***57.04***
P&L, M2Mkt (mil€)	−1.88	***4.72***	***3.95***	***11.25***	***1.31***	***19.36***	−11.38	−4.80	***5.77***	***3.97***	***7.48***	***1.04***

(continued)

Table 8.1 (continued)

	Forward						Backward					
	2008	2009	2010	2011	2012	08–12	2008	2009	2010	2011	2012	08–12
No of Buys	24	14	8	16	7	69	16	17	9	13	10	65
No of Sells	17	18	10	14	11	70	25	15	8	17	7	72
End Inventory (‘000)	470	(4)	(20)	120	(100)	(100)	(420)	218	288	148	376	(420)
Panel C: DAX 3-AUCTION Sample												
No Tapering												
P&L, realized (mil€)	−27.73	***21.98***	***14.58***	−3.36	***27.16***	***32.64***	***82.61***	−4.14	−5.16	***17.05***	−15.67	***74.68***
P&L, M2Mkt (mil€)	−2.44	***11.56***	***2.41***	***16.91***	***6.97***	***35.42***	−8.11	−19.14	***2.86***	***9.46***	***6.83***	−0.55
No of Buys	32	19	9	20	8	88	23	22	12	16	12	84
No of Sells	24	23	11	17	12	89	34	20	10	20	8	92
End Inventory (‘000)	1,032	668	552	904	608	608	(548)	776	464	232	448	(548)
With Tapering												
P&L, realized (mil€)	−11.99	***22.20***	***6.80***	−0.26	***21.44***	***38.18***	***43.90***	***6.41***	−1.72	***23.19***	−14.05	***57.73***
P&L, M2Mkt (mil€)	−1.68	***4.44***	***4.00***	***13.98***	***1.27***	***22.02***	−11.71	−6.30	***5.85***	***7.15***	***6.86***	***1.85***
No of Buys	32	19	9	20	8	88	23	22	12	16	12	84
No of Sells	24	23	11	17	12	89	34	20	10	20	8	92
End Inventory (‘000)	464	(42)	(30)	114	(84)	(84)	(396)	222	340	140	414	(396)

Note: This table presents simulation results by year, using 100,000 shares as the SL order size, and 5% as the SL spread. The italicized bold cells indicate the positive P&L scenarios. P&L realized and P&L M2Mkt denote, respectively, the realized and marked-to-market profit/loss values in million dollars/euros for each simulation run. No of Buys and No of Sells indicate the number of buy and sell order executions during each simulation run. End Inventory is the number of long or short shares in the SL inventory by the end of each simulation run denoted in thousands. No Tapering means that the SL order size is fixed at 100,000 shares regardless of the inventory level. With Tapering indicates that the SL buy order size is halved to 50,000 shares when the inventory exceeds long 500,000 shares, and that the SL sell order size is halved to 50,000 shares when the inventory exceeds short 500,000 shares

Table 8.2 Simulation results by SL spread, averaged across 2008–2012

	Forward										Backward									
	1%	2%	3%	4%	5%	6%	7%	8%	9%	10%	1%	2%	3%	4%	5%	6%	7%	8%	9%	10%
Panel A: DOW Sample																				
No Tapering																				
P&L, realized (mil$)	***285.05***	***143.33***	***96.25***	***78.81***	***61.95***	***46.57***	***40.12***	***39.28***	***32.05***	***27.66***	***216.22***	***80.22***	***39.34***	***27.37***	***23.08***	***15.72***	***15.09***	***8.08***	***9.63***	***9.26***
P&L, M2Mkt (mil$)	***62.34***	***28.93***	***18.99***	***12.29***	***9.81***	***10.61***	***8.78***	***6.32***	***6.02***	***6.12***	−2.09	−0.68	−0.18	−0.15	−0.08	−0.02	−0.04	***0.01***	−0.01	−0.03
No of Buys	299	168	105	73	52	39	30	25	20	17	315	174	109	76	55	42	33	26	22	18
No of Sells	317	179	113	80	58	44	35	29	23	19	301	169	108	75	55	42	33	26	22	18
End Inventory ('000)	(2,873)	(1,640)	(1,063)	(893)	(660)	(507)	(440)	(443)	(340)	(277)	(2,093)	(677)	(180)	(147)	(83)	(20)	(40)	10	(13)	(27)
With Tapering																				
P&L, realized (mil$)	***63.05***	***44.52***	***39.65***	***37.80***	***35.63***	***33.46***	***32.08***	***31.82***	***28.16***	***25.93***	***50.01***	***33.62***	***28.15***	***26.07***	***20.38***	***16.65***	***16.26***	***12.40***	***11.28***	***10.16***
P&L, M2Mkt (mil$)	***48.60***	***18.43***	***8.11***	***2.72***	***1.41***	***2.37***	***1.77***	***1.35***	***2.08***	***3.08***	***19.13***	***3.82***	***0.28***	−1.27	***0.06***	***0.82***	−0.68	***0.83***	***0.82***	***0.53***
No of Buys	299	168	105	73	52	39	30	25	20	17	315	174	109	76	55	42	33	26	22	18
No of Sells	317	179	113	80	58	44	35	29	23	19	301	169	103	75	55	42	33	26	22	18
End Inventory ('000)	(163)	(357)	(440)	(492)	(485)	(450)	(423)	(408)	(348)	(297)	(283)	(395)	(397)	(370)	(273)	(210)	(193)	(127)	(118)	(100)

(continued)

Table 8.2 (continued)

	Forward										Backward									
	1%	2%	3%	4%	5%	6%	7%	8%	9%	10%	1%	2%	3%	4%	5%	6%	7%	8%	9%	10%
Panel B: DAX 1-AUCTION Sample																				
No Tapering																				
P&L, realized (mil€)	***133.99***	***67.21***	***46.43***	***40.70***	***32.71***	***28.55***	***23.75***	***17.70***	***14.51***	***15.32***	***445.07***	***210.14***	***127.20***	***91.58***	***74.19***	***57.47***	***52.35***	***48.40***	***42.39***	***35.95***
P&L, M2Mkt (mil€)	***178.20***	***80.35***	***56.38***	***38.79***	***32.62***	***28.06***	***25.58***	***20.93***	***19.75***	***16.45***	−4.31	−1.93	−1.00	−0.65	−0.60	−0.38	−0.39	−0.35	−0.28	−0.29
No of Buys	330	195	130	92	69	53	43	34	29	24	330	194	126	88	65	50	41	33	27	22
No of Sells	332	197	131	93	70	53	43	34	28	24	330	198	132	95	72	55	46	38	32	26
End Inventory (‘000)	3,768	1,796	1,088	780	584	456	436	432	420	300	(4,312)	(1,928)	(1,000)	(652)	(600)	(376)	(392)	(352)	(284)	(288)
With Tapering																				
P&L, realized (mil€)	***157.02***	***81.95***	***55.57***	***41.58***	***36.56***	***30.74***	***28.33***	***23.86***	***21.20***	***20.64***	***197.45***	***109.70***	***78.41***	***68.65***	***57.04***	***47.54***	***41.85***	***38.31***	***34.24***	***30.43***
P&L, M2Mkt (mil€)	***133.61***	***62.19***	***34.47***	***22.81***	***19.36***	***19.90***	***18.50***	***16.13***	***15.98***	***14.05***	***63.01***	***24.27***	***10.02***	***5.44***	***1.04***	***0.36***	***0.07***	−1.20	−0.06	−1.69
No of Buys	330	195	130	92	69	53	43	34	29	24	330	194	126	88	65	50	41	33	27	22
No of Sells	332	197	131	93	70	53	43	34	28	24	330	198	132	95	72	55	46	38	32	26
End Inventory (‘000)	380	70	(48)	(52)	(100)	(34)	(14)	32	56	20	(302)	(362)	(466)	(410)	(420)	(326)	(312)	(280)	(226)	(230)

Panel C: DAX 3-AUCTION Sample																				
No Tapering																				
P&L, realized (mil€)	***121.50***	***78.62***	***55.81***	***43.12***	***32.64***	***26.97***	***22.93***	***19.62***	***17.02***	***12.99***	***471.09***	***195.89***	***127.25***	***89.30***	***74.68***	***66.05***	***59.86***	***49.96***	***46.44***	***40.76***
P&L, M2Mkt (mil€)	***175.66***	***89.06***	***55.56***	***42.63***	***35.42***	***27.37***	***23.26***	***19.86***	***17.99***	***14.76***	−4.62	−1.50	−0.92	−0.56	−0.55	−0.48	−0.44	−0.36	−0.32	−0.36
No of Buys	639	310	185	122	88	66	51	41	34	28	657	313	183	122	84	63	50	38	31	25
No of Sells	657	316	189	124	89	67	52	41	34	27	649	315	192	128	92	70	56	44	37	30
End Inventory ('000)	4,040	1,548	924	696	608	512	472	420	384	356	(4,616)	(1,500)	(916)	(560)	(548)	(476)	(444)	(360)	(324)	(356)
With Tapering																				
P&L, realized (mil€)	***150.93***	***88.20***	***62.52***	***46.23***	***38.18***	***32.67***	***30.13***	***26.27***	***23.74***	***19.11***	***186.49***	***106.95***	***77.21***	***63.06***	***57.73***	***51.45***	***45.65***	***40.11***	***36.55***	***31.69***
P&L, M2Mkt (mil€)	***127.20***	***64.39***	***39.68***	***27.06***	***22.02***	***18.57***	***17.02***	***15.37***	***15.58***	***12.53***	***81.73***	***29.38***	***12.09***	***5.63***	***1.85***	***0.36***	***0.13***	−0.93	−0.64	−2.22
No of Buys	639	310	185	122	88	66	51	41	34	28	657	313	183	122	84	63	50	38	31	25
No of Sells	657	316	189	124	89	67	52	41	34	27	649	315	192	128	92	70	56	44	37	30
End Inventory ('000)	418	10	(98)	(96)	(84)	(78)	(54)	(22)	0	24	(86)	(276)	(418)	(350)	(396)	(380)	(332)	(300)	(268)	(246)

Note: This table presents simulation results over January 2, 2008–December 31, 2012, by SL Spreads ranging from 1% to 10%, using 100,000 shares as the SL order size. The italicized bold cells indicate the positive P&L scenarios. P&L realized and P&L M2Mkt denote the realized and marked-to-market profit/loss values in million dollars/euros for each simulation run. No of Buys and No of Sells indicate the number of buy and sell order executions during each simulation run. End Inventory is the number of long or short shares in the SL inventory by the end of each simulation run denoted in thousands. No Tapering means that the SL order size is fixed at 100,000 shares regardless of the inventory level. With Tapering indicates that the SL buy order size is halved to 50,000 shares when the inventory exceeds long 500,000 shares, and also that the SL sell order size is halved to 50,000 shares when the inventory exceeds short 500,000 shares

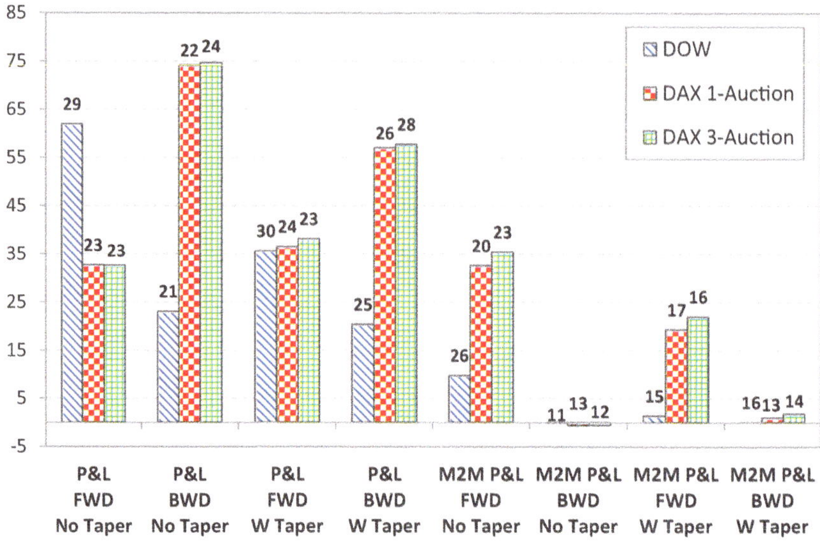

Fig. 8.1 Simulation results: average profitability for DOW (mil $), DAX 1-Auction (mil €), and DAX 3-Auction (mil €) for all five years combined. (*Note:* This chart presents the average profitability for DOW (in million dollars), DAX 1-Auction (in million Euros), and DAX 3-Auction (in million Euros) samples using 100,000 shares as the SL order size, and 5% as the SL spread. P&L is the realized profit & loss, M2M P&L is profit & loss marked-to-market. FWD and BWD denote the simulation results from forward and backward simulation runs, respectively. No Taper and W Taper indicate simulation results with tapering off and on, respectively. All P&L values are in millions. The numbers above each column indicate the number of stocks out of 30 that have a positive P&L value)

when prices are marked-to-market, the negative profits are far smaller in magnitude than the positive profits which are observed across the board.

Figure 8.1 presents a summary, based on a 5% SL spread, of all five-year combined P&L and M2M P&L values for all four scenarios of our simulations (forward and backward, each without and with tapering). The numbers above each column show the number of stocks in each sample of 30 that have a positive P&L for the scenario.

The columns, being predominantly positive, indicate that the SL mechanism is mostly profitable. The only negative profits we observe are the marked-to-market profits for the backward runs without tapering for all three samples. Even in that scenario, over one third of the stocks in each of the samples table positive profits.

Relatively definitive conclusions for the sensitivity analysis are more difficult to achieve, but we point out that the different profit/loss measures give generally consistent results, and that tapering does, as one would expect, control the maximum absolute inventory accumulations.

Regarding the parameter settings, the 5% spread appears reasonable for the representative stock in our three data sets. However, the optimal SL spread and tapering parameters would undoubtedly differ from firm-to-firm depending on the general level of volatility for the firm's stock, on the profitability measure that the firm feels is most relevant, on whether or not (and how) a firm may wish to include tapering to control its SL inventory fluctuations, and so on.

The SL Program Vis-À-Vis Traditional Market Maker Operations

By posting bids and offers, the program brings liquidity to the market much as would a market maker. And, as would a more traditional market maker, the corporate fund profits as prices bounce between lower bids and higher offers. There are important differences, however. We next consider these, and suggest why the listed companies are better situated to be the suppliers of supplemental liquidity.

Traditional market maker operations, on the other hand, are designed for continuous market trading, not call auction trading. In contrast, SL purchases and sales will be made in call auctions only, a feature that brings liquidity to the market without forcing the SL orders to execute at disequilibrium prices as typically occurs in the continuous market. The purpose of the corporate purchases and sales is not to generate market maker profits per se, but to bring meaningful liquidity and stability to the market, and the primary benefit should be that a corporation's shares will be more attractive to investors (and, accordingly, its cost of capital will be lower). Further, the SL market maker benefits as its orders, by their very presence, curb excessive price moves, and an SL fund can realize this benefit without actually trading. A traditional market maker firm, on the other hand, can profit only when its bids are hit and its offers lifted and, accordingly, it wants to trade. Traditional market makers like opacity; in contrast, the corporate share buyback and issuance procedure should be maximally transparent for one reason in particular: the value of the SL procedure lies in good part in the public knowing that a company will be in the market as a buyer of its shares if the share price falls to a buy trigger, and that it will be in the market as a seller of its shares if the share price rises to a sell trigger. Consequently, all parameters of the corporation's trading algo should be publicly known (most importantly, the prices at which its buy and sell orders have been entered, the sizes of its orders, and the length of time that it is committed to adhering to its stated parameters).

For four reasons in particular, a listed company should step forward and take on a market maker-type role:

1. The listed companies are better positioned than traditional market makers, for their own private incentives, to support an optimal provision of the key public good that attends enhanced liquidity: sharper price discovery.
2. The company's shareholders would be the program's primary beneficiaries. Bringing supplemental liquidity to the market will translate into higher share values and, consequently, into a lower cost of equity capital for the listed company.

3. The capital required to run an SL fund should be relatively small. Moreover, the very market dynamic that calls for the institution of an SL fund (i.e., excessive share price volatility) will, through the mean reversion that excessive volatility implies, yield returns for the fund, as cash obtained from selling shares in a rising market will be used to buy back shares in a falling market when price mean reverts. Equivalently, shares bought in a falling market will be sold in a rising market when price mean reverts. By buying low and selling high, the program can generate positive revenues, as our empirical findings presented in the preceding section suggest. Thus the program can be largely self-financing.
4. As we have noted, traditional market maker operations are geared for the continuous market while a periodic, price discovery call auction is the appropriate venue for the provision of SL capital.

Conclusion

We have considered a supplemental liquidity (SL) procedure that does not attempt to distinguish, on a case-by-case basis, between price changes attributable to new information and price changes attributable to noise. The procedure simply states, in a totally transparent, informationless way, that prepositioned SL buy orders will execute in a falling market, and that prepositioned SL sell orders will execute in a rising market.

To get a better sense of how the SL procedure can dampen accentuated volatility, consider the following. Assume that a stock has been trading at the $42 level, that the company has entered an SL buy order for 100,000 shares at $40, and that price is declining toward $40 and possibly below. Public knowledge that the corporation has an order to buy 100,000 shares at $40 can encourage other potential buyers to step forward and enter their own purchase orders in the close neighbourhood above $40. Consequently, price in the continuous market may not fall to $40. However, if the share price does cross the $40 level and a clearing price of $39 is set in the next call auction, the company's SL order will execute at $39, not at $40 (as will all other buy orders submitted to the call that were priced at $39 or higher). Importantly, if the corporate order had not been entered at $40, the clearing price at the next call could have fallen below $39. Note that the power of the corporate order to retard a price decrease will not have been wasted; that is, the benefit of the corporate stabilization effort will not have been squandered by making purchases at a disequilibrium price (i.e., a price above $39). It is largely for this reason that we propose that the SL orders be entered for execution in a call auction only.[8]

[8] In call auction trading, liquidity provided stability and reasonably accurate price discovery are brought into alignment in a way that is not possible to achieve in continuous market trading, as we discuss in Section C of the appendix. It is important to emphasize that, when this alignment is

An SL order entered in a call auction will set neither a price floor nor a price ceiling; it is simply another input into the determination of a market clearing price. Like any other order, an SL order is of limited size (for our simulation analysis, we have taken the order size to be 100,000 shares). As might any large order, an SL order can effect price (this is indeed the intention), but it will not *peg* price. For instance, if a price decrease from \$40 to \$39 (or a rise from \$40 to \$41) is justified following a major news release, the clearing price in the call auction should (and will) move to \$39 (or \$41).

In the short-run, prices at times over-adjust to fundamental information change and, at other times, they under-adjust. When price over-adjusts, an SL order will dampen the short-run price volatility; in a falling (rising) market, a pre-positioned SL buy (sell) order will help to stabilize price. This is the main objective of the SL program. However, when price under-adjusts, an SL order can slow the attainment of a new equilibrium value. This effect, which can attend an SL program, is undesirable. Which of these two effects outweighs the other is an empirical question. Our tests (along with a number of academic studies) indicate that, in the short-run, over-adjusting (and mean-reversion) is more dominant than under-adjusting (and trending).[9] This is why the supplemental liquidity procedure, without distinguishing on a case-by-case basis between news-justified price changes and price changes that are noise, keeps short-run prices, on a probability basis, in better alignment with longer-run equilibrium values.

Our tests are comprehensive in that they were run for five years, for thirty DOW and 30 DAX stocks, and both forward and backward, for a total of 600 different stock/year observations. As shown in Table 8.1, for the forward runs without tapering, over the period 2008–2012, realized profitability (in millions) is \$61.95 (DOW), €32.71 (DAX 1-Auction), and €32.64 (DAX 3-Auction). The results are similar when we run the simulations backward, and/or with tapering.

In light of these findings, exchange listed companies should consider supplying supplemental liquidity to the markets for their shares. The superior quality of price formation that can be achieved when adequate supplemental liquidity is provided is a public good, and the listed companies are in a far better position to supply this public good than is any third party, broker-dealer intermediary. The listed companies should have a clear incentive to participate, and they ought to have sufficient capital for their efforts to produce economically meaningful results.

While our empirical analysis has shed light on the net cash flows realized from running an SL program, we are not able to quantify the impact that SL orders would have on realized transaction prices; live trading would be required for this assessment to be made. Moreover, for such a test to be properly conducted, a

achieved, excess volatility can be dampened without perturbing a proper adjustment of prices to new information.

[9] The SL tests derive power because they do not presuppose any specific pattern of mean reversion or trending (such as would a more standard autocorrelation test). This is important because correlation patterns shift over time, both in terms of sign and duration, and because stock returns can reflect a mixture of autocorrelation patterns of first and higher orders.

sufficient number of firms would have to be actively running an SL program. This is because the desired impact of SL orders on the dynamic behaviour of share prices would be more substantial, the larger the number of firms that undertook such a program.

Four constituencies will benefit from the institution of an SL program: Issuers from their share prices being more stable and, accordingly, their cost of equity capital being lower; the investing public from enhanced liquidity and sharper price discovery; an exchange from the more consolidated order flow that will be directed to its call auctions, and from the improved quality of the markets for its listed stocks; and third party broker/dealer firms from revenues gained from advising on and running an SL fund.

In conclusion, listed company involvement in liquidity provision is critical. Our empirical findings are encouraging, and we suggest that additional steps be taken to refine, further test, and implement the SL procedure.

Appendix: Further Considerations

In this appendix we turn to four further topics of considerable importance.

A. Additional Rules for Implementing an SL Program

The parameters of the SL procedure should be established individually by each participating company, and be made public. To have the intended stabilizing effect, traders must know in advance that a listed company will be participating in the next auction. This knowledge can temper herding and over-reacting, while encouraging contrarian orders to be more forthcoming. Moreover, transparent and publicly known parameters will help guard against market manipulation and other forms of foul play (we discuss the possibility of gaming in section D of this Appendix).

Participants in the supplemental liquidity program should adhere to the following:

1. **Neutrality**: Execution is managed by a third party.
2. **Predictability**: The parameters for execution that are selected by the listed company must be publicly known.
3. **Transparency**: Advance notice of a parameter change is required. Once instated, a parameter should be maintained without change for an extended period of time (e.g., 6 months).
4. **Reliability**: The supplemental liquidity fund is supplied with capital from the company in an amount sufficient to cover repurchases if the price were to decrease to zero (or to an otherwise pre-specified amount). This assures the market that executions will occur as announced. Sufficient shares have to be kept available "on the shelf" to support sales as price rises to higher levels.

5. **SRO Regulation**: Program should be under surveillance by the listing exchange.
6. **Value Retention**: Cash contributions to the stabilization fund may be invested in host nation bonds, if necessary, as a means of securing shareholder value (i.e. avoid/minimize opportunity costs).
7. **Profitability**: A company may withdraw funds if its cash account sufficiently exceeds the minimum required to cover a potential price decrease.
8. **Investment Vehicle**: Cash raised from the sale of shares in a rising market is deposited in the listed company's stabilization fund. Each firm must have its own, separate fund. Likewise, shares are repurchased using capital from the stabilization fund. Adjustments to the fund may be necessary to ensure sufficient capital for price decreases (i.e. to cover the minimum number of repurchases).

B. Compliance with Local Regulations

Depending upon the Accepted Market Practices of a host nation, certain aspects of the liquidity program should be evaluated to ensure compatibility with local regulations:

New Share Issuance and Repurchase: Companies wishing to issue new shares or to buy back existing shares could possibly utilize the apparatus established by the stabilization program as a mechanism to do so.

Free Float: To ensure that rules governing minimum free float requirements are not violated, a constant calculation should be maintained to assure that a company buy back will not violate a free float constraint.

Market Manipulation: Having the SL order placement algorithm established and publicly announced well in advance ensures that order placement under prescribed conditions will be predictable, cannot be manipulated, and that the main effect will be a dampening of excess volatility.[10]

Insider Trading: To avoid any potential violations of insider trading, listed companies would be required to engage a third party to conduct the execution of the SL orders.

Unprofitable companies: A company whose fortunes have turned and could be heading towards bankruptcy will not want to be committed to buying back its shares as its share price declines. No attempt should be made to prop up the company's share price, or to impose a cost that could increase the probability of its demise. Under clearly specified conditions, a company in such as position should be relieved of its SL commitment.

[10] Vulnerability to gaming is considered further in Section D of the appendix.

C. Call Auction Prices and Equilibrium Values

As SL orders execute, they do not prevent price changes from achieving equilibrium values. This essential property of the procedure is achieved precisely because SL orders are entered for execution in the call auction facility only. To better understand this, it is necessary to distinguish between short-run and long-run equilibrium.

A well-known economic reality is that short-run responses are generally less elastic than long-run responses and, accordingly, that demand and supply shifts result in larger price changes in the short run than in the long run. This result holds for an equity market: in the short run, the relative thinness of a book (i.e., illiquidity) results in accentuated price changes and, accordingly, in heightened price volatility.

In call auction trading, buy and sell orders are cumulated to obtain downward sloping buy curves and upward sloping sell curves that are analogous to the demand and supply curves of economic theory. The intersection of these two curves establishes a clearing price that is an equilibrium value. As the curves shift, the equilibrium value changes. As it does, various short-run dynamics that characterize the order flow cause short-run price equilibrium to differ from long-run price equilibrium. For instance, momentum trading causes prices to over-react in the short run, and then to mean revert back to more sustainable long-run values. Further, contra-side buyers step back when price sharply drops and, similarly, contra-side sellers step back when price sharply rises. Additionally, effective demand (orders actually conveyed to the market) is generally less than *latent demand*, the volume of orders that would be placed in a frictionless environment. Lower effective demand translates into buy/sell curves that are less elastic and, accordingly, this causes accentuated price volatility.

Call auctions naturally control volatility, and the price improvement that limit order placers can receive in a batched trading environment incentivizes more aggressive order placement. Nevertheless, in a world replete with trading frictions, potential traders do not all participate in any specific auction and, consequently, the price set in any call is a short-run, not a long-run, equilibrium. Accordingly, the SL program can be understood as a procedure that, through the liquidity it supplies, bolsters the elasticity of the short-run buy/sell curves. In so doing, this keeps short-run equilibrium prices in closer alignment with longer-run equilibrium values.

One might question how it is possible for an SL order to change a call auction clearing price without preventing that clearing price from achieving an equilibrium value. The answer is that the SL orders *change* equilibrium values. How might this be? In an environment characterized by divergent expectations, the short-run equilibrium price is not an exogenous, fundamental value (and neither is a long-run equilibrium price, for that matter). Rather, it is the price that best balances all buy and sell orders that have been submitted to the auction. In standard economic terms, equilibrium is the value given by the intersection of the (effective) downward sloping buy curve and the (effective) upward sloping sell curve. If the inclusion of an SL order shifts a buy/sell curve, it alters the intersection point and, in so doing, it changes the equilibrium price.

To clarify further, it is important to emphasize that, in an environment where participants in possession of the same fundamental information form divergent expectations, shares do not have exogenously determined fundamental values (if some participants think that shares are worth $45 while others think that they are worth $50, what is *the* fundamental value?). In a divergent expectations environment which is devoid of exogenously determined fundamental values, market clearing values can be determined only by participant orders meeting in the marketplace, and the SL orders would simply be one more input into price determination. Just as these orders might impact a call auction's clearing price, they can also affect the underlying equilibrium values. They can do so because they are one of the determinants of the equilibrium value.

Because of the malleability of an equilibrium price, an order that supplies supplemental liquidity to the market is able to dampen excessive short-run volatility (noise) without preventing share prices from achieving short-run equilibrium values. By bolstering buying (selling) in a falling (rising) market, the SL orders add elasticity-preserving liquidity to the market's buy and sell curves. The greater elasticity tempers short-run price swings and, in so doing, dampens excessive short-run price volatility.

D. An SL Program and Gaming Possibilities

While gaming is always a major consideration, we find it difficult to see how the SL procedure could be gamed in a way that would have undesirable consequences. However, we caution that, when it comes to gaming, one should never say never.

The possibility of gaming should be considered for two times in an SL cycle in particular: (1) when an SL order has been posted, and (2) when, via its SL trading, a company has either purchased or sold a large number of shares, and the market has come to anticipate that the company will be undertaking a rebalancing transaction(s).[11]

The initial posting of an SL order should not be game-able because these orders are totally informationless, the procedure is fully transparent, and the prices at which the orders are pre-positioned are public information. No trading halt is triggered when an SL order price is reached, and an SL order does not attempt to peg price. Thus an SL order does not establish an absorbing barrier. And, because it is entered for call auction execution only, if it does execute, it executes at the auction's clearing price, not at its own limit price (that is, the SL order can be price improved).

Because of the affect it may have on the placement of other orders, an SL order could, however, establish a reflecting barrier. Suppose an SL buy order has been entered at $40. Some public buyer, viewing this large order as a free put option,

[11] Given that the program executes based on price movement and not on inventory, there should be no cause for concern regarding any rebalancing activity. Additionally, cause for concern in the event of a hostile takeover and/or short-squeeze situation is also unwarranted, as this can be adequately addressed by the inclusion of a tapering function.

would be encouraged to enter a more aggressive buy order in the neighbourhood of \$40 in the continuous market preceding the auction; if his order executes and he so wishes, he could (possibly) flip out of the position at a good price in the next call because of the SL order. Plus, if he wishes to buy and hold, he will have to price his order more aggressively so as to get the merchandise. On the other side of the market, a public seller will be encouraged to seek a higher price than he or she otherwise would in the continuous market preceding the call. And so, the presence of the SL buy order at \$40 acts to increase both buy and sell prices in the continuous market, and thus it operates as a reflecting barrier. This response is desirable, however, and we do not consider it gaming.

Regarding the unwinding of an SL position, the procedure is structured so that a company need never have to unwind a position. This is critically important. A traditional market maker firm that has acquired an unduly large inventory position (long or short) will be looking to rebalance its portfolio. The market maker firm, of course, does not want public participants to know that it will be doing this and, accordingly, keeps its inventory positions hidden. In contrast, the inventory of the SL fund should be public knowledge. It can be totally transparent because, unlike a traditional market maker, an SL fund need never rebalance. Hence, the procedure cannot be gamed from this perspective.

To satisfy the no-rebalance condition, enough cash must be kept in a firm's SL fund to repurchase shares if its share price were to fall without bound, and the firm should maintain sufficient shares "on the shelf" to issue new shares if its price were to rise to ever higher levels. Because the SL orders, although large in the marketplace are small relative to the total value of shares outstanding, a company can acquire ever larger long/short positions at relatively low cost.[12]

Consideration needs also be given to the procedure by which a firm might periodically change the parameters of its SL program or, if it so chooses, terminate the program entirely. Our suggestion here is that the firm commit to the program and set its parameters with a specified frequency (e.g., quarterly), and that it preannounce its forward commitment.[13] Other issues concerning the integration of an SL program with standard share issuance and buyback programs require further consideration.

[12] In one benign way, however, a company can, if it so wishes, rebalance its portfolio without decreasing the size of its publically announced SL orders: if it has an undesirably large short position, the company can rebalance by augmenting its SL buy orders; similarly, if it has an undesirably large long position, the company can rebalance by augmenting the size of its SL sell orders. Alternatively, it can taper its order sizes as we have done in our empirical tests.

[13] Under certain conditions (e.g. the advent of potential bankruptcy or an unexpected hostile takeover), a company should be allowed to alter the parameters of its SL program without delay.

References

Alan, N. S., & Schwartz, R. A. (2013). Price discovery: The economic function of a stock exchange. *Journal of Portfolio Management, Fall, 40*, 124–132.

Bessembinder, H., & Rath, S. P. (2008). Does market structure matter? In *Stock market liquidity: Implications for market microstructure and asset pricing* (pp. 149–172). John Wiley & Sons.

Fleming, M. J., & Remolina, E. M. (1999). Price formation and liquidity in the U.S. Treasury market: The response to public information. *Journal of Finance, 5*, 1901–1915.

Hasbrouck, J., & Schwartz, R. A. (Spring 1988). Liquidity and execution costs in equity markets. *Journal of Portfolio Management, 14*, 10–16.

Lo, A. W., & Craig MacKinlay, A. (1988). Stock market prices do not follow random walks: Evidence From a simple specification test. *Review of Financial Studies, 1*, 41–66.

Schwartz, R. A. (Fall 1988). A proposal to stabilize stock prices. *Journal of Portfolio Management, 15*, 4–11.

Schwartz, R. A. (2009). Dark pools and fragmented markets. In *Annual report and statistics* (pp. 16–21). World Federation of Exchanges.

Schwartz, R. A., & Whitcomb, D. K. (1977). The time-variance relationship: Evidence on autocorrelation in common stock returns. *Journal of Finance, 32*, 41–55.

Stoll, H. R. (2000). Friction. *Journal of Finance, 4*, 1479–1515.

The manufacturer's authorised representative in the EU is Springer Nature Customer Service Centre GmbH, Europaplatz 3, 69115 Heidelberg, Germany. If you have any concerns regarding our products, please contact ProductSafety@springernature.com

Printed and bound by CPI Group (UK) Ltd, Croydon, CR0 4YY
30/09/2026
02225259-0014